No Escape

For a fellow
fan of N. Elias

Paul Sands

No Escape

Freedom of Speech and the Paradox of Rights

Paul A. Passavant

NEW YORK UNIVERSITY PRESS

New York and London

NEW YORK UNIVERSITY PRESS
New York and London
www.nyupress.org

First published in paperback in 2003

Library of Congress Cataloging-in-Publication Data
Passavant, Paul A. (Paul Andrew)
No escape : freedom of speech and the paradox of rights / Paul A. Passavant.
p. cm.
Includes bibliographical references and index.
ISBN 0–8147–6695–1 (cloth : alk. paper)
ISBN 0–8147–6696–X (pbk. : alk. paper)
1. Freedom of speech—United States—History.   I. Title.
KF4772 .P37 2002
342. 73'0853—dc21   2002005469

Manufactured in the United States of America
c 10 9 8 7 6 5 4 3 2 1
p 10 9 8 7 6 5 4 3 2 1

To my mother, Jean, and my father, Francis,
I dedicate this book with love

In the camp of the Left, one often hears people saying that power is that which abstracts, which negates the body, represses, suppresses, and so forth. I would like to say instead that what I find most striking about these new technologies of power introduced since the seventeenth and eighteenth centuries is their concrete and precise character. . . . In the seventeenth and eighteenth centuries a form of power comes into being that begins to exercise itself through social production and social service. It becomes a matter of obtaining productive service from individuals in their concrete lives. And in consequence, a real and effective 'incorporation' of power was necessary.
—Michel Foucault, "Truth and Power"

This triple exergue is intended not only to focus attention on the ethnocentrism which, everywhere and always, had controlled the concept of writing. . . .

Perhaps patient meditation and painstaking investigation on and around what is still provisionally called writing . . . are the wanderings of a way of thinking that is faithful and attentive to the ineluctable world of the future which proclaims itself at present, beyond the closure of knowledge. . . . For that future world and for that within it which will have put into question the values of sign, word, and writing, for that which guides our future anterior, there is as yet no exergue.

—Jacques Derrida, *Of Grammatology*

Contents

Preface

Most scholarship describes legal rights as possessing atomizing power, protecting the individual against the social forces of a political majority or a suffocating community sentiment. While liberals appreciate rights for preserving the priority of the individual to the community, communitarians criticize rights on the very same basis that liberals value them—for giving priority to the individual over the community. Various forms of critical scholarship also see rights as problematic—as creating abstract and formalistic equalities that distract from real, substantive inequalities. Disembodied rights do not correspond very accurately to the embodied and socially embedded lives that we lead, do not provide us with an adequate language by which to pursue justice, and may even make matters worse, either by obscuring reality or by doing further damage to the social fabric that ought to be the real subject of justice.

This book argues that the conventional perspectives on rights neglect how recognizing rights for subjects also requires the production of subjects for rights. Under the conditions of "modernity," rights have been protected through national constitutions. In the context of the United States, the American people is the referent for the rights recognized in the Bill of Rights. The sovereign American people has authorized the government to exercise certain powers while reserving certain rights to itself. When rights are claimed and contested within the framework of the U.S. Constitution, the subject position to which rights attach is the American people. Thus, when one claims a right like freedom of speech in this context, one also claims identity with the American people. While this enables the possibility of a successful rights claim, it also defines the limits of such rights claims according to the logic of American–non-American. The conditions of legal inclusion are, necessarily, exclusive grounds.

Because claiming rights incorporates the politics of national identity, we can see that liberal government does not escape the politics of identity.

Indeed, liberal legal rights can work hand in hand with nationalism. Therefore, paradoxically, neither the liberal nor the communitarian position on rights is correct. In fact, they can be shown to be two sides of the same coin when they posit, mistakenly, the inherent hostility between rights and community. Practices of rights help to generate forms of social identity that sustain a rights claim. Rights claims, in addition to repressing certain forms of identity, *produce identities.*

When I prepared to send this manuscript to the publisher as the summer of 2001 was coming to a close, I was led to consider the historical contingency of the main argument of the book—that legal rights are not inherently opposed to the politics of nationalism—by a variety of developments. Not only has capitalism become increasingly and more powerfully global, with processes of governance and legalization following close behind, but protests against the hegemony of global capital are also globalized. A protestor, armed with a fire extinguisher, was shot dead by police in Genoa, Italy, at the G-8 meetings in July. Academia was abuzz over Michael Hardt and Antonio Negri's recently published book *Empire,* in which they argue that a new form of global sovereignty and new opportunities for global resistance have taken hold in the world today. And the U.S. Supreme Court had just decided *Zadvydas v. Davis,* arguing that the indefinite detention of non-Americans would violate the Constitution since the Fifth Amendment protects the due process rights of all *persons.*[1]

It seemed like change was afoot. I hoped that rights practices might become dislodged from the exclusionary and biopolitical tendencies of nationalism and linked to other practices that would enable greater justice to be done. I feared, based on a passage in *Zadvydas* that refers to the "conduct of all civilized nations" as a normative guide for congressional legislation, that the national basis of rights would be rejected, only to install an even more unfortunate racial practice of discriminating in the matter of rights according to the discourse of Western civilization versus the savage or barbarian. The aftermath of September 11 makes my hopes seem out of place and my fears incompletely realized, with the incompletion making, if possible, the situation even worse.

As the aftermath of September 11 has shown, we now live in a world where the worst of both the nationalism and the racism I discuss in this book have come to govern conduct.[2] Leaders in the United States and around the world frame global problems and proper responses in the racial discourse that defends Western civilization against barbarism. In the United States, America is forthrightly constituted as the exemplar of Western civilization and its rights are regulated according to the strictest, most exclusive logic of a racially based nationalism. President George W. Bush, in his 2002 State of the Union Address, says in the opening sentence that "the civilized world faces unprecedented dangers."[3] In Sacramento, California, a graduation speaker was booed off the stage for urging citizens to safeguard their rights to free speech and habeas corpus.[4] Near Charlotte, West Virginia, a student had her suspension from school for insufficient patriotism upheld in the state courts, in seeming contradiction to the Supreme Court's holding in the famous First Amendment case of *Tinker v. Des Moines* (she wore a shirt that read, "When I saw the dead and dying Afghani children on TV, I felt a newly recovered sense of security. God Bless America.").[5] University faculty and staff are being punished for their speech while state supported institutions of higher education are having their funding threatened by state governments for harboring faculty deemed insufficiently nationalistic.[6] Lynn Cheney, wife of Vice-President Dick Cheney, is acting as a present-day American Protective Leaguer in her renewed efforts to police the speech of academe.[7] Attorney General John Ashcroft, behaving like a present-day A. Mitchell Palmer, the World War I attorney general who undertook the "Palmer" or "Red" Raids of 1919–20 to rid the nation of the Industrial Workers of the World (IWW) through mass detentions and attempted deportations of aliens, directed the Federal Bureau of Investigation (FBI) and other law enforcement officials to interview at least 5,000 men solely on the basis of national origin. In the wake of September 11, there has been the detention of over 1,000 persons, the overwhelming majority of whom are "Muslims or Arabs, come from Middle Eastern countries, and are noncitizens."[8] President George W. Bush, through executive order, has created military tribunals for the trial of noncitizens and Congress has passed, with only one dissenting vote in the Senate, the U.S.A Patriot Act, that further jeopardizes rights for many.[9] To illustrate the dominance of nationalist discourse, the leading critic of these measures, the American Civil Liberties Union (ACLU), has condemned them as being "unconstitutional and un-American."[10] Rights continue to be denied and claimed according to the logic of what it means to be an American, as I discuss in this book. Also, unfortunately, we find my diagnosis of post–cold war American nationalism to be confirmed in the response to September 11— America sees itself and the world in terms of the racialized moral geography of the West versus the Rest.

There is a genealogy of support for this project that reaches back to the University of Wisconsin, Madison. I would like to acknowledge the contributions of Marion Smiley, Benjamin Marquez, Kathryn Hendley, and John Fiske. I particularly benefited from Joel B. Grossman's wise counsel, open mindedness, and good humor. There are too few like him in academia today. I also benefited from conversations with Boa Santos, Patrick Riley, and Dick Merelman. Mike Shapiro and I met in Madison. While the project benefited from his wealth of knowledge, I benefited from his friendship. I would like to express gratitude to Julie White, Tina Chen, Kevin Glynn, and Dan Smith for listening to or reading the first versions of my arguments. I would also like to thank Bert Kritzer, Chuck Epp, and Dan for their help in locating sources right up to the end of the project. Of course, where would I be in terms of my sanity if it weren't for Jonathan Goodman and Ian Verstegen? Peace, E!

I would like to acknowledge the support, suggestions, and friendly arguments of Austin Sarat, Cornelia Klinger, and Costas Douzinas. I presented chapters one and two at Birkbeck College's School of Law as a visiting fellow during the fall of 2001, and I would like to thank Birkbeck's faculty, staff, students and the other Visiting Fellow, Morris Kaplan, for providing such a rich intellectual environment. From this group, however, I must single out Peter Fitzpatrick for his generosity without limit, friendship, intellectual companionship, and for encouraging my efforts from the earliest moments of the project to its ends.

I am very lucky to be employed doing what I do. In the Department of Political Science at Hobart and William Smith Colleges, Mel Joyce makes things run smoothly, for which I am deeply grateful, and I have received last-minute research assistance from Amanda Cortese. I would like to thank Hobart and William Smith for faculty research money that enabled me to complete this project. My newest department colleagues, Cedric Johnson and DeWayne Lucas, valiantly tried to answer last-minute source questions. I enjoy the arguments I have had with Steven Lee in Philosophy—somehow their recurring nature is comforting. Christine de Denus, in the spirit of interdisciplinarity that lives at Hobart and William Smith Colleges, made sure I didn't embarrass myself when using the natural sciences to illustrate a point. I am also grateful to Lee Quinby and especially to John Shovlin for reading my work. John has been particularly helpful in paring three arguments down to one that can actually be presented and perhaps make sense to someone other than me. Chapter six was especially improved by his eye.

But no one helped me more to bring this project to a close than Jodi Dean. Everyone should have a reader like Jodi. Jodi's comments are notably honest—critical or enthusiastic, they are always helpful. Moreover, Jodi is always fast at just about everything she does. Her turnaround time as I was revising the manuscript was phenomenal. Thanks, Jodi, for this and for everything else that you continue to give me. You're really, really great.

Three of the chapters had previously published lives. Chapter 3 was originally published in *Social and Legal Studies* 6 (1996); chapter 4 previously appeared in *Studies in Law, Politics, and Society* 18 (1998); and an earlier version of chapter 6 appeared in *Cultural Studies and Political Theory*, edited by Jodi Dean (Ithaca: Cornell University Press, 2000). I thank Sage, Elsevier Science, and Cornell University Press for permission to include these essays here. Paula Durbin Westby compiled an excellent index, and I thank her.

NOTES

1. *Zadvydas v. Davis* 2001 Lexis 4912 (2001).

2. For a discussion of the novelty of the response to the event of September 11, see Paul A. Passavant and Jodi Dean, "Representation and the Event," *Theory and Event* (2002) (online: http://muse.jhu.edu/journals/theory_and_event/v005 /5.4passavant.html).

3. "The State of the Union; President Bush's State of the Union Address to Congress and the Nation," *New York Times*, January 30, 2002, 22A.

4. Timothy Egan, "In Sacramento, a Publisher's Questions Draw Wrath of Crowd," *New York Times*, December 21, 2001, B1.

5. *Tinker v. Des Moines Independent Community School District* 393 U.S. 503 (1969); Emily Wax, "The Consequences of Objection: Students Who Speak Out against War Find Themselves Battling to Be Heard," *Washington Post*, December 9, 2001, C1.

6. David Glenn, "The War on Campus: Will Academic Freedom Survive?" *Nation*, December 3, 2001, 11–14.

7. Anne Neal and Jerry Martin, *Defending Civilization: How Our Universities Are Failing America and What Can Be Done about It* (Washington, D.C.: American Council of Trustees and Alumni, November, 2001). This report was a project of the "Defense of Civilization Fund." The American Protective League was a World War I hyperpatriotic citizens organization that was sanctioned by the Department of Justice to police, especially, cities with high alien populations. See Joan Jensen, *The Price of Vigilance* (New York: Rand McNally, 1968).

8. Nadine Strossen, "The Massive, Secretive Detention and Dragnet Questioning of People Based on National Origin in the Wake of September 11," testimony of Nadine Strossen, Submitted to the Senate Judiciary Committee, December 4, 2001.

9. Aryeh Neier, "The Miliary Tribunals on Trial," *New York Review of Books*, February 14, 2002, 11–15; Ronald Dworkin, "The Threat of Patriotism," *New York Review of Books*, February 28, 2002, 44–49. Unfortunately, the use of military tribunals for civilians was largely supported by the leading American constitutional analyst Laurence Tribe in "Trial by Fury," *New Republic*, December 10, 2001, (online: www.tnr.com/121001/tribe121001.html).

10. ACLU Press Release, "ACLU Files First Post–September 11 Challenge to Closed Immigration Hearings on Behalf of MI Congressman and Journalists" (online: www.aclu.org/news/2002/n012902a.html).

Introduction

Freedom of Speech and the Paradox of Rights

Freedom of speech is the classic liberal right. Controversies that involve the question of free speech have also been key chapters in the political and legal history of the United States. Such conflict has influenced American political and legal development as the memories of earlier struggles become part of the contemporary national fabric and constitute the sociolegal parameters within which current challenges to the boundaries of America's tolerance are adjudicated. Having said just this much, however, we have traveled far. We have treaded a path from liberalism's seemingly abstract rights to the substantive commitments of nationalism. While this is a road often traveled, how we get from point A, liberalism, to point B, nationalism, is not well understood. In this book I shall elaborate the route whereby liberal rights are connected with nationalism.

Ronald Dworkin famously describes rights as "trumps" for the individual against the community.[1] Communitarians appropriate this description of liberal rights to suggest what is wrong with the excessive rights consciousness of the liberal legal culture that predominates, unfortunately in their view, in the United States.[2] Liberals and communitarians, therefore, invoke an instrumental conception of legal rights by calling them "trumps." Liberal legal rights, according to this view, are nonsocial forms that can be used instrumentally within society to preserve a space of freedom for an individual to believe or speak to beliefs contrary to what the community considers to be its welfare. Where liberals and communitarians differ is their judgment of where final commitments should lie. Liberals value legal rights because they are thought to protect the individual against temporarily impassioned majorities. And communitarians argue that legal rights ought to be limited for the good of the community—when individuals assert legal rights, they fray the social bonds that hold

1

together the community. Interestingly, scholars who are influenced by various forms of critical theory tend also to share this conceptualization of rights.[3] In this book I will argue against this very common understanding of rights as asocial trumps for a disembodied subject.

If these analysts of various stripes are correct to describe rights like free speech as trumps for abstract individuals, then there is an apparent paradox. Most theorists lead us to believe that liberalism constrains or weakens a collective subject like the nation on behalf of the individual, and yet historically liberalism and nationalism have shared a coeval existence. The familiar communitarian critique of the U.S. legal order is that it has failed to balance properly individual rights against the needs of the national community and that it has veered dangerously toward the individualism of liberalism since the founding of the Constitution.[4] This critique and others like it are faced with a historical problem: the high points of liberal legalism have coincided with the high points of nationalism, the archetypically "modern" form of community power. For instance, it is a staple of courses on U.S. constitutional law that *Lochner v. New York* (1905), in which the Supreme Court struck down maximum hours legislation for bakers, symbolizes the extreme liberalism of the "night watchman state" of early-twentieth-century jurisprudence.[5] Paradoxically, the late nineteenth and early twentieth centuries are also known as a period of extreme if not chauvinistic American nationalism. Interestingly, the very same year that *Lochner* was decided, the Court came to a rather different decision regarding individual rights in *Jacobson v. Massachusetts*. In this case, the Supreme Court noted the judgment of "most civilized nations," by which it meant "most nations of Europe," that vaccinations are legitimate means to prevent the spread of disease, and argued that a man does not have the right to refuse a forcible invasion of his body by the state—the right to refuse to be vaccinated—because of the overriding interests in public health. Moreover, shortly after the Court decided *Lochner*, it ruled in *Muller v. Oregon* that maximum hours legislation for women is constitutional because of a public interest in healthy mothers to "preserve the strength and vigor of the race" and to ensure the "future well-being of the race."[6] Rather than an abstract, disembodied juridical subject, the Court during this high point of liberal legalism seems to be elaborating a national grammar within which different substantive national subject positions fit, with each playing a specific role in the overall functioning of the system to reproduce this national formation.

So if we follow conventional theory, we have a seeming contradiction. If liberal rights are so abstract and disembodied, then why is there such a historical intersection between liberalism, which is advertised as being so abstract and universal on the one hand, and nationalism, which is advertised as being so substantively committed to a particular social group, on the other? In this book, I will show how liberalism and nationalism are correlated under "modern" conditions, and in fact may function to intensify each other. This challenges the typical assessments that lead us, falsely, to describe liberalism as antithetical to nationalism.

When we study legal rights, we should treat them the way we would any other piece of textual evidence and study the context in which the invocation of such rights is meaningful. In the United States, part of the context for claiming rights like freedom of speech is the U.S. Constitution. Rather than locating sovereignty in the state, the U.S. Constitution reflects and creates a new sovereignty—the American people. The rights guaranteed by the Constitution and by the Bill of Rights are properly understood as the "rights of the people." The First Amendment, for example, protects the "right of *the people* peaceably to assemble." Others of the Bill of Rights also indicate "the people" as the referent of the relevant right. Furthermore, Supreme Court jurisprudence also refers to free speech (among other rights) as a right of the "people."[7] This fact has important implications for the practice of rights in the United States. One becomes legally authorized to speak by becoming embodied as a national subject—as an American— and not as an abstract or disembodied subject.

When one claims a constitutional right like freedom of speech, one is incorporated within legal discourse as an American because such rights are *reserved for the American people.* This is not, however, an instance of a passive subject being acted upon or repressed by power. One gains a subject position that allows conduct. One seeks to invoke this form of discursive power in order to gain recognition as one who exercises a right to free speech legitimately. In the moment of claiming a right, one also refers to others as the American public with the aspiration that this call will result in a public that will recognize the practice in question as an instance of "free speech" rather than as a social problem that must be governed differently to promote the welfare of the people. In this process of discursive struggle, much depends upon which elements that might constitute an American are constellated together, which are cast off, and whether a given articulation can foster a self-recognition in one exercising judgment.

Finally, much depends upon what sort of an identity the law fixes upon the one claiming a right.

In this way, we are faced with the paradox of rights. The American Constitution announces the judgment of the American people that its right to free speech should be protected. But the same gesture that establishes the possibility for claiming a right to free speech in this context limits the recognition of this right according to the logic of American and non-American. Thus, one gains a platform to claim rights at the very moment when liberal claims to abstraction and universality are contradicted. But this very platform, which also contradicts the communitarian position that rights practices necessarily dismember the body politic, constitutes the limit to legitimate rights claims, making plain the unfortunate exclusivity of the communitarian position.

In the U.S. context, rights are connected with national identity, and this is illustrated by the Supreme Court's jurisprudence. For example, the Supreme Court finds that to punish a military deserter with the loss of citizenship violates the Constitution's Eighth Amendment protection against cruel and unusual punishment. By losing his status as one of the American people, the expatriate has "lost the right to have rights," becoming invisible in a world organized around national states.[8] One's existence as a rights-bearing subject is inextricably linked to one's national identity. Moreover, we can see how being one of the American people regulates the perception of legitimate speech rights by taking the particularly obvious example of cases where immigrants are deported or excluded from entry to the United States for political reasons.

In 1903, Congress enacted legislation providing for the exclusion and deportation of alien anarchists. John Turner, a subject of Ireland and Great Britain who was to give a number of lectures in the United States, was arrested in New York City, imprisoned at Ellis Island, and ordered deported on the basis of this immigration legislation for being an anarchist. Turner challenged his imprisonment and deportation order. When the case reached the Supreme Court, it upheld his removal and exclusion despite Turner's contention that the law violated his First Amendment right to free speech. In *U.S. ex rel. John Turner v. Williams*, Chief Justice Fuller argued that the Court was "at a loss to understand" how this legislative act violated the First Amendment. According to Fuller, Turner "does not become one of *the people* to whom these things are secured by our Constitution by an attempt to enter, forbidden by law."[9] Because the American people's rights are protected from governmental usurpation by the Constitution, one must be an American to claim *this* people's rights.

These issues were replayed when Ernest Mandel, a journalist and Marxist scholar, was denied a temporary visa to attend various academic conferences in the United States. In this case, we can see how the terrain of legal debate is structured by the American people. The Supreme Court upheld Mandel's exclusion because the power to exclude aliens is "inherent in sovereignty, necessary for maintaining normal international relations and defending this country against foreign encroachments and dangers."[10] In dissent, Justice Douglas argued that even assuming those on the outside seeking admission "have no standing to complain" about their exclusion, "those who hope to benefit from the traveler's lectures do." Thus, Douglas accepted that one must be part of the American people to claim that one's speech rights have been infringed upon. He disagreed with the majority in this case by arguing that the government sought to assume "guardianship over the public mind," in violation of the First Amendment.[11] In other words, the government violated the First Amendment by seeking to control the American public's beliefs, not by violating Mandel's rights. Justice Marshall also dissented, finding a violation of the "liberty of American citizens"—a violation of "Americans' First Amendment rights." For Marshall, the "rights of Americans" were involved because they wished to hear Mandel.[12] Thus, regardless of support for or opposition to the constitutionality of the application of the 1952 Immigration and Nationality Act to this case, the argument turned on American identity in each instance. The rights at stake were those of *Americans*, not of an abstract, disembodied juridical subject.[13]

While the force of nationalism is particularly obvious at the borders where insider and outsider are distinguished by the state's policing of immigration, I contend that this force pervades the practice of First Amendment rights. In *Young v. American Mini Theatres*, Justice Stevens describes a "profound national commitment to the principle that debate on public issues should be uninhibited, robust, and wide-open." He goes on to argue, however, that society's interest in protecting indecent sexual expression is of a "wholly different, and lesser, magnitude than interest in untrammeled political debate." Because, as we shall see in chapter 6, Americans are identified as civilized and decent, it does not violate the First Amendment rights of Americans for governments to regulate sexually indecent expression. Few of us, Stevens argues, "would march our sons and daughters off to war to preserve the citizen's right to see 'Specified Sexual

Activities' exhibited in the theaters of our choice."[14] By constituting the legitimate American citizen's interests in accordance with norms of decency, Stevens is able to uphold the regulation of sexual expression without violating the right of the people to speak freely. Sexual expression, on this view, is a problem to be addressed for the welfare of the people since *this* people is identified by its decency and civility. *Stevens is securing the subject who has a First Amendment right to speak.* Thus, questions regarding the power to exclude in order to preserve the sovereignty of the nation extend beyond immigration law because a nation is an imagined community, meaning that its security must be perpetually reachieved; because humans constantly engage in interpretive acts, their identities are never fully established once and for all.[15]

Despite the fact that the American people is the sovereign and the referent of rights in the U.S. constitutional system, the word *person* does appear in the Constitution. Does this indicate that an abstract subject of rights is truly at the heart of the U.S. Constitution? My answer is no, although I will complicate this answer slightly in the Conclusion. For now, I must emphasize that the meaning of constitutional rights is nothing other than the way that they are materialized through various legal interpretive practices, and as I have shown through the cases already cited, the question of rights is closely articulated to the problem of national identity. Although the Supreme Court has acknowledged in various circumstances rights for noncitizens, their rights have been limited in U.S. constitutional history. For instance, the Court recognizes that Congress has plenary power over immigration and naturalization. Thus, it holds congressional action in this domain to very deferential levels of scrutiny, meaning that the Court will defer to whatever Congress judges to be in the nation's interest.[16]

When a state, rather than Congress, attempts to regulate matters relating to noncitizens, the Court heightens its scrutiny, in part because the state is understood as potentially infringing upon the powers and responsibilities of Congress in violation of the Supremacy Clause of the Constitution. Despite this, the Court has permitted states to discriminate against aliens in favor of citizens when there are core public interests at stake. For example, citizenship has been held to be a valid qualification for employment in a police force because the police function is a "most fundamental obligation of government to its constituency." The exclusion of aliens has also been upheld when extended to public school teachers because of the importance of public schools to the "preparation of individuals for participation as citizens" and the "preservation of the values on which our society rests," and because of the significance of the teacher as a "role model for his students, exerting subtle but important influence over their perceptions and values." The teacher, according to the Court, can influence the "attitude of students toward government, the political process, and a citizen's social responsibilities. This influence is crucial to the good health of a democracy."[17] Thus, when it comes to securing national subjects and their reproduction in a variety of registers—legal, political, or social—citizenship-based discriminations are allowable despite the Court's "sometime" treatment of alienage as a suspect criterion of classification in the context of state legislation.[18] The good health of a democracy rests in part upon there being a *people* to exercise the powers of the people.

Could it be the case that the schizophrenia that the Court exhibits in its jurisprudence regarding noncitizens is a reflection of ambivalence over what constitutes a nation? There are many signifiers of nationality—language, territory, and blood are three customary ones—and it is possible that the shifts in jurisprudence that we see may reflect shifts from a biopolitical conceptualization of America as a people to a conceptualization of America defined territorially.[19] Although a territorially based notion of America can easily fold back into a biopolitical conception when the Court refers to the norms of "civilized nations" as it looks for guidance on how to govern and secure America's territorial boundaries, the fact that there is a gap or play between different conceptualizations of what it means to be American is worth emphasizing. No single conceptualization of the American nation could totally control all questions of nationality, precisely because the nation is an "imagined community"—a construct—rather than something that really and objectively exists separately from attempts to represent it.[20] Any one invocation of the nation, then, will be found lacking in some way and will have to be supplemented for the nation to continue to be viable in changing circumstances. Rather than being something totally solid, the nation exhibits a certain indeterminacy in the varied ways that it is brought to life in representational form. The very fact of these gaps, however, means that in the short term there are spaces that may be strategically appropriated in the interests of justice, as the Court did in its decision invalidating a Texas statute denying free public education to the children of illegal aliens.[21] Longer term, the maintenance of the nation is a struggle to overcome the fact of these gaps, and thus these gaps represent the possibility that something better might one day emerge from popular efforts, that change in a nonnationalistic direction is possible.

But even if the word *person* is used in the Constitution, how does this influence the adjudication of disputes? The norms by which the legal significance of *person* is interpreted extend a disciplinary effect beyond the question of visa status to that of general social government. For example, Reconstruction-era civil rights legislation defines the standards by which violations of rights shall be recognized. According to civil rights law, "All persons within the jurisdiction of the United States shall have the same right in every State and Territory to make and enforce contracts . . . [etc.] as is enjoyed by white citizens."[22] In the Civil Rights Act of 1866, a key part of the legal foundation for the current protection of civil rights, we can see how the rights of "persons" are protected based on the norm of "white citizens" within the jurisdiction of the United States. Thus, in order not to appear out of place in America, governing one's self according to the basis of "whiteness" helps.

In sum, to adjudicate a question of rights is in some measure, then, to adjudicate the identity of the American people. What identity is given to the "American people," I find, helps to determine whether a given act is an instance of "free speech" that is protected by the Constitution's First Amendment, or whether it constitutes a social problem that is policed legitimately in the social interests of the American body politic. As long as the American Constitution provides the relevant context of rights claiming, the possibility of having one's speech rights protected is contingent upon being recognized as an American. This possibility of recognition, in turn, is inextricably linked to the normalizing and exclusive patterns of national identity politics. Rather than wholesale utopianism or cynicism, this book is poised at a constant three-dimensional awareness of possibility, incompletion, and danger in its assessments of the practice of rights.

The book is organized historically. Chapter 1 is devoted to the claims of early Americans that the British were violating the "rights of Englishmen" and the founding of the U.S. Constitution to protect the "rights of the people." This chapter shows that the protection of rights and the founding of the nation occurred simultaneously, and that the rights claimed in the Declaration of Independence and inscribed within the Bill of Rights are the rights of a national people, not of abstract, generic persons. Arguing against those who posit a mutually hostile separation between nationalism and legal rights, I show how law and society, the latter figured nationally, are mutually constitutive, such that national identity is a basis on which to justify rights claims, and rights claims like the Declaration of Independence function to constitute a national people.

Chapter 2 takes up the tendency to frame First Amendment controversies over free speech as a face-off between liberal rights and nationalism. In particular, this framework is used to understand the emergence of the "modern First Amendment" as President Wilson sought national conformity in wartime through legislation that is commonly perceived today to have violated the First Amendment rights of those penalized under the Acts of 1917 and 1918. First Amendment scholarship attempts to portray opposition to Wilson's policies by John Burgess, the founder of the first U.S. graduate program in the social sciences and of political science as an academic discipline in the United States, as a libertarian response to Wilson's nationalism. Against this view, I demonstrate how such scholarship misunderstands the controversy because of a misplaced reliance on the idea that liberalism and nationalism are antithetical. Rather, I show how Burgess's views on constitutional law capture the logic of the U.S. Constitution such that the question of national sovereignty is not opposed to but inhabits the practice of rights like freedom of speech.

Chapters 2 and 3 focus on the racial genealogy of the opposition of Western civilization to savagery and barbarism, which is often used to identify what it means to be an American. Although this racial perception figures heavily in Burgess's definition of Americans who have a right to enjoy rights, free speech discourse has largely forgotten him. But free speech discourse has not forgotten John Stuart Mill. In fact, First Amendment jurisprudence uses Mill as a philosophical standard to measure and govern U.S. legal practices regarding freedom of speech, and Mill also utilized the racial opposition of Western civilization and the savage or barbarian to justify why speech rights were appropriate in the West but out of place in the non-West. Thus, American free speech discourse also incorporates a racialized moral geography whereby standing to claim a right to free speech legitimately is regulated according to the racialized norms of civility and savagery.

Although racial identifications of the American people pervade U.S. law, the racial formation of the American people is not constant over time—indeed, there were important differences between the racial formation of the late nineteenth and early twentieth centuries and the racial formation that emerged during World War I, as I discuss in chapter 2. Yet the governing national formation of the United States has also been organized in opposition to the ideological enemy communism, as it was during the cold war. Chapter 4 compares rights claiming in the cold war and post-1989, indicating how "America" and the "people" were constructed differently in these different periods, and demonstrating how these differences in turn have produced differing patterns in the practice of rights. As America's landscape changes from a global imaginary constructed around communism and anticommunism to a nation located within the civilized West, a change symbolized by the significance of the Rushdie affair to America, the practice of claiming rights becomes racialized such that racially defined minorities suffer burdens that disqualify their voices.

Chapter 5 builds upon the discussion of the Rushdie affair in chapter 4 and extends its analysis of the increasingly racial basis of the post–cold-war American national formation to the controversy over multiculturalism and hate speech codes in the late 1980s and early 1990s. Beginning with the insight of critical legal studies (cls) that law is indeterminate, I find that hate speech codes bear an ambiguous relation to First Amendment values. But such regulations were widely considered to violate the First Amendment in the early 1990s. In chapter 5, I go beyond the cls insight that law is indeterminate to examine how the legal conclusion that hate speech regulations necessarily violate the First Amendment became determined. I find that the simultaneously occurring debates over multiculturalism constructed the American people racially in such a way that American rights were perceived to be violated by hate speech codes, while the rights claims of racialized minorities were dismissed. Then, the now-determined legal conclusion was circulated to undermine multicultural efforts. Thus, identity was used to establish legitimate rights claims and the invocation of rights functioned to construct what it means to be American.[23]

Chapter 6 deals with the recent regulatory interest in nonobscene "indecent" sexual expression, the racial anxieties such legal policies rely upon for their legitimacy, and the race and gender norms they promulgate. This chapter suggests an understanding of rights that extends the insights of Michel Foucault beyond his own published statements on rights as well as much of the scholarship by political and social theorists who have been influenced by his work. Building upon the historical research of the book, the final chapter challenges those who place juridical rights and the governance of populations in separate intellectual categories. Moreover, drawing upon the racial import of a concern for civility that animated so many of the legal controversies discussed in the book, this chapter brings forward more explicitly than much Foucauldian scholarship the way that techniques for governing populations are driven by racial interests.[24] Finally, by highlighting the racial genealogy of "civility," the entire book indicates the subtle ways that unexceptional legal discourse builds upon racial distinctions to motivate citizens to behavior consistent with a population capable of exercising the powers of self-government and to promote an American national identity derivative from racial norms.

There are many studies in which their authors give a preassigned meaning to "free speech" and then impose this external standard upon current events either to castigate or to celebrate the principals involved for their failure or success to act in accordance with this standard. In this book, I argue that there are no legal principles that are self-evident across time and space. Thus, the meaning and applicability of law must be claimed and are inherently contestable. But the stability that the law lacks will not be found in society, despite communitarian efforts. Because of the plural, decentered nature of the social field, efforts must be made to establish social "unities." Thus, claims about the fundamental nature of a national community often tell us more about the interests of those making these proclamations and the temporary constellations of power within a particular location than about the existence of a true and primary community that could serve as reliable referent to solve a given dispute. Therefore, neither law nor society offers an escape route from politics. Instead, law and society are mutually constitutive, such that legal meaning relies on a stable empirical situation while a particular form of social being is defined and distinguished by the law of its existence.

The tendency, however, by both liberals and communitarians to invest legal rights and community with distinct, positive, and preconstituted values that should serve as reference points to solve current controversies, a tendency in mainstream theory that I challenge here, may help to account for the ease with which the insights of liberals and communitarians have been synthesized into a "liberal republicanism" or "liberal communitarianism." But another reason for the ease of synthesis may be that the participants in these debates, unintentionally perhaps, were never far apart to begin with, because recognizing rights for subjects entails producing subjects for rights; liberal rights are given by a national constitution, and the national community's presence is called into being by legal forms. This theoretical insight, however, is not a compromise that solves our problems. Some of the synthetic work of mainstream theory promotes a version of American exceptionalism as it invents a phony coherence for the U.S. system by suggesting that the framers of the Constitution created a unique system in which rights and community are in balance and that a return to these principles would solve contemporary problems.[25] The question of liberal rights is unavoidably linked to the problem of the national community within the U.S. constitutional system, and while claims regarding American identity enable rights to be recognized, such claims are a source of danger from which there is no escape as long as the logic of this system continues to operate. In brief, the way that liberal rights are haunted by the specter of nationalism should be a source of anxiety, not unqualified celebration.

To sum up, I do not shy away from the lack of resolution inherent in the practice of rights under contemporary conditions. Instead, I describe this lack of resolve as fueling ongoing rights practices and use historically situated legal events as means for diagnosing the U.S. national formation at specific junctures. At the same time, I point out the unjust effects that correlate with the way in which rights are adjudicated in historically specific junctures. The discourse of rights I analyze here enables justice to be pursued while constraining at the same time the ways in which justice may be sought according to the parameters of the national people brought to life in a particular claim of right. In this way, I recognize and balance the hopefulness inspired by the perpetual openness of rights in their discursive nature with an awareness of the dangerousness of the mechanisms by which we seek justice or seek to forestall greater oppression presently in the United States.

1

Liberal Legal Rights and the Grounds of Nationalism

Liberalism, a theory of politics beginning from the premise of individualism, and communitarianism, a theory of politics beginning from the premise of an organic social whole, define the opposed poles of "modern" political and legal understanding. While liberals seek to establish universal rights, abstracted from particular social conditions, in order to protect the individual's independence to decide how to make his or her life meaningful, communitarians seek to preserve and strengthen their privileged community because they perceive the welfare of individuals to derive from the health of their community. The primary form of political community within the paradigm of modernity is the nation. This means that the polarity of liberalism and communitarianism is often played out as an opposition between liberalism and nationalism.[1] Many, particularly liberals, portray privileging social group ties like nationalism as "ancient" or "premodern," and suggest that the trend of history is a movement away from such affiliations and toward universal human rights.[2] Communitarians, in fact, often agree with this diagnosis while bemoaning its consequences.[3] Although theory posits an opposition between liberalism and nationalism, I suggest that liberalism and nationalism have coincided historically. Indeed, the very declaration that formed the American nation continues to be invoked as a basic legal document requiring the protection of individual rights. This book examines this coincidence between liberalism and nationalism in the United States by exploring a specific area of constitutional law—the right to freedom of speech.[4] This chapter, however, sets the stage for that effort by investigating constitutional discourse of the eighteenth century more broadly.

Law and legal rights are valuable for liberals because they protect the liberties of the individual against an oppressive community. In one influential formulation, rights are conceptualized as "trumps" for the individual.[5] To describe rights as legal forms that can "trump" community interests in unity is to suggest that rights are instrumental—they are instruments the individual can use to protect him or herself against social or political forces. In this light, liberalism understands law and legal rights in an asocial if not an antisocial manner. Law stands apart from society and can insulate the individual from social and political forces. Indeed, for law to be legitimate in liberal eyes, it must be neutral and therefore refuse to be compromised by political or social interests.[6]

For communitarians individual rights are a problem for the same reason that liberals find them valuable. The communitarian literature also considers rights to be trumps, and this is its problem with rights.[7] When individuals assert their rights, they disrupt the social bonds that hold the community together. Excessive rights claiming can fragment the community, instill alienation among its members as they become divorced from their true identity, and thus lead to a weakening of the social organism. Indeed, for one conservative, the rights revolution in the United States has led to the "disabling of America."[8] Legal rights are asocial if not antisocial instruments that privilege the individual and threaten to weaken the national community.

Giorgio Agamben extends this argument by perceiving a total suspension of legal rights where nationalism is most extreme. In the drive to create a "pure" nation—which entails practices of exclusion or enforced normalization and implies Nazism and genocide generally as its logical extremes—Agamben describes the central space of the Holocaust, the concentration camp, as a place where law is meaningless. He finds contemporary analogues to the concentration camp in spaces that perform nationalism's sifting of impurities to maintain or strengthen the health of the body politic, such as the *zones d'attentes* in French international airports where foreigners may be held. Agamben describes these spaces as zones outside of the legal process where law fails to rise above a factual or social situation.[9] Agamben suggests an opposition between legality and the social practice of nationalism by declaring law's absence from those places where the nationalist logic of inclusion and exclusion is vividly and violently materialized.

In this chapter, I challenge the simple opposition between liberal legal rights and the social formation of the nation. I do so by investigating the discursive patterns of rights claiming during the transition from the late colonial period to the early national period in U.S. history. My examination shows how the fates of liberalism and nationalism have become linked such that liberal rights and the national community are better understood as historically joined partners in justice and its lack. Before proceeding, however, I consider in more detail Agamben's contrast between the biopolitical aspects of nationalism and the rule of law. In so doing, I suggest the possibility of a more complex relationship between law and nationalism, which in turn will become empirically manifest in my treatment of late-eighteenth-century American politics.

The Law of Peoples

In his ambitious study, Agamben describes spaces like concentration camps and *zones d'attentes* where national identity and difference are sifted as places where "law is suspended" in a permanent state of exception:

> [The] camp is thus the structure in which the state of exception—the possibility of deciding on which founds sovereign power—is realized *normally....* This is why in the camp the *quaestio iuris* is, if we look carefully, no longer strictly distinguishable from the *quaestio facti*, and in this sense every question concerning the legality or illegality of what happened there simply makes no sense. *The camp is a hybrid of law and fact in which the two terms have become indistinguishable.*[10]

For Agamben, the camp and other such zones where "biopolitics" is carried out most obviously—the Italian stadium in Bari where Albanian refugees were gathered before being returned to their country is yet another example—are places central to modern politics. Zones like the death camps, according to Agamben, are spaces where "power confronts nothing but pure life, without any mediation." Agamben's adoption of Michel Foucault's term "biopolitics" refers to the way that politics no longer is just about *a way of* life but has centered on *biological* life itself (which the Greeks excluded from political space), making the life and health of the population a central political preoccupation. When mass life is a constant political question, mass death is a constant political possibility.

The dangers of biopolitics, however, are not limited to special zones devoted to such purposes. In one section devoted specifically to Carl Schmitt, the well-known German legal philosopher who became a supporter of the Nazi regime, Agamben suggests that whenever concepts such as "good morals," "public security and order," or a "concept such as the National Socialist notion of race" invade law, the latter becomes "indeterminate," and a judge, civil servant, or anybody who must deal with such notions is faced with a situation in which "the distinction between life and politics, between questions of fact and questions of law, has literally no more meaning."[11] Here Agamben is drawing upon Schmitt's theory of the sovereign decision and arguing that its dangerous implications have pervaded modern political life. Agamben's attempt to put the fear of the biopolitical devil in us, however, does not give due emphasis to some of Schmitt's insights, and in this failure implies an inadequate opposition between law and nationalism whereby human rights can be saved and nationalism contained by a return to a formalistic rule of law. In making this critique, I am not downplaying the dangers of biopolitics; rather, I am suggesting that they are not escaped as easily as Agamben's framing of the issue might suggest.

According to Schmitt, all law is situational law because chaos has no law.[12] The sovereign is the one who produces a factual situation or a given social order and guarantees its existence. Only when there is a "normal" situation can a norm define this state of affairs and distinguish it from other possible situations or social orders. A normal situation is therefore a prerequisite for legal validity, and the sovereign is the one who decides whether this normal situation indeed exists. Correspondingly, an "exception" is a situation of extreme peril or a danger to the existence of the state. Under such emergency conditions, the state's sovereign will suspend ordinary law to exercise the state's right of self-preservation. Agamben argues that during such states of exception, there is no law, only the unmediated sovereign power to decide what is necessary to preserve the state. Nevertheless, we should realize that sovereign power and decision making continue to exist *in relation* to law during a state of exception.[13]

Schmitt puts sovereignty and the state of exception in relation to law. In his 1922 study *Political Theology*, Schmitt describes sovereign power in the state of emergency as follows: "[The sovereign] decides whether there is a state of emergency as well as what must be done to eliminate it. Although he stands outside the normally valid legal system, *he nevertheless belongs to it*, for it is he who must decide whether the constitution needs to be suspended in its entirety."[14] Moreover, Schmitt argues that because "the exception is different from anarchy and chaos, order in the juristic sense still prevails even if it is not of the ordinary kind."[15] Indeed, there must be an underlying rule or principle that guides decision making even in a state of exception. Sovereignty and sovereign decisions cannot be a case of "anything goes," because that would be chaos, something incompatible with a given state or decisions made with the purpose of protecting the state's fundamental nature. Decisions will be made in accordance with preserving a particular state. Therefore, the exercise of sovereign power in a state of exception cannot be described the way Agamben does as power unmediated by law or as a simple suspension of law. Sovereignty must remain bound by law or else it disappears and no longer exists because only in chaos can law of any sort be lacking totally. Sovereignty is both political and juristic, but not purely one or the other. We should describe the sovereign's existence paradoxically as being *before* the law—as giving the law while also having been given by the law.[16]

While it is beyond the scope of this chapter to engage directly with Agamben's empirical claims or theoretical argument as a whole, this paradoxical nature of sovereignty provides a key to a more sophisticated understanding of America's foundation than does the simple opposition of law and the biopolitical drives of nationalism.[17] In many ways, the paradox of sovereignty and the complex relationship between liberal legal rights and nationalism are condensed within the American Declaration of Independence, which both founds a nation *and* serves as a source for ongoing rights claims.[18] In what follows, we shall see that, on the one hand, Americans of the second half of the eighteenth century justified their rights claims based on their *identity*—as the posterity of Englishmen, they claimed the rights of Englishmen as their birthright. On the other hand, legal declarations are constitutive of the distinctiveness of the American people; Americans are born in their claim to rights. Law and society—in this case, law and nation—are not opposed categories; they are linked. This is not to say, however, that they are identical—there is a gap of difference just as there is a gap between a signifier and signified that constitutes the possibility of communication.[19] This gap creates the possibility and the need to *claim* one's rights because there is always the possibility, as the British Americans of the 1760s and 1770s learned, that such claims may not be successful at winning over their target audience.[20] Moreover, as many concerned with civil rights are learning today, unless one continues faithfully to outperform one's detractors, one risks losing one's hard-won audience, hence one's rights.

The Ancient Constitution, Norman Yoke, and the Rights of Englishmen in British American Discourse

The British Americans claimed that their rights under the British constitution were being infringed upon by acts of Parliament in the 1760s and 1770s. If the British government did not recognize these rights in the colonies, then English constitutional history provided the Americans a script to follow, into which the Americans narrated themselves.[21] The script was familiar: British Americans widely consumed the stories of the British struggle during the seventeenth century to reclaim their ancient constitution and constitute themselves properly as English by recovering their free origins against a tyrannical monarchy. Ultimately, the British Americans would invoke and extend this narrative by breaking their ties with the British government in order to preserve their identity as a people to whom freedoms are legitimately entrusted.

The rights the British Americans claimed in the period leading up to the American Revolution were "British liberties" or the "rights of Englishmen." By claiming *these* rights, the British Americans were drawing upon British constitutional discourse. Constitutional argument in England from the sixteenth through the eighteenth centuries (if not earlier) was dominated by variations upon the theme of an ancient constitution, Norman Conquest, and a reconnection of the English with their ancient Anglo-Saxon liberties. In broad strokes, the story goes as follows. Before 1066 the Anglo-Saxon inhabitants of England enjoyed great freedoms and were self-governing through representative institutions. At the hands of William and the Norman Conquest, however, all of this was set at naught, and the English were deprived of their liberty at the hands of a tyrannical foreign power that brought feudal social arrangements to the island. The English, being a freedom-loving people, did not forget the rights they had lost and fought with varying success to retrieve their ancient liberties. The Magna Carta, for example, is one such instance of the English winning back portions of their heritage.[22]

The Norman Conquest was thus an apparent breach in the continuity of English history. This led to struggles over how to interpret this event. These struggles, in turn, had important implications for the status of rights and privileges. Common law lawyers interested in preserving the continuity of England's law often denied the fact of a conquest or asserted that William I had confirmed various rights rather than imposed foreign laws. Moderates and radicals, however, tended to associate whatever was not conducive to liberty with the Norman Conquest—a foreign imposition. Therefore, arguments for various liberties generally took the form of rediscovering ancient Anglo-Saxon rights and privileges while eradicating corrupt foreign (French) influences from English law. One moderate form of Whig history identified the Glorious Revolution and its aftermath of parliamentary sovereignty within a balanced constitution as the reachievement of the ancient Anglo-Saxon constitution. This, in fact, was Thomas Jefferson's interpretation of British history. In sum, claiming rights and protecting the British constitution were linked to questions of the nation, English identity, and a hardening of boundaries between inside and outside.[23]

American political science and legal scholarship conventionally interpret the process of asserting rights against the British in the period leading up to the American Revolution and culminating in the Declaration of Independence as a process of putting John Locke's defense of natural rights in his *Second Treatise* into political and legal practice.[24] Since the publication of Bernard Bailyn's *Ideological Origins of the American Revolution* and Gordon Wood's *Creation of the American Republic*, however, the important influence of the Whig view of history, republican political thought, and ancient constitutionalism on the revolutionaries and framers of the U.S. Constitution has been uncovered. The discursive diversity of this period is significant because it suggests that the American Revolution was not an immaculate conception. That is, various American constitutional documents such as the Declaration of Independence and the Bill of Rights are not representations of natural rights inscribed upon a blank album, justified through their basis in a universal reason abstracted from particular historical circumstances. The British Americans appropriated the same discourses of ancient Anglo-Saxon liberties protected by the British constitution as the Whigs in Britain did. The British Americans relied upon their identity with the English in common origins predating written history to justify their claims upon rights.

The narrative of the ancient constitution was not an entirely unproblematic means for justifying rights for the British Americans—this constitutional narrative justified the sovereignty of the British Parliament. Though in England a Whig might plausibly argue that to defend parliamentary sovereignty was a sign of defending the rights of Englishmen, in North America the sign and its referent were disarticulated because of the Parliament-imposed burdens the Americans believed violated their rights. How, then, did the British Americans derive their rights from the British constitution while marking their difference from the English represented in Parliament?

Gaps and Indeterminacy Incite the Need to Claim

The repeated assertions of the rights of Englishmen on the part of British Americans should indicate if nothing else an anxiety about a relationship so tenuous that it needed to be continuously reaffirmed and recreated. At first blush, there was an apparent contradiction in the American position. While the Americans attempted to claim the rights of Englishmen, they also denied the legitimacy of the British Parliament to tax them or to regulate their internal polity, and only grudgingly conceded, through tacit consent, British power to regulate their external trade. Somehow they needed to forge an identity that would allow them to maintain their position rightfully.

The main complication, constitutionally speaking, for the relation between the American colonies and the English Parliament came with the celebrated Glorious Revolution. Its aftermath established parliamentary sovereignty, signified by the new coronation oath by which monarchs swore to govern the kingdom of Great Britain and its dominions according to the "Statutes in Parliament agreed on."[25] This result was celebrated by many as the restoration of the ancient constitution. With the monarch subordinated to Parliament, denying parliamentary sovereignty was to deny the British constitution, something for the Americans to negotiate very carefully since the Whig view of history held a position of major significance in America as well as in England.

The stakes were significant. If the Americans did not obey the law, in the eyes of one British observer, then "they say in effect that they will no longer be a part of the British Empire." The Americans, however, based their rights claims of consensual governmental authority, opposition to taxation, and other measures on the rights of Englishmen. Furthermore, they did not necessarily want to cut themselves off from the world's greatest tradition of liberty, the British constitution. John Dickinson, a reluctant revolutionary, expressed the latter sentiment when he attempted to create this middle position of protesting the violations of rights yet endeavoring to dissuade from actual severing of ties: "Torn from the body, to which we are united by religion, liberty, laws, affections, relation, language, and commerce, we must bleed at every vein." And as John Adams understood it, "England has been a principal bulwark . . . of civil liberty and the Protestant religion in all Europe." The Americans saw themselves as the same people, part of the same national body, as the English, such that any severance would cause severe bleeding, if not death. Furthermore, this was not just any people, but one on which the world's liberty and enlightenment depended.[26]

The Americans attempted to negotiate this quandary by using feudal concepts of personal "legeance," asserting their allegiance to the king's natural person rather than the crown in Parliament. John Adams's arguments to this effect won him Charles McIlwain's praise as one of the intellectual founders of the twentieth-century theory of the British Commonwealth. But this move, while eluding, theoretically, Parliament's power, did so at the risk of giving up claim to the rights of Englishmen. As McIlwain states, discussing various key precedents relating to the issue, "The post-natal Scots were not subject to English laws or an English parliament. They were subject only to the King and their own laws and parliament, but they had no rights of Englishmen."[27]

For a variety of reasons, not least of which was the issue of tacit consent to the coronation and the fact that various acts of Parliament had been consented to, the Americans were in a very indeterminate position. They needed to mark out precisely in what ways they were the same as the English, and in what ways they were different, without becoming an absolute Other. They could not be the same as the English, or else Parliament would have sovereignty over them. The theory of virtual representation would suggest that the members of the political community are fundamentally similar such that coming to a consensus representing a general will, as opposed to a negotiated compromise between several independent, different, or antagonistic wills, ought to be possible; according to republican theory shared by the English and the British Americans, even necessary. Americans saw British members of Parliament, however, as legislating at "so great a distance" from them that they were "little acquainted with our circumstances, and not immediately affected with ye taxes laid upon us."[28] British law misfires on North American grounds.

Claiming Identity to Claim Rights

When arguing for their rights, the British Americans used a narrative of a people migrating to a new land, suggesting both connection to the origin of rights and a spatial relation of difference from the government that sought to rule over them. John Adams, in his *Novanglus* letters, frequently referred to "British" or "English" liberties. For Adams, the emigration of the colonists' ancestors both constituted and bridged a gap between England and America:

> English liberties are but certain rights of nature, reserved to the citizen, by the English constitution, *which rights cleaved to our ancestors, when they crossed the Atlantic,* and would have inhered in them, if instead of coming to New England they had gone to Outaheite, or Patagonia, even although they had taken no patent or charter from the king at all. *These rights did not adhere to them* the less, for their purchasing patents and charters, in which the king expressly stipulates with them, that they and their posterity should forever enjoy all those rights and liberties.[29]

Americans had rights because rights adhered to the bodies of the ancestors of the Americans who then populated North America.

On the one hand, Adams saw in England corruption leading to a decline practically to Roman depths. On the other hand, English liberties cleaved to the bodies of those who traveled to America. In this light, the migration allowed the possibility that the essence of the British constitution might be saved from corruption in America. Adams taunted the British:

> [I]f we enjoy, and are entitled to more liberty than the British constitution allows, where is the harm? Or, if we enjoy the British constitution in greater purity and perfection than they do in England, as is really the case, whose fault is this? Not ours.[30]

The Americans had brought the British constitution to a greater degree of purity than the English themselves because these embodied rights were taken from one environment where there was decline and implanted in another untouched by foreign corruption. Adams, therefore, argued that nipping the shoots of arbitrary power in the bud was necessary to preserve the liberties of any people and that British oppression was a cancer encroaching upon the virtue of the American people.[31]

Adams recognizes, in his discussion of the Welsh, that a country can owe allegiance to the natural person of the king but that this does not guarantee the enjoyment of the rights of Englishmen. Yet he can maintain the position that "Americans are entitled to all the liberties of Englishmen, and that they are not bound by any acts of parliament whatever . . . excepting those for the regulation of trade, which they have consented to and acquiesced in."[32] Considering the Welsh precedent, it seems that the weight of his arguments in favor of recognizing the rights of Englishmen for Americans rests on ancestry and migration.

The tendency for Americans to assert their Englishness as a mechanism for claiming rights by telling varieties of stories about their ancestors deriving from England and migrating to America was widespread.[33] In "The Bill of Rights [and] a List of Grievances" (1774), the American colonists began with the constitutional quandary: "Whereas, since the close of the last war, the British parliament claiming a power, of right to bind the *people of America*, by statute in all cases . . ." Then they listed various grievances and violations of constitutional right (from their perspective), which they declared to be "contrary to the rights of the *people*." The meaning and legitimacy of this declaration rode in part upon the construction given to the word *people*. Who was this "people"? The colonists gave an answer that also put their Declaration into the tradition of the ancient constitution, using the Whig view of history as the narrative context for their actions and therefore their identity:

> Whereupon the deputies . . . do in the first place, as *Englishmen their ancestors* in like cases have usually done, for asserting and vindicating their rights and liberties, DECLARE . . .

The Americans described their territory as "English colonies in North-America," derived their rights from the "laws of nature, principles of the English constitution, and the several charters or compacts," and resolved that

> our ancestors, who first settled these colonies, were at the time of their emigration from the mother country, entitled to all the rights, liberties, and immunities of free and natural born subjects, within the realm of England.

The Americans then went on to argue that "by such emigration they by no means forfeited, surrendered, or lost any of those rights," and that their descendants were now entitled to those rights.[34] In "A Declaration . . . Setting forth the Causes and Necessity of their Taking up Arms" (1775), a Dickinson and Jefferson collaboration, the Americans argue:

Our forefathers, inhabitants of the island of Great Britain, left their native land, to seek on these shores a residence for civil and religious freedom. At the expense of their blood, at the hazard of their fortunes, without the least charge to the country from which they removed, by unceasing labor and an unconquerable spirit, they effected settlements in the distant and inhospitable wilds of America, then filled with numerous war-like nations of barbarians.

Furthermore,

Honor, justice, and humanity forbid us tamely to surrender that freedom which we received from our gallant ancestors, and which our innocent posterity have a right to receive from us.[35]

Thus, a narrative of rights claiming derived from British constitutional discourse provided the British Americans with a structure within which to situate their arguments in a manner that would be comprehensible and compelling to their British and American audiences. By appropriating the resources this discourse provided in different circumstances, the Americans could empower themselves against the British government, a government that also derived its legitimacy from this discourse. To borrow the language of John Dickinson, "Changing the word *Stuarts* for *parliament* and *Britons* for *Americans*, the arguments of the illustrious patriots of those times . . . apply with inexpressible force and appositeness, in maintenance of our cause."[36] In order to make the discourse apply in the different geographical circumstances of America, however, the Americans invented themselves as part of the same bloodline as the British by invoking a common Anglo-Saxon past transmitted through descent. The Americans were innovating a racial basis to their national identity, however ambiguous and unstable at that historical moment.[37] The roots of America's most rigidly racial nationalism of the late nineteenth and early twentieth centuries, which I shall discuss in chapter 2—what is known as "Teutonic origins theory"—can be found in Thomas Jefferson's arguments of the late eighteenth century.

Like Adams, Jefferson depended on the authority of ancestral heritage and migration to legitimize the rights he claimed on behalf of British America. Jefferson argued, in "A Summary View of the Rights of British America" (1774), that America was conquered by the ancestors of British Americans, who, "before their emigration to America, were free inhabitants of the British dominions in Europe." The ancestors of the British Americans were acting just like England's ancestors, the Saxons, who "in like manner left their native wilds and woods in the North of Europe," took possession of "the Island of Britain," and "established there that system of laws which has so long been the glory and protection of that country." Jefferson argued that Germany never attempted to claim power over England. If it did, however, Britons would "have too firm a feeling of the rights derived to them from their ancestors, to bow down the sovereignty of their state." Jefferson used the Germanic variant of the Whig view to mark America's similarities and differences from Britain. Just as it would be ludicrous for England to submit its sovereignty to Germany, so it was just as ridiculous for Americans to lay down their forms of self-government before Parliament.[38]

Jefferson believed in the small, independent farmer as the basis for the free republic. Consequently, feudalism was contrary to such republican values. Because, according to Jefferson, the Norman Conquest brought feudalism to England, something that was considered foreign to the laws and values of the "original" Saxons, migration to America meant that America could realize these values to a more pure extent than England. After all, "America was not conquered by William the Norman."[39] Therefore, Americans' claims to their rights cannot be divorced from a simultaneous invention of a national identity that, in resting upon the authority of a people's migration, inaugurated racial concerns with purity and corruption, inside and outside, identity and difference.[40] Claiming rights, on this view, is a moment of deterritorialization and reterritorialization of social identities, in contrast to the usual understandings of rights as antithetical to social identity.

Claiming Rights and Producing a National People: The Declaration of Independence

Not only did the British Americans claim an identity in order to claim rights, as shown in the previous section, but, as I shall demonstrate here, the constant invocation of rights and legal principles called forth a new identity formation—the American nation. This formulation challenges Hannah Arendt's claim that the American Revolution was "unprecedented"—a claim that has received significant scholarly attention.[41] Even Arendt herself, however, is forced to recognize that in fact the founders did cite precedents upon which to base their actions constituting the new nation. The framers were bound to the ancients not by tradition, according to Arendt, but because they needed "models and precedents." A beginning as such is saved from arbitrariness because it carries its own "principle" within itself. Beginning and principle, Arendt states, are *related* to each other and are coeval. One who begins something, Arendt argues, starts by laying down "the law of action for those who have joined him in order to partake in the enterprise and to bring about its accomplishment." In like fashion, we can say that a nation and its fundamental law are born simultaneously and in relation to each other. While in the previous section I emphasize how the British Americans used a narrative of ancestry to create an identity justifying their rights, here I highlight how claiming legal rights produces a corresponding form of subjectivity. By citing legal precedent, the framers of America produce a distinctive national people. Thus, although a certain body politic provided the grounds for rights, this people was identified by their rights and was called into being through the law and legal declarations.[42]

Gordon Wood argues that for most Americans, an "uncorrupted English constitution" was the "model of what a constitution should be." The Americans, according to Wood, were so absorbed in the Commonwealth tradition of English radicalism that "even the destruction of monarchy and the institution of republicanism did not signify a repudiation of the ancient constitution." Rather, the Americans' actions could be perceived as the "greatest glory" of the "British constitution."[43] This argument indicates how the American nation was called into being by legal incantation. For example, John Adams, through his repeated legal citations and invocations of rights, helped to call the American people into existence. Adams argued in his "Dissertation on the Canon and the Feudal Law," "Let us recollect it was liberty, the hope of liberty for themselves and us and ours," that carried the early Americans through their hardships. In this, Americans claimed a legally inspired ancestry: "Let the bar proclaim, 'the laws, the rights, the generous plan of power' delivered down from remote antiquity,—inform the world of the mighty struggles and numberless sacrifices made by our ancestors in defence of freedom." Adams's *Novanglus* letters, moreover, were rife with citations of British precedent. The actions of the British Parliament, according to Adams, were "inconsistent with the right of British subjects." In the face of mounting hostility between the colonies and the British, Adams argued that the patriots desired "nothing new," they wished only to "keep their old privileges."[44] Thus, Adams's arguments invoked not only a social body to which rights could be attached, as discussed in the previous section, but rights that would inspire a corresponding subject.

The Declaration of Independence, however, is perhaps the most celebrated instance of a national people called into existence through the law.[45] From one perspective, the Declaration of Independence marks a failure in the American attempt to claim the rights of Englishmen. From another perspective it represents a successful performative speech act. The rhetorical conventions marking relations of identity and difference with Britain facilitate the legal construction of an American counternation out of the cultural resources provided by the discourse of British constitutionalism. The performative utterance of the Declaration is enabled by the staging provided by the spatial difference of America in relation to Great Britain, the negotiation of these relations of identity and difference through the narrative of migration, and the discourse of the ancient constitution. In order to recognize these ancient rights, the Declaration as a legal action dismembers one population, "British America," and forms an American national body. The Declaration breaks and founds.

Jefferson's version of the Declaration of Independence enacts a painful process of cutting and reconstituting. After a series of protests that the Declaration lodges against the king, the document turns to the British people.

> Nor have we been wanting in attentions to our British brethren. . . . We have reminded them of the circumstances of our emigration and settlement here . . . we have appealed to their native justice and magnanimity [as well as to] the tyes of our common kindred to disavow these usurpations, which [were likely to] interrupt our connection & correspondence. They too have been deaf to the voice of justice and of consanguinity, [and when occasions have been given them . . . of removing from their councils the disturbers of our harmony, they have by their free election reestablished them in power. . . . These facts have *given the last stab to agonizing affection; and manly spirit bids us to renounce forever these unfeeling brethren.*] We *must* [*endeavor to forget our former love for them*, and hold them as we hold the rest of mankind, enemies in war, in peace friends. We might have been a free and a great people together. . . . Be it so since they will have it. . . . We will climb (the road of happiness and glory) apart from them, and] acquiesce in the necessity which denounces our eternal separation![46]

This portion of Jefferson's Declaration indicates that the Revolution involved more than merely throwing off a government. It was also a rejection of a people—a reformation of the body politic through the severance of ties to create a new identity as a new national people. The pain, anticipated by Dickinson ("we must bleed at every vein"), is evident in Jefferson's legal text calling forth a new national-legal people ("These facts have given the last stab to agonizing affection").

Jefferson's America endeavors to follow Ernest Renan's insight that in the process of forming a nation, sometimes it "is good for everybody to know how to forget."[47] Jefferson admonishes: "[W]e must endeavor to forget our former love for them." Indeed, Jefferson so succeeded in this endeavor to forget that he would later forget the role of Whig history in the American Revolution. When he wrote to Major John Cartwright toward the end of his life, Jefferson praised his treatment of the English constitution for having deduced it from "its rightful root, the Anglo-Saxon." An encapsulation of the Whig interpretation of history based upon ancient constitutionalism, the violation of these "ancient rights" by "Norman force," and the "re-conquest of [these] rights from the Stuart[s]" then erupted from his pen. Writing in 1824, however, Jefferson forgot the importance Americans placed upon this historical narrative to justify their claims to the rights of Englishmen. At this point, he interjected that "[o]ur Revolution commenced on more favorable ground. It presented us an album on which we were free to write what we pleased."[48] I suggest that this forgetting on the part of Jefferson anticipates a tendency of liberal theory to forget its inheritances and its debts. Indeed, it forgets the paradoxical grounds that enable the sociolegal practice of claiming rights.

Remainders

Of course what is repressed may return with reconstituted force. And so it is with the American people and those who have been excluded to constitute this nation. After a brief and confusing period of governance under the Articles of Confederation, the Americans redeclare themselves a national people through the Constitution. While sovereignty technically remained lodged in the several states under the Articles, a new form of sovereignty is invented in the Constitution—the sovereignty of the people. This move makes the legal basis for national government and the protection of rights consistent with the nationalist claims used to declare rights in the 1770s. Both in the U.S. Constitution and in the declarations leading to the American Revolution, the focus is upon the *rights of the people*. Here I elaborate the boundaries used to identify a distinctive American people and the exclusions produced by these boundaries.

In his opening address to the Pennsylvania ratifying convention, James Wilson reviews the traditional theory of sovereignty—that it must exist in some singular place in a given system—in order to explain the proposed Constitution. Citing William Blackstone, Wilson states that in Great Britain sovereignty resides in Parliament. Where does it lie in the new U.S. Constitution? While some might say it resides in the states, Wilson corrects this misapprehension of the new system. Sovereignty under the Constitution "remains and flourishes with the people."[49]

The "people" is now the foundational referent of power and rights in the American system. The Bill of Rights protects *the people's* liberties—those powers that the people have decided not to delegate to the national government. Echoing the 1774 "Bill of Rights [and] A List of Grievances," which refers to the "people of America" and the "rights of the people," the First Amendment to the Constitution refers to the "right of the people peaceably to assemble." The Fourth Amendment refers to the "right of the people to be secure in their persons, houses [etc.]." Thomas Jefferson in a letter refers to the Constitution as an "instrument of security for the rights of the people."[50] The Constitution secures rights in part by securing a national subject position from which to claim these rights. Neither God nor Philosophy, therefore, is the guarantor of these rights or provides the conditions of justice. This is the function of the people, an entity that is *before the law*, that is both inside and outside this constitution. As I have shown in the previous sections, the people is both legally constituted and a national condition of possibility for claiming rights in this context.

A national people is being invented through these paradigmatic instances of recognizing individual rights. This discourse of rights generates the following logic: to claim rights under the U.S. Constitution, one must declare one's self an American. For this claim to be successful, however, one must be recognizably American. How does one identify an "American"? What are the signs? Many of the Euro-American legal arguments against the British give substance to the "people" on whose behalf rights are being claimed. The signs that function to designate who is included in a claim on rights also function at the same time to designate who is excluded from such a claim. Not just anybody is an American or else the term is meaningless. Consistent with this insight, the Americans distinguished themselves through their rights claims.

While the Declaration castigates the king for behavior "totally unworthy the head of a *civilized* nation," it also locates a boundary, distinguishing the American people from other possible peoples. The Declaration complains that the British have brought upon the inhabitants of "*our* frontiers, the merciless Indian *savages*." (italics mine). Here we can see that the Americans use a discourse that categorizes peoples according to the opposition of civilization versus barbarism and savagery in order to differentiate Americans who are claiming their rights from the indigenous peoples who also happen to live on the continent. Similarly, the "Declaration . . . Setting Forth the Causes and Necessity of Their Taking up Arms" (1775) places the migration of British Americans in the context of America's previous identity as a space filled with inhospitable wilds inhabited by warlike nations of "barbarians." Adams's "Dissertation on the Canon and the Feudal Law" effects the deterritorialization and reterritorialization of this space to which the British Americans migrated: remarking upon the civility amongst the common people of America, Adams goes on to recollect how their ancestors labored in "clearing their grounds . . . amidst dangers from wild beasts and savage men."[51] The drive to create a national people inevitably requires exclusions that produce remainders, and here we can see that the process of identifying the American people as a civilized people excludes the indigenous population from the national imaginary based on the opposition of the "civilized" and the "savage."

Moreover, although observers frequently note that Jefferson's version of the Declaration included a long passage condemning slavery that was edited out by Congress, this effort hardly indicates a racially inclusive vision of the American people in terms of black-white relations. Indeed, this passage betrays Jefferson's great fear of a race war. He condemns the British for inciting insurrections by the slaves against whites, "thus paying off former crimes committed against the *liberties* of one people, with crimes which he urges them to commit against the lives of another."[52] Jefferson may have proposed various ways to bring slavery to an end, and his views on whether blacks were inferior to whites may have been complex, but he doubted very deeply that blacks and whites could become submerged in the same national body. Indeed, Jefferson advocated the removal of blacks from America upon emancipation in his "Notes on the State of Virginia," a position endorsed by Adams and put forward by others. This doubt that blacks and whites could be joined within the same national body became manifest in the Declaration that inscribes several racially distinctive peoples, but declares independence and claims rights for only one of these entities. Thus, when the Declaration refers to the "rights of the people," this is a distinctively bounded social body.[53]

Incorporation

The shift in the location of sovereignty from the state to the people politicizes the American sociolegal body. When we refer to something as political, we suggest that it is in question, that a decision must be made to resolve the question in one way rather than another, and that an effort must be made to resolve the question in one way precisely because its resolution could be otherwise if one does not exert the effort and another does in a contrary manner. In other words, there is conflict and the application of force. For example, the atomic weights of most elements occur naturally, and thus they are open to scientific inquiry but they are not in themselves political. If, however, it becomes possible to manipulate or to alter atomic weights and hence invent new elements, then this process can become political precisely because a decision must be made and justified against other courses of action. A political question can be formed when a space of decision is opened up, created by the possibility of different courses of action and a consideration of the consequences of different courses of action with respect to some standard of interest or value.[54]

The American people is political precisely because it is invented and things could have been otherwise. Furthermore, because new humans can come within the space over which the American people seeks sovereignty (through travel and birth, for example), and because humans constantly are in a process of interpreting themselves and their surroundings (hence the constant possibility of interpreting one's self differently than one did earlier), force must be brought to bear in order to insure the continuation of the "American people," and decisions must be made and defended regarding what it means to be an American. Many Americans are so deeply subjected that it is hard to conceive of themselves as existing otherwise, and thus they have difficulty perceiving the force that is constantly brought to bear to maintain their incorporation as Americans. For others, perhaps those especially who have been excluded from prior acts of incorporation and are contending for inclusion, the force is unmistakable.

A necessary condition for national sovereignty is that a singular national people must be constituted and maintained against the ever-present possibility of social diversity. As is so often the case, Thomas Jefferson's voluminous writings address the question of national unity in an exemplary way. Jefferson identifies three main threats to America's sociolegal security. These perceived threats illustrate the forcefulness of incorporation because of the obvious contingency of perceiving something as a threat and the way that defining a threat reciprocally defines a value or an identity to be secured. Deciding upon a threat to the nation both opens and attempts to foreclose the question of national identity.[55]

According to Jefferson, America's sociolegal security is threatened by immigration, slavery, and the Native Americans. Jefferson's response to these threats is *either* to incorporate new elements within the body politic on the condition that such new elements can be normalized sufficiently, *or* to exclude that which is constructed as different from American identity. Jefferson's treatment of the Native Americans in particular exemplifies this either-or logic of identity.

Jefferson, in his "Notes on the State of Virginia," addresses the "present desire of America" to increase its population as quickly as possible and to that end encourage immigration. By examining census records, Jefferson finds that the population's current rate of increase is to double every 27 1/4 years. Using four and a half million as a "competent" population goal, under generous assumptions Jefferson calculates that encouraging immigration would populate America adequately only twenty-seven years and three months earlier than merely relying on a "natural" rate of increase. He then argues that to seek adequate population through immigration rather than waiting twenty-seven years is shortsighted in light of the dangers of unrestricted immigration.

Jefferson recognizes that locating sovereignty in the American people necessitates the maintenance of this social body according to the norms that make it capable of self-government. As he puts it elsewhere, "our republicanism" is found not just in legal constitutions but also in the "spirit of our people." Therefore, protecting American sovereignty requires protecting the American people. Jefferson fears the effects immigrants socialized under monarchy will have on this free republic. Equally as bad as monarchists, however, are those who throw off monarchy and go too far to the side of "unbounded licentiousness, passing, as is usual, from one extreme to another." Jefferson argues that it would "be a miracle were they to stop precisely at the point of temperate liberty." Good government depends upon the constitution of normative subjects, and unrestricted immigration therefore places the good government of the American people in jeopardy, particularly if these new immigrants pass on their poorly disciplined practices to their children. The outcome of unrestricted immigration, therefore, will be to infuse into American legislation a foreign spirit that will "warp and bias its direction, and render it a heterogeneous, incoherent, distracted mass." American government, Jefferson concludes, would be "safer" and "more homogeneous, more peaceable, more durable" if the nation follows the course of patience rather than the path of open borders. Locating sovereignty in the people incites a politics of identity because it is necessary to identify "the people" out of a heterogeneous social flux and to maintain this national body by force in the face of diverse or contrary social forces. Since the nation is the condition of possibility for American law, failing to defend the American people against unrestricted immigration would result in the destabilization of American law.[56]

Jefferson displays the same attention to unity and the security of American identity in his proposed policies toward blacks as he exhibits in his proposed policy for governing the American population's future increase. In his "Notes on the State of Virginia," and elsewhere, Jefferson counsels the exclusion of further importations of slaves, the emancipation of those who are enslaved, and their removal from America and their colonization elsewhere. To balance the loss inflicted upon the inhabitants of America, equal numbers of whites must migrate to America.[57] "Why not retain and incorporate the blacks into the state?" he asks. Jefferson answers his own question:

> Deep rooted prejudices entertained by the whites; ten thousand recollections, by the blacks, of the injuries they have sustained; new provocations; the real distinctions nature has made; and many other circumstances, will divide us into parties, and produce convulsions which will probably never end but in the extermination of the one or the other race.[58]

Because of the threat of factions and parties to a unified American public posed by irreconcilable difference, fueled in part by memories of oppression too vivid to forget, Jefferson advocates the removal of blacks from America. They cannot be incorporated within America.

Jefferson's treatment of the indigenous peoples in North America particularly exemplifies the either-or logic of identity. The presence of diverse peoples in the same territory challenges Jefferson's efforts to secure the

American people and thus to defend the rule of American law. Jefferson addresses this challenge by encouraging those whom he calls "savage Americans" to discipline themselves and conform to those social norms that Jefferson took to be fundamental to the well-being of the American people if they were to be capable of self government. Those who would agree to adhere to this civilizing process and govern themselves according to these social norms would come within American law and enjoy the rights of the people—they would, that is, become part of the American sociolegal body. Those who resist this call to govern themselves in this manner would have to be removed from national space.[59]

As mentioned above, Jefferson believed that it is "the manners and the spirit of a people which preserve a republic in vigor. A degeneracy in these is a canker which soon eats to the heart of its laws and constitution." Jefferson saw manufacturing, and cities which were associated with it, as corrupters of his free republic's virtue. "[L]et our workshops remain in Europe," Jefferson argued, because the "mobs of great cities add just so much to the support of pure government, as sores do to the strength of the human body." For Jefferson, the way to prevent degeneracy, therefore, was to build upon the social basis of the independent farmer. He argued, "[C]ultivators of the earth are the most virtuous and independent citizens." Jefferson constantly invoked culturally specific farming practices as a norm by which incorporation of various tribes within the national body could be measured.[60]

Jefferson measured the progress various tribes made in entering "modernity" and the American national imaginary by the extent to which they accommodated themselves to Jefferson's idealized farming practices—the independent freehold. As president, Jefferson charted the progress of the Native Americans in many of his messages and addresses to the nation. For Jefferson, if tribes of indigenous peoples would practice these methods of farming, then they could be considered members of the American nation; and the greater their success at these particular farming practices, the more American they were. Thus, in his third annual message, he noted that with "many other Indian tribes, improvements in agriculture and household manufacture are advancing, and with all our peace and friendship are established on grounds much firmer than heretofore."[61]

For these social norms to take effective hold in their target populations, as we have learned from Foucault, the targets themselves need to evaluate and discipline themselves according to these norms.[62] Jefferson sought to incite such self-surveillance amongst various tribes by encouraging a comparative perspective by which tribes and members of tribes would measure their proximity and deviance from Jefferson's Anglo-Saxon ideal of the independent farmer. Jefferson addressed the Choctaw nation:

> I rejoice, brothers, to hear you propose to become cultivators of the earth for the maintenance of your families. Be assured you will support them better and with less labor, by raising stock and bread, and by spinning and weaving clothes, than by hunting. Compared with you, we are but as of yesterday in this land. You see how much more we have multiplied by industry, and the exercise of that reason which you possess in common with us. Follow then our example, brethren, and we will aid you with great pleasure.[63]

In this way we can see how Jefferson's praise is subtly linked to implanting a Euro-American exemplar within the consciousness of the objects of his praise so they can measure future progress.

Jefferson also sought to instill a form of self-surveillance by which tribes and members of tribes would compare themselves and measure their comparative achievements in conforming to particular agricultural practices against the achievements and failures of other tribes, members of their own tribe, and themselves over time. He also made them aware that others were evaluating their progress as much as they were.

> Our brethren, whom you have happened to meet here from the West and Northwest, have enabled you to compare your situation now with what it was formerly. They also make the comparison, and they see how far you are ahead of them, and seeing what you are they are encouraged to do as you have done.[64]

In this way, Jefferson sought to produce a certain form of self-consciousness within members of the Cherokee.

Racism can take many forms. One form of racism that legitimizes colonialism for the good of the colonized includes a temporal dimension. That is, the savage or barbarian represents an earlier point in historical time for the colonizer, and colonialism is justified as a way of civilizing the savage or barbarian and bringing this premodern subject into the modern world. Manifestations of this practice are the tendencies to refer to non-Europeans as backward or as children, implying that the path of development and modernization is the path defined by a European *telos*.[65]

Jefferson participates in this racial practice by referring constantly to various tribes as "my children." The more that the Cherokee, for example, govern themselves by the norms of a particular agricultural practice, the more the Cherokee will have "grown up" and become more American. And becoming American means being able to claim the rights of the American people. Jefferson displays this form of reason in a message to the Cherokee:

> You propose, my *children*, that your nation shall be divided into two, and that your part, the upper Cherokees, shall be separated from the lower by a fixed boundary, shall be placed under the government of the United States, become citizens thereof, and be ruled by our laws; in fine, to be our *brothers* instead of our *children*. My children, I shall rejoice to see the day when the red men, our neighbors, become truly one people with us, enjoying all the rights and privileges we do.[66]

Thus, the process of becoming incorporated within the American nation is represented temporally as the difference between being one's child and being one's brother. Furthermore, as we can see from Jefferson's message to the Cherokee, the enjoyment of rights is tightly linked to the question of being part of the American people.

Of course, the problem with children is their lack of self discipline. This is one factor that distinguishes a child from an adult. Jefferson proceeds to lecture the Cherokee as if they were his own children:

> But are you prepared for this? Have you the resolution to leave off hunting for your living, to lay off for each family to itself, to live by industry, the men working that farm with their hands, raising stock, or learning trades as we do, and the women spinning and weaving clothes for their husbands and children? All this is necessary before our laws can suit you or be of any use to you.[67]

One must be willing to govern one's self in accordance with specified norms in order to gain standing as an American legal subject.

By relying on a temporal narrative to give extra force to the process of normalization, Jefferson can then "predict" the future by continuing along this particular narrative path:

You will find your next want to be mills to grind your corn. . . . When a man has enclosed and improved his farm, builds a good house on it and raised plentiful stocks of animals, he will wish when he dies that these things shall go to his wife and children, whom he loves more than he does his other relations, and for whom he will work with pleasure during his life. *You will, therefore, find it necessary to establish laws for this.* When a man has property, earned it with his own labor, he will not like to see another come and take it from him because he happens to be stronger, or else to defend it by spilling blood. You will find it necessary then to appoint good men, as judges, to decide contests between man and man, according to reason and to the rules you shall establish.[68]

Once he has caught up to the present, the Cherokee man becomes like any civilized American man. He has the same sentiments (preference for wife and children over other relations), the same needs (mills, for instance), and the same selfishness and individualized understanding of interest (he will want to exclude others from his property, rather than engage in cooperative modes of farming). We finally have produced a normal American subject. Other social forms are not dealt with as alternative ways of organizing life that are due a measure of respect. Rather, they become a past out of which the present has grown.

Once they have been formed as certain types of modern subjects, Jefferson states that the Cherokee will "find it necessary to establish laws." *Law*, as we learned from Schmitt above, emerges from and governs the stability of what has become a recognizably normal situation in which a given social practice is able to monopolize a given territory.[69] The stability of this situation is produced jointly by law and social discipline.

Through this disciplinary process of normalization according to the values of the American social body, indigenous peoples can become American. Approximation to these norms indicates incorporation within the American national body. Incorporation is key when the national people is sovereign. It preserves the unity of the national will and guards against factious heterogeneity, which the framers identified as the bane of republicanism's existence.[70] Success in the disciplinary process of normalization results in social commonality. As Jefferson writes, the "great tribes on our south-western quarter, much advanced beyond the others in agriculture and household arts, appear tranquil, and [identify] their view with ours, in proportion to their advancement."[71] Governed by common social norms, this territorialized nation could achieve unification. Consonant with such relations of identity, those tribes who agree to discipline themselves by Jefferson's social norms come within the limits of the law and come to enjoy the same rights as any other American—the rights of the people.

According to the norms suggested by his favored variant of Whig history, Jefferson created a standard upon which to measure Native American likeness to Euro-Americans. If Native Americans were willing to engage in these practices, then they were within the realm of Euro-American comprehension, and Jefferson could then document and measure deviation from this norm within a community of value. But a refusal to submit to social discipline, however, meant that they were outside this community. If not subject to Jefferson's and other Americans' knowledge of historical development, then they could not be American subjects, they were not within American law, and they could not claim American rights. They became, in that case, absolute Others. In the latter case, those Cherokee who refused to govern themselves by American norms should remove to another place, "beyond the Mississippi."[72] The Mississippi had become the boundary between the national territory and the "or else" of the either-or logic of identity—the point of forceful distinction between American and not American.

Conclusion

In this chapter, I have argued that contemporary liberal and communitarian political and legal theorists share the same paradigm for conceptualizing rights. These theorists tend to understand individual rights instrumentally. Working like "trump cards," rights intervene in the social order from outside it to create spaces of freedom that allow individuals to abstract themselves from society. This paradigm of thought understands nationalism and liberalism to be opposed to each other. In contrast, by examining the early history of American rights claiming, I have argued that rights enjoy a paradoxical existence that neither liberals nor communitarians fully appreciate. Practices of rights and national formation have a common history. Legal practices of claiming rights in the United States have been coextensive with the constitutional project of inventing and defending the sovereignty of the American people. Hence the legal discourse through which one claims rights like free speech implies the American national people as the subject position from which one claims rights. Therefore, rights that the Americans claimed in their revolutionary period and subsequently are not as abstract or universal as liberals may suggest. Paradoxically, however, for the very reason that rights never achieve the universality that liberals claim for them, rights cannot be as destructive to "community" or the national formation as communitarians claim. As one places a claim upon the "rights of the people," one simultaneously claims identity with the people for whom such rights are reserved. The adjudication of rights claims is in part a process of adjudicating one's claim for incorporation. This is one reason why claiming rights is simultaneously legal and political.

The problem of identifying the people, with which the framers grappled in the cases of Native Americans, blacks, and immigration, is a common theme in controversies over rights throughout American history. While the problem of rights and identity is perhaps most obvious in the area of immigration and naturalization, as I discussed in the introduction, we should be attentive to the more subtle ways in which incorporation within the national people continues to inform the practice of rights. Agamben is correct to note the proliferation of zones such as those dealing with immigration where the national people is constructed through a production and sifting of difference, and the grave dangers associated with this process since questions of the "people" carry with them biopolitical implications. Building on the insights of this chapter, in the rest of this book I suggest that, without taking anything away from the unique intensity and horrible violence of specific places where national purity is determined, this question of the "people" is hardly contained within specific local zones.[73] Indeed, this is the fate that follows from making the American people the fundamental political and legal subject. Once the nation is the condition of possibility for claiming rights, not only is it possible for someone like Martin Luther King Jr. to make a successful rights claim based on a simultaneous claim on American identity (see chapter 4), but exclusions such as the one suffered by John Turner (see introduction) also become a real possibility.

This correlation between liberal rights and the nation gives rise to a certain ambivalence that we can see on display in Hannah Arendt's work. Arendt, in *On Revolution*, criticizes the French practice of making the national people sovereign, fearing the exclusionary and normalizing tendencies exhibited here in the case of America. Different insights, however, emerge from her discussion of rights in *The Origins of Totalitarianism*. There, Arendt finds that once one loses one's national identity, one also loses standing to make a rights claim. As she puts it, losing one's national citizenship results in finding one's self "out of legality altogether."[74] Being able to claim a national identity is a precondition to a successful claim to rights. But this means that the practice of rights is inescapably related to the politics of nationalism when the people is the legal sovereign and its rights are inscribed within the nation's constitutional law, as is the case with the U.S. Constitution. Arendt's ambivalence seems to be the fate to which our ethical sensibilities are condemned as long as law and politics are nationally organized. It is an ambivalence that haunts the question of free speech in America due to the nature of the legal discourse within which "free speech" is framed.

2

John Burgess Is to Woodrow Wilson as Individual Rights Are to Community?

Nation, Race, and the Right of Free Speech

Scholars understand modern First Amendment legal doctrine to have emerged during the early twentieth century. Despite repression by governments and private police forces of speech-related activities in the late nineteenth and early twentieth centuries, not until radicals voiced opposition to World War I did the Supreme Court begin to hand down key decisions in the area of the First Amendment. At this time, the opinions of the Court did not protect the First Amendment rights of the individuals concerned—indeed, the well-known socialist Eugene Debs won almost a million votes for president in 1920 while sitting in jail serving a ten year sentence for having delivered an antiwar speech. Beginning in the fall of 1919, however, Justices Oliver Wendell Holmes and Louis Brandeis began to issue dissenting opinions that the Court would later accept as the rule of law for the First Amendment in the area of radical speech. Holmes, who wrote the opinion of the Court supporting conviction of radicals in the earliest cases of 1919, had a change of heart later in the year. In *Abrams v. U.S.* (1919), he wrote a now famous dissent joined by Brandeis that laid the groundwork for later, more speech-protective First Amendment jurisprudence.

Why the change of heart? How did the First Amendment become more tolerant of dissenting speech? The legal scholar David Rabban points to Zechariah Chafee, calling him the "key figure" in a "heroic effort" to redirect First Amendment jurisprudence.[1] Chafee, a Harvard University law professor, wrote several articles on free speech in this period and met with Holmes in the summer after Holmes wrote opinions to uphold convictions in *Schenck v. U.S.* (1919), *Frohwek v. U.S.* (1919), and *Debs v. U.S.* (1919) and before he wrote his dissent in *Abrams*. Moreover, Chafee's *Freedom of Speech* (later revised as *Free Speech in the United States*) rationalized Holmes's shift. In the book, Chafee suggested that the rest of the Court had actually misapplied Holmes's "clear and present danger" test for unprotected speech in cases following *Debs* that continued to uphold convictions and that it was Holmes who remained consistent by dissenting from those rulings. According to Rabban, then, we could understand Chafee as a sort of mythic inventor of a libertarian First Amendment jurisprudence who "spun" restrictive legal decisions into speech-protective precedents. The Court has integrated Chafee's spin into constitutional law, developments that have led to the current legal test for "incitement." Established in 1969, the test puts a heavy burden of proof on governments that wish to punish incendiary speech. Rabban describes these developments as a process of the law working itself "pure."[2]

Historian Paul Murphy situates the emergence of civil libertarian protests, which in turn generated a First Amendment jurisprudence, in a context of "modernization" whereby the United States became nationalized and political power became increasingly centralized. Murphy links this process of nationalizing and centralizing power to those organized politically under the banner of "Progressivism." According to Murphy, the well- intentioned if paternalistic Progressives sought national standards administered by national agencies to address such issues as food safety, child labor, and the eight-hour workday. The consequences of this attempt to set uniform standards included institutional developments in the state structure that increased and centralized political power in national and elite hands. As Murphy also notes, the Progressives sought to Americanize newly arrived immigrants. Thus, he describes Progressive social policy as "anti-pluralistic" and "anti-individualist" because the rights of the individual must be balanced against the welfare of the larger social whole of the nation.[3]

Murphy argues that the developments in the field of civil liberties associated with U.S. entry into World War I were consistent with the spirit of the Progressive era.[4] By 1916, Woodrow Wilson had shepherded through "virtually every important domestic plank in the Progressive party platform of 1912." With war approaching, the Wilson administration turned its attention toward pushing through Congress a number of pieces of legislation to manage domestic opposition to the war in order to foster national unity against those who might impede military victory or threaten national security.[5] In President Wilson's 1916 State of the Union address, he warned that the foreign born were "pouring the poison of disloyalty into the very arteries of our national life" and cited the need for legislation to suppress disloyal activities. Murphy also describes Wilson's lead role in drafting a "loyalty" plank for the Democratic party platform of 1916 to defend the solidarity of the American people and his urging Congress in 1916 and in a special session in 1917 to pass espionage legislation that would curtail freedom of speech and press.[6]

On April 2, 1917, Wilson asked Congress for a declaration of war and instruments to repress disloyalty coming from German-American quarters. Legislation was introduced, and on June 15, 1917, Congress passed the Espionage Act. On October 6, 1917, Congress passed a Trading with the Enemy Act giving the president control over international communications and the postmaster general censorship powers over the foreign language press. The Espionage Act was amended the following year with the passage of the Sedition Act of May 16, 1918. In sum, according to Murphy, Progressive efforts to improve the welfare of the national community and increase social solidarity socioeconomically on one hand, and the Wilson administration's antipathy to dissent and sensitivity to "disloyalty" on the other, were two sides of the same coin: the Progressives' turn away from laissez-faire policies and toward an attempt to promote the national welfare against disruptive individual behavior, be that behavior prostitution, harsh labor contracts, or political dissent from the war.

Mark Graber also blames the lack of protection given to civil liberties during the World War I period and its aftermath on the intellectual perspective that informed Progressivism. Progressivism, according to Graber, was supported philosophically by pragmatism and in legal theory by sociological jurisprudence. These theories, by attacking absolute principles of law, truth, and natural rights, redirect governmental action away from a laissez-faire concern for individual rights protected by an unelected "impartial" judiciary. They lead to public policies that promote the social interests of the entire community as decided by elected officials and experts because the community is understood as being prior to the individual and absolute truths are understood as being nonexistent.[7] Graber argues that Progressives, guided by these theories, emphasized the general welfare over individual rights in their policies and legitimized judicial deference to legislatures institutionally. This theoretical conjuncture allowed Progressives to justify their opposition to the laissez-faire jurisprudence of the late-nineteenth- and early-twentieth-century Supreme Court, which had struck down a variety of socioeconomic reforms supported by Progressives. Most famously, New York's maximum hours legislation for bakers in *Lochner v. New York* (the case that has come to symbolize the era) was struck down as a violation of the individual's right to freedom of contract. Although justifying judicial deference to legislatures enacting Progressive economic reforms, the intellectual formation behind Progressivism presented a theoretical difficulty for those seeking to justify judicial intervention on behalf of an individual's right to free speech. While Graber is in accord with other scholars like Murphy in his description of Progressivism's emphasis on social interests over individual rights, Graber differs from those like Rabban who paint Zechariah Chafee as a libertarian savior of the First Amendment in the face of nationalist hysteria.

Rather than describing Chafee as a First Amendment *hero*, Graber presents Chafee as a First Amendment *villain* for having constructed a defense of free speech from the intellectual resources that Progressivism itself relied upon. Graber argues that Chafee, by overlooking an earlier "conservative libertarian" tradition, saddled later generations with a defense of freedom of speech that is incapable of addressing today's most pressing threats to the exercise of those rights. This earlier tradition, according to Graber, valued individual rights in the area of property and contract, on the one hand, and freedom of speech and press, on the other.

Graber describes the difference between the conservative libertarians and the Progressives as the difference between a libertarian sensitivity toward individual rights and a social interest in the national community's welfare. In so doing, Graber conforms to a conventional theoretical framing of controversies over rights and to traditional criticisms of the Wilson administration during World War I and the red scare. My discussion of the late colonial and early national period of U.S. legal history in chapter 1 demonstrating the mutually reinforcing relationship between liberal rights claiming and nationalist politics, however, should make us hesitate to accept the way that Graber and others frame the issues of this period as an opposition between a liberal concern for individual rights and the politics of nationalism.

In this chapter, I argue that those who describe the repression of free speech during the early twentieth century as an instance of excessive nationalism for which the proper antidote is a sufficiently pure liberalism that will protect the rights of the individual in a legally neutral manner, untainted by social context or political bias, are putting forward an antidote that does not exist. Therefore, just as Graber presents an unveiled

Zechariah Chafee who is not the libertarian hero liberals have come to embrace and instead argues that the conservative libertarians are the true defenders of individual rights, I will argue that John Burgess, a member of this conservative libertarian tradition who lived long enough to condemn the Wilson administration's wartime policies, is not the defender of abstract individual rights Graber makes him out to be. I will not, however, put forward my own candidate for the role of intellectual superhero who can defend an individual's right to free speech in any context with a single theory or principle. I find, instead, Graber's mischaracterization of Burgess's defense of free speech to be symptomatic of a misdirected tendency within political and legal scholarship to consider nationalism as necessarily antithetical to liberal rights.

The late nineteenth and early twentieth centuries were a period in which extreme nationalism coexisted with laissez-faire legal liberalism. This should be an unlikely event if liberalism and nationalism are as opposed as contemporary scholarship assumes. As we have seen in the previous chapter, because the U.S. Constitution makes the American people sovereign and reserves certain rights like freedom of speech to the people (while delegating other powers to the government), questions of rights like free speech are discursively joined to the problem of nationalism. By examining certain shared characteristics between Burgess on one side, and Wilson and others who supported repressive actions during this period on the other, and by studying the basis on which Burgess defended a right to free speech against the Wilson administration, we will gain a better understanding of why it is a mistake to perceive controversies over rights through a prism that posits an inherent hostility between nationalism and claiming a right to free speech.

I shall demonstrate that Burgess and Wilson, rather than representing opposed intellectual traditions as Graber argues, in fact draw from a shared conceptual universe and a shared paradigm of rights known as "Teutonic origins" theory. Indeed, I will show how support for the repression of radical speech during World War I and its immediate aftermath can be understood as an extension of the very rights paradigm that informed Burgess's positions on free speech. In other words, rather than creating an opposition between Burgess and Wilson's administration (which represents the opposition between liberal legal rights and nationalism), I will paint Wilson and Burgess with the same brush to illustrate how they in fact shared a similar discursive terrain. Although I do not treat other members of Graber's "conservative libertarian tradition," a proper portrayal of Burgess is critical for Graber's argument that this earlier free speech tradition would have provided better protection to radical critics of the war and U.S. economic policies, since he was the only member of this tradition to have explicitly criticized Wilson's policies as unconstitutional.[8] Although Burgess and Wilson shared the same conceptual universe, they did not use its resources in the same way as each negotiated the new challenges presented by World War I. *This* explains why Burgess and Wilson took contrasting positions on the question of free speech and national security. Contrary to Graber's contention that Burgess's criticism of Wilson derived from a libertarian defense of individual rights against a homogenizing nationalism, I shall argue that both Burgess and Wilson operated within a racialized nationalism, but they would come to differ in their interpretations of what should follow from this racialized nationalism during World War I.

Graber's book is an important revisionist treatment of what might be considered the founding period of contemporary First Amendment protections for free speech.[9] The study, moreover, is significant methodologically for the nature of its empiricism. Graber argues that scholarship focusing narrowly on legal conclusions, tests, and rules is inadequate. A narrow focus on conclusions can miss how a superficial agreement on legal outcomes can proceed from vastly different worldviews that would lead to divergent conclusions in other circumstances. Following Quentin Skinner, Graber argues that to gain a proper understanding of legal developments, one must examine the reasons put forward in legal argument in order to reconstruct the intellectual context from which the argument in question proceeds.[10] On this point, Graber's work dovetails with other law and politics scholarship that returns to legal texts not for the formalistic purposes of "mechanistic jurisprudence," but to gain a better empirical grasp of legal patterns, changes, and institutional developments.[11]

I agree with this project. I simply argue here that Graber has missed an important dimension of the political and legal context that is significant for the controversies Graber seeks to understand—the hegemonic nature of "Teutonic origins" theory, a racial theory of American national greatness. Teutonic origins theory constitutes the discursive terrain for legal and political interventions during the late nineteenth and early twentieth centuries, and I will show how scholars, activists, and politicians acted within its parameters. Because I agree that legal conclusions must be situated within their intellectual context in order to understand their significance, I will not be content to falsify Graber's claims regarding Burgess's libertarian concern for individual rights by documenting Burgess's "illiberal" positions on legislation or theories of individual rights, though I will bring forward such evidence. Rather, I will go further and reconstruct Burgess's thought, linking it to the dominant intellectual formation of the period and the political controversies produced and negotiated using the resources of this intellectual formation, in order to understand not only the repressive measures Burgess endorsed, but to provide a more adequate understanding of Burgess's criticisms of Wilson's wartime policies than Graber's approach can give. A proper grasp of Burgess's constitutional thought shows why it is a mistake to consider liberal rights like freedom of speech as necessarily antithetical to even the most extreme forms of nationalism. Burgess's exposition of the U.S. constitutional system's logic illustrates how liberal government can coexist with the most racist biopolitical drives. I shall suggest that the work of Michel Foucault and others on governmentality may provide us with a better language to appreciate these tendencies than political and legal theory's inclination to oppose liberalism to nationalism.

Graber's Conservative-Libertarian Tradition

Scholarship on the early twentieth century argues that individual rights were violated because a nationalist "hysteria" overtook the country. It suggests that if the nation had not lost its senses and if the principles of legal liberalism had been followed, such as independent and objective preservation of legal rights by the courts, then the abuses of the period would not have occurred.[12] In this vein, Graber notes that Progressive interests in national unity "were responsible for the restrictions placed on political debate during the second decade of the twentieth century," and he goes on to argue that Progressive members of the Wilson administration were responsible for the Espionage and Sedition Acts.[13] For Graber, however, the problems of Progressivism persist in the First Amendment legacy bequeathed by most people's free speech hero, Zechariah Chafee.

At root, the problem Graber finds with Chafee is that "he was a mainstream progressive" who thought that "judges had no business protecting their idiosyncratic notions of individual rights" because an unelected judge should not "determine the fundamental values of his community." Graber's treatment of Chafee is scathing. Indeed, he calls Chafee's arguments to expand First Amendment protections "unnecessary" and "a failure."[14]

Chafee's defense of free speech focused, according to Graber, on the social interest in free speech rather than the individual interest in self-expression. Graber states that Chafee believed the First Amendment was a declaration of a "national interest in free speech" and represented the idea that the "nation would be best served by unregulated debate on matters of public interest." By viewing free speech instrumentally, as a procedural prerequisite for democratic society, Chafee gave birth to a tradition that continued through the 1940s, 1950s, and 1960s to justify free speech based on social needs and the public interest rather than on a theory of individual liberty. The weakness of this approach, Graber argues, is that if debate is not perceived as promoting the public interest or a social good such as truth, then free speech will not be protected. In accordance with this logic, Graber describes how Chafee believed the Espionage Act to be a constitutional exercise of national power and was willing to uphold the long prison sentence for Angelo Herndon, the black communist organizer in Georgia, because the "unrest of Negroes" could have led to "some sort of disorder." These views, for Graber, were rooted in the "structure of the new constitutional defense of free speech" put forward by Chafee. Thus, Graber argues that Chafee and the free speech tradition he initiated compare unfavorably with the arguments of John Burgess and the rest of an older free speech tradition that Graber disinters.[15]

John Burgess, according to Graber, was a member of a free speech tradition that preexisted Chafee and that Chafee ignored to the detriment of twentieth-century First Amendment jurisprudence. This conservative libertarian tradition understands freedom of speech to be an aspect of a more general right of personal liberty that includes the liberty of contract. In other words, it does not separate the system of free expression from the system of private property. Graber states that conservative libertarians were the late nineteenth century's leading proponents of the "night watchman state" who supported "laissez-faire policies" for economic *and* intellectual development. The highest value for the conservative libertarians is the autonomy and self-development of the individual. In contrast to the Progressives who emphasized the social interest in free speech, the conservative libertarians take an "individualist approach" to free speech that proceeds from a theoretical basis in individual liberty. Moreover, the conservative libertarians differ from Progressives on the proper role of judges by arguing that "the fundamental freedoms . . . could be secured in practice only if placed in a constitution whose final interpreters were an unelected judiciary."[16] In sum, in Graber's telling, the conservative libertarians are philosophically consistent liberal legal individualists.

Graber waxes nostalgic about the conservative libertarians throughout *Transforming Free Speech*. They are the good guys done wrong by Chafee and his intellectual followers. The conservative libertarians were forgotten, and Graber views this as unfortunate. Graber blames what has come to be known as the civil libertarian tradition in the United States for ignoring and distorting the earlier conservative libertarian approach to free speech. He notes that Burgess found the Espionage Act of 1917 an unconstitutional infringement of the right to free speech and argues that the conservative libertarian tradition would have "afforded better protection to those radical critics of American war and economic policies who were punished during World War I and the red scare" than the civil libertarian tradition that emerged with Chafee. Throughout the book, Graber uses conservative libertarianism as a standard by which to measure subsequent First Amendment developments.[17]

Are Burgess and the conservative libertarian tradition really "all that"? Would Burgess and the legal tradition he represents truly have given us stronger protections of freedom of speech? Is it really unfortunate that the nation wound up following a different legal path than the one laid down by Burgess? Even from what Graber tells us, we have reason to be skeptical. Despite the rose-colored glasses through which Graber views the past, he occasionally qualifies in significant ways his positive statements on the conservative libertarians. For example, he concedes that the conservative libertarians did not believe that obscenity was protected by the First Amendment.[18] He also acknowledges that there is a difference between saying, as the conservative libertarians did, that the Fourteenth Amendment protects free speech, and interpreting that guarantee broadly.[19] In other words, one could protect "speech" very strongly but have a very narrow definition of "speech."[20] Graber has also been taken to task by reviewers for arguing that the conservative libertarian perspective would permit us to address the grave threat that economic inequality presents to freedom of expression today since this perspective strenuously defended property rights against government intervention.[21]

But there are more fundamental problems with Graber's presentation of the conservative libertarians, at least when John Burgess is considered. These are problems that should make us think twice about whether to revive Burgess and his legal tradition or to leave them where Graber found them—dead and buried. Because questions of constitutional rights simultaneously raise the problem of interpreting what it means to be part of the American people, Burgess's vicious racism, which I discuss below, should make us hesitate before reviving him as a representative of a legal paradigm that should guide First Amendment practices. Because Burgess has such a racially constricted view of who counts as an American, many would be excluded from being able to call on the First Amendment's protections. Most significantly, the basis of exclusion is a biopolitical meter— one that posits different types of human beings. This concern with the sociobiological purity of America is shared by those like President Wilson who had a xenophobic concern with immigrants in the early-twentieth-century United States and the racial threat that they posed to national unity and security. Such a racially narrow view of what it means to be an American would not ameliorate but worsen the impediments to justice in the United States and the world today.

John Burgess and the Teutonic Historians

Both John Burgess and Woodrow Wilson worked within a tradition known as Teutonic origins theory. Important historical studies of the late nineteenth and early twentieth centuries emphasize this tradition as providing the ideological support for the anti-immigrant agitation prominent during this era—agitation that was linked to popular support for repressive measures during and immediately after World War I. I suggest that this connection undermines the notion that Burgess's intellectual paradigm necessarily provided strong support for free speech during this period. To the contrary, this paradigm created the conceptual universe that made the repression described by Graber and others make sense as a reasonable course of action.

The Teutonic origins thesis presented a narrative of history that racialized the capacity to exercise freedom and self-government and used a "moral geography" to express this form of racism. Teutonic origins theory traced the origins of England's free institutions to the woods of Germany. The history of the movement of Germanic peoples west to England became the history of the development of free institutions. Americans inserted themselves into this narrative by emphasizing that the same spirit that led the "Goths" or "Teutons" to leave the woods of Germany led their more immediate forefathers to cross the Atlantic and set up similar institutions on America's shores. This history insisted that liberty was justified for the Germanic people because as a people they were particularly capable of exercising liberty, and it often emphasized this point by making derogatory contrasts with "southern" or "eastern" peoples who were considered either not ready for, or incapable of, exercising liberty due to various defects in their nature.

The racial discourse of Teutonic origins generated a further series of oppositions that could be used to imply the differential capabilities and value of various peoples: liberty versus luxury; cold (or temperate) versus hot; Protestant versus Catholic; masculine versus feminine; civilized persons versus barbarians. The point of such contrasts was to suggest that Latin peoples or southern Europeans, for example, were too effeminate or weak—degenerates due to excessive luxury—to maintain liberty. The hardy, vigorous Germanic peoples, however, were found to be the only ones capable of properly exercising freedom by protecting it from despotism on one side and license on the other. Teutonic origins theory was a discursive mechanism whereby different races were invented and then located spatially.

Teutonic origins theory provided a series of traits by which to identify a white race suited to the exercise of liberty and other races doomed to despotism. For example, William Hickling Prescott exclaimed, "What a contrast did these children of Southern Europe present to the Anglo-Saxon races who scattered themselves along the great northern division of the western hemisphere!" For Prescott, while the Anglo-Saxons took care to preserve the tree of liberty, the communities of the neighboring continent exhibited even in their prime, a prime that Prescott likened to "tropical vegetation," the "sure symptoms of decay."[22] The Germanic race, and particularly the Anglo-Saxon branch of it, was "peculiarly masculine," according to the historian Francis Parkman, "and, therefore, peculiarly fitted for self-government."[23] In this way, the exercise of liberty was linked to the racial identity of a people, which, in turn, was linked to other norms such as patriarchy or to geographic location.

British Americans of the eighteenth century often used narratives, such as the ancient constitution and the ancient rights of Englishmen, in which emphasis fell upon an insular nationalism that perhaps could be distinguished from a racialized logic in a "modern" sense. Nevertheless, they could be said to have functioned as a "hinge" that opened out toward modern racism.[24] But Americans like Jefferson invoked a Germanic variant of this narrative, inserting America into this story of liberty as the latest chapter of a continuing westward migration in order to justify

American rights claims in protests made to the English Parliament and king.[25] These latter narratives within which rights of Englishmen or Gothic freedoms were situated underwent a racial intensification beginning in the early nineteenth century.[26] By the 1880s and 1890s, some of the most important American political scientists and historians took the deeply racist Teutonic view of history, differing only on their relative affinity for the English or the Germanic aspects of the story.[27]

John Burgess was not just one of these Teutonic political scientists and historians. Gossett describes him as the "real fire-eater" of the bunch.[28] Burgess founded the first graduate program in the social sciences in the United States at Columbia and is considered the founder of American political science as an academic discipline.[29] Burgess received an undergraduate education at Amherst, engaged in further study in Germany with his friend Elihu Root, and, after a short teaching stay at Amherst, where he had to battle the theological forces that still dominated American higher education and resisted his efforts to create a graduate program, accepted a job offer from Columbia to replace Francis Lieber (a German ex-patriate and another Teutonic historian). In addition to training many of America's leading academic social scientists and founding the journal *Political Science Quarterly*, Burgess also taught Theodore Roosevelt.[30]

Teutonic origins theory forms the theoretical basis of Burgess's writings. In an article published in *Political Science Quarterly*, Burgess argues that the people of Germany, Great Britain, and the United States are "substantially of Teutonic stock." For Burgess, "Germany is the motherland of Great Britain, as Great Britain is the motherland of the United States. Moreover, Germany is not merely the motherland of our motherland; she is in some degree, racially, the immediate motherland of the United States." Burgess admits that this relation would not count for much if it referred only to blood. But, he continues, "if it has produced and maintains a substantial consensus of opinion concerning rights and wrongs, liberty and government . . . it counts for very much. It has then become an ethical as well as an ethnical bond." Burgess finds such a bond to exist between Germany, Great Britain, and the United States. Making use of the symbolic oppositions between west and east and north and south to produce the discursive effect of entirely different populations, Burgess argues that the racial bond tying the Teutonic nations together also separates them from "the Romanic, Celtic, and Slavic peoples of Europe, and from all other peoples in other parts of the world." Thus, using Teutonic origins theory to map out the world and America's place in it racially, and then arguing that the relations of identity and difference stand for ethical relations and differences, Burgess produces a moral geography that others might consult as a handbook of sorts to gain direction in contemporary politics.[31]

Burgess's major work, *Political Science and Comparative Constitutional Law*, relies on Teutonic superiority as its major assumption. Burgess argues that the

> highest talent for political organization has been exhibited by the Aryan nations, and by these unequally. . . . [T]he Teuton really dominates the world by his superior political genius. . . . The political subjection or attachment of the unpolitical nations to those possessing political endowment appears, if we may judge from history, to be as truly a part of the course of the world's civilization as is the national organization of states. I do not think that Asia and Africa can ever receive political organization in any other way.[32]

Moreover, Burgess's Teutonic supremacy informs his comparative methodology. His study applies only to European nations and the United States because they are the only nations to have developed "such political organizations as furnish the material for scientific treatment." He chooses Great Britain, Germany, France, and the United States for his case studies because he must be "systematic, not encyclopaedic," and these are the most important states of the world. Furthermore, their constitutions represent all the species of constitutionalism yet developed. The attempt to derive general principles of public law will be most trustworthy, Burgess argues, if the "less perfect systems" are excluded from generalization, the "less important states" disregarded, and those species "not typical" are excluded.[33] In this way, we can see that the normative standards that for him define value, progress, the typical, and the deviant are informed by a Teutonic variant of white supremacy. Burgess's Teutonic theory defines the case selection for deriving universal principles and yielding scientific knowledge.

For those who may be considering the advantages of comparative study of courts and law, Burgess and his Euro-American bases for generating political *science* should cause a moment, at least, of reflection, particularly in the design of such studies. We should be very careful in how we use Burgess's Euro-American centrism as the point of departure for developing models of courts and law. Emerging scholarship, fortunately, has inaugurated a research approach that focuses on a more complex interaction between colonial powers and their colonies in the experimentation with and advance of new forms of governance.[34]

Race, Nationalism, and Rights

In Burgess's view, each race has a role to play in the world's history. For instance, Asians contribute to the history of the world through theocracies and despotisms. The first requirement for civilization is to develop reverence and obedience because without this quality, according to Burgess, "the reign of law can never be attained." Therefore, Asia's contribution to world history, Burgess argues, is to have "subject[ed] barbaric liberty to law," which is the "first problem in the development of the state everywhere."[35] Other races play their own role in the world's history before reaching their limits. While Burgess concedes that the Romans demonstrated great political and legal genius when they contributed "universality" to the world's development, this contribution entailed sacrificing individual liberty to the overriding principle of uniformity, local autonomy to the goal of empire, and the suppression of "all ethnical differences." Reconciling "uniformity with variety, sovereignty with liberty" was not the "mission of the Romans. . . . This work was reserved to the Teutonic nations."[36]

Burgess praises Teutonic nations as "the political nations *par excellence*," the founders of national states. National states, for Burgess, come closer to solving all the problems of political organization than any other system because the national state "solves the problem of the relation of sovereignty to liberty," thereby allowing the realization of the "truest liberty." Because the national state is historically, practically, and scientifically the most modern and complete solution to the problems of political organization, because it is the creation of Teutonic political genius, and because it could not have been the creation of any other race since "education can only develop what already exists in seed and germ," the Teutonic nations are thereby "authorize[d] . . . to assume the leadership in the establishment and administration of states."[37] Teutons racially signify modernity and the path of future development for other races, and the nation-state is the form of political and legal organization that is the model by which Teutons should organize the modern world in Burgess's eyes.

Burgess has a teleological view of history that uses Teutonic identity as the standard by which to measure progress and refers to other races as representing various stages in the world's development. In other words, various races signify different temporal moments in the process of development from barbarism to civilization. The nation state, then, represents for Burgess the most modern form of political development, while other forms of political organization are alternatively either anachronistic or appropriate only for less developed races. Hence, he concludes that "national unity is the determining force in the development of the modern constitutional states." Burgess also concludes that the "prime policy" of such a state "should be to attain proper physical boundaries and to render its population ethnically homogeneous. In other words, the policy in modern political organization should be to follow the indications of nature and aid the ethnical impulse to conscious development."[38] Burgess clearly exemplifies the biopolitical impulse of modernity in the way he posits races with natural dispositions and then advocates national political organization to "aid" the production of "natural" tendencies. In light of this evidence, Burgess cannot be classified as a libertarian rather than a nationalist.

Not only is Burgess a nationalist, he is also quite explicit regarding his opposition to theories of universal, abstract, transcendent, or timeless human rights. As Burgess puts the matter himself:

> The elements of individual liberty cannot be generally stated for all states and for all times. All mankind is not to be found, or has not yet been found, upon the same stage of civilization. The individual liberty of the Russian would not suffice for the Englishman, nor that of the Englishman at the time of the Tudors for the Englishman of to-day. As man develops the latent elements of his own civilization he becomes conscious of the need of an ever-widening sphere of free action, and the state finds its security and well-being in granting it.[39]

Rather than understanding individual rights in a universal manner, Burgess states that the same sphere of individual liberty is not appropriate for all races or nations. Rights are contingent upon identity. In this example, the racially and nationally distinctive Russians occupy a temporally parallel position to the Tudor-era English, and in this way represent the past out of which Teutons have developed. Correspondingly, Teutons represent the future for other races and nations, and hence provide a normative standard for political and legal development. This discursive move involving temporal narratives produces three effects. It justifies a more narrow berth of liberty for nonwhites. Second, it displaces other peoples from the Teutonic present, thereby making these peoples objects of knowledge (from a Teutonic perspective) rather than fellow human beings existing in the same moment of time. Third, it implies that non-Teutons are not as mature as the civilized Teuton—much as Jefferson referred to Indian nations as his "children"—and it justifies relations of paternalism rather than relations of equality that would imply dialogue as the ethical relation between different subjects. In other words, Teutons should lead and non-Teutons should follow or risk the consequences.[40]

Burgess distinguishes between barbaric liberty that must be disciplined by law and true liberty that comes with civilization.[41] And civilization comes with the Teutons, who have the world-historical mission of leading the less civilized races along the path of development. Again, Burgess puts it best: "[T]he mission of the Teutonic nations must be that they are called to carry the political civilization of the modern world into those parts of the world inhabited by unpolitical and barbaric races; *i.e.* they must have a colonial policy."[42] The temporal nature of Burgess's racial discourse indicates that political and legal organization according to the model of Teutonic modernity is an offer that cannot be refused. It acquires the force of an injunction that may not be opposed by those "barbaric races."

On Burgess's assessment, most of the world is inhabited by populations that are incapable of establishing "civilized states." Therefore, they must remain "in a state of barbarism or semi-barbarism, unless the political nations undertake the work of state organization for them." The barbaric condition of these populations authorizes the Teutonic nations "to force organization upon them by any means necessary . . . to accomplish this result. There is no human right to the status of barbarism." Indeed, Burgess argues that the "civilized state may righteously go still further than the exercise of force in imposing organization." If the "barbaric populations" resist the civilized state, then the latter may "clear the territory" of the former's presence and inhabit the territory itself without violating any rights that are not "petty" in comparison with the "transcendent right and duty" of the civilized to "establish political and legal order everywhere." Against those who may object to his argument, Burgess claims that such "sentimentality" derives from a "misconception of the origins of the rights to territory, and a lack of discrimination in regard to the capacities of races." Against this sentimentality, Burgess states that the "politically unorganized" have no rights that "a civilized state, pursuing its great world-mission, is under any obligations, legal or moral, to respect."[43]

These arguments show that Burgess discriminates rigorously in the matter of rights, at least in his reflections upon comparative constitutional law and U.S. imperial policy. Burgess makes civilization a precondition for "truest liberty," and bringing "civilization" to "barbarians," even as a forced gift if necessary, is part of the "mission" of a Teutonic nation like the United States. Creating the justification, even the obligation, to use force against barbarian populations in order to enforce civilization requires an argument about rights—who has rights, what "righteous" behavior entails, and that to which one does not have a right—an argument that Burgess does not avoid as he pushes his point to its violent conclusion. Hardly a libertarian, Burgess justifies rights upon a racial basis.

Burgess's racial standard of progress, in addition to his nationalism, leads him to advocate policies with genocidal implications as opposed to policies that make "abstract" individual rights their centerpiece. Burgess's political and legal theory maps the world into nation-states and maps nations and states in a one-to-one relation of identity. Should a state include more than one nationality, Burgess argues that the "sound policy" is for "the state to strive to develop ethnical homogeneity." If Burgess sounds as if he is advocating a policy of "ethnic cleansing," that is because ethnic cleansing is exactly what he is advocating. For instance, should a state have a "naturally exposed boundary," the state must rely on its border population to possess the most intense nationalist spirit in the interest of national security. If, however, a portion of a frontier population is ethnically hostile, then the state is "in perfect right" if, failing to nationalize these troublesome elements, "it deports them." The state "cannot safely or righteously give way, in such a case, to sentimental politics and the claim of an inalienable right to fatherland." To do otherwise, for Burgess, is to threaten to render the nation "incapable of fulfilling its mission or maintaining its own existence," which would lose the greater moral imperative in the "petty."[44] These are not the arguments of one who places individual rights above the security of the nation.

Anticipating Carl Schmitt, who suggests that ultimate political questions of national security cannot be solved by a prior norm or disinterested third parties but instead must be solved by the actual participants of a conflict, Burgess argues that the state follows an "ethnically obligatory" policy when it "protects its nationality against the deleterious influences of foreign immigration." Burgess claims that the state itself represents the highest good, and that the duty of a state to the world is a duty of which the state itself is the highest interpreter.[45] For Burgess, "common consciousness is the state consciousness," which, in the modern national state, is called "national consciousness." Burgess argues that the "so-called laws of God, of nature, of reason, and between states are legally, and for the subject, what the state declares them to be," particularly since the world has no organization for making its interpretations or for intervening between the state and its citizens to nullify the state's interpretation. Therefore, the national state is "the organ for the interpretation, in the last instance, of the order of life for its subjects."[46] In an argument that also echoes Jefferson's opposition to foreign immigration for its potential to warp and bias law, Burgess argues that "national harmony" is the social condition that makes possible the existence of a democratic state. That is, the mass of the population of a given state must have a consensus of opinion in reference to rights and wrongs, in reference to government and liberty. They must be able to understand one another, share a common interest, and rise in their mental development to the consciousness of the state and be truly national.[47] In defense of this national identity, this national sovereignty over the interpretation of right, wrong, and common interest, Burgess argues that there can be no higher "right" than that defined and interpreted by the national state. Therefore, the national state possesses absolute sovereignty to exclude or to deport "foreign" elements, and there can be no legal principle above the nation-state that anyone could call upon to check a state pursuing the goal of national security. For Burgess, to reiterate, legal protections of individual rights cannot transcend national imperatives.

If a state comprises more than one racial group, which one should be able to control the state? If Graber is correct that Burgess is a libertarian, then we would expect that everyone would have an equal right, or at least an equal chance, to participate in government regardless of identity. Contrary to Graber's portrayal, Burgess's racism intersects with his nationalism as he argues that "in a state whose population is composed of a variety of nationalities the Teutonic element, when dominant, should never surrender the balance of political power." Indeed, under certain circumstances, the Teutonic element "should not even permit participation of the other elements in political power." While conceding that the Teutonic element should try to secure individual liberty, he qualifies this advocacy by stating that "under certain circumstances, some of which will readily suggest themselves to the mind of any observing American, the participation of other ethnical elements in the exercise of political power has resulted, and will result, in corruption and confusion most deleterious and dangerous to the rights of all, and to the civilization of society. The Teutonic nations can never regard the exercise of political power as a right of man. . . . [I]t must not hasten the enfranchisement of those not yet ethnically qualified for reasons outside of such qualification."[48] Here, Burgess is alluding to the Reconstruction era of U.S. history and is trading on the racial presumptions of his reading audience to carry his point that the recognition of rights, such as the right to vote, must be contingent upon racial and national identity. On this point, Burgess is more explicit in his book on Reconstruction, in which he argues that "from the point of view of sound political science the imposition of universal negro suffrage upon the Southern communities, in some of which the negroes were in large majority, was one of the 'blunder-crimes' of the century. There is something natural in the subordination of an inferior race to a superior race, even to the point of the enslavement of the inferior race, but there is nothing natural in the opposite."[49] For Burgess, it is self-defeating to allow non-Teutonic elements to enjoy rights on an equal basis with Teutons in America since America is fundamentally a Teutonic nation. Such a grant could threaten the security of the basis for the recognition of any rights at all—the sovereignty of the American national state. In other words, nothing could be further from Burgess's legal theory than to suggest that the recognition of rights should proceed from a libertarian disregard of identity—racial or national.

The Shared Racial Presumptions of Woodrow Wilson and John Burgess

There were several important similarities between Woodrow Wilson, the U.S. president during World War I who demanded that public opinion be controlled in part by censorship for the nation's security, and John Burgess.[50] Both idolized Abraham Lincoln, were academic political scientists, were Southerners, and had Whig political affinities. And most significantly, both worked within the framework of Teutonic origins theory and therefore perceived similar threats to American security. Thus, as I shall demonstrate, both approached the question of free speech using similar intellectual resources. If there was a difference between them that was potentially significant, Wilson's intellectual debts tended to be biased toward the English while Burgess illustrated a Germanic bias, although Burgess's hopes for world civilization lay, as I shall discuss below, in a Teutonic triumvirate of Germany, Great Britain, and the United States.

Wilson's greatest intellectual influence is Walter Bagehot (tempered by a measure of Edmund Burke), the English public law scholar, political journalist, Social Darwinist, and editor of the *Economist*.[51] Bagehot, Wilson, and Burgess, I suggest, all share a similar narrative of law, politics, and history in which races and nations are the primary explanatory variables, and all three think about free speech within the same paradigm. Bagehot marks the progress of civilization in a manner that parallels Burgess. For Bagehot, as for Burgess, the first important step toward civilization is discipline: the problem of fixing law and cementing a "cake of custom." Of course, this is the stage at which the "Orient" stagnates. "Discussion," for Bagehot, is what breaks the cake of custom and allows progress without throwing off law. Reproducing the moral geography that underwrites Burgess and the discursive formation of Teutonic origins theory, Bagehot introduces his chapter "The Age of Discussion" by arguing that the "greatest living contrast is between the old Eastern and customary civilizations and the new Western and changeable civilizations."[52]

According to Bagehot, "discussion" is the reason why some nations progress. It marks modernity. Moreover, it also marks a geographic difference between East and West. Thus, it works as a signifier that articulates time, place, and people. And "discussion" itself is constituted by Bagehot's distinction between civilization and the savage. When he describes "discussion," he contrasts the verbal utterances of savages to verbiage that rises to the level of discussion. As he argues, "[T]he oratory of the savages led to nothing. . . . It is a discussion not of principles, but of undertakings. . . . [Such discussions] do not excite the speculative intellect." Referring to political "discourses," Bagehot exclaims that "no Asiatic ever thought of such things." Meanwhile, "government by discussion," where the subjects of discussion are in some degree "abstract" or "matters of principle," is initiated, among other places, in England and Europe thanks to the "Germanic tribes" who brought with them the elements of popular government "wherever they went," thereby enabling the breakdown of the customs of the Middle Ages.[53]

Wilson picks up this thread and follows it to the same paradigm of speech, a paradigm that Bagehot and Wilson call "government by discussion" and that resurfaces in the 1990s, as I discuss in chapter 6. In his essay "Character of Democracy in the United States," Wilson acknowledges the relation of freedom of thought and press to the spread of democracy. By themselves, however, Wilson finds that such forces cannot produce "a government such as ours." The influences of popular education, the press, travel, commerce, and other means by which knowledge and thought are spread "through every part and member of society" are concededly "mighty," yet they may only "confuse and paralyze the mind" without more. In contrast to those societies presently seeking democracy or the excesses of the French Revolution, Wilson argues that "[v]ery different were the forces behind us." "Our democracy" is a "stage of development," a "piece of developed habit," and it came, "like manhood, as the fruit of youth. An immature people could not have had it," since it was the result of "freedom and self-control." "Such government as ours," Wilson argues, "is a form of conduct, and its only stable foundation is character." A particular form of government, like a particular character, cannot be "adopted," according to Wilson. Both must be "developed by conscious effort and through transmitted aptitudes." In sum, the notable characteristic of American democracy is, well, *character*. A form of government is linked to a form of character, which is, in turn, biopolitical in its formation—the product of biological transmission (aptitudes) that is then politically developed (conscious effort). Self-government refers equally to popular sovereignty and to a specific governance of the self.[54]

One may not be totally surprised that Wilson, who as president would question the loyalty of "hyphenated" Americans, places the foundation of democracy not in an abstract legal principle of free speech but in the identity of the American people, who are capable of exercising this right beneficially. The form of Wilson's nationalism and his approach to free speech, we must note, are indebted to Teutonic origins theory. Echoing Walter Bagehot on the merits of government by discussion and John Burgess's race-based view of world history, Wilson argues,

> Governments such as ours are founded upon discussion, and government by discussion comes . . . late in political . . . development. It . . . is possible for a nation only in the adult age of its political life. The people who successfully maintain such a government must have gone through a period of political training which shall have prepared them for gradual steps of acquired privilege for assuming the entire control of their affairs . . . . They must have acquired adult self reliance, self-knowledge, and self control. . . . It is the heritage of races purged alike of hasty barbaric passions and of patient servility to rulers, and schooled in temperate common counsel. . . . It . . . strengthens through long heredity. It is poison to the infant, but tonic to the man.[55]

Which nations are "man" enough for government by discussion? This is a question Wilson answers with Teutonic origins theory supplemented by an Anglophilic twist. Wilson finds deep significance in the fact that only in those governments "begotten of the English race," and in Switzerland, "where old Teutonic habit" persists as it does in England, can one find examples of successful, modern democracies.[56] Discussion, properly understood, derives from a racially and nationally inflected subject position. The rules of recognition for this subject position are simultaneously rules that justify a refusal of standing to participate in government by discussion to those positioned within this discourse as non-Aryan subjects. They must be tutored and trained before enjoying "democracy of the modern type."

This moral geography of Wilson's matches Burgess's moral geography and its spatialization of world-historical progress. We have already seen how for Burgess the recognition of rights is contingent upon the status of being "civilized"—the cultural practices of the Teutonic racial group. This precondition for the recognition of rights allows Burgess to value freedom of speech. Burgess argues that "freedom of individual thought and expression . . . and the free interchange of the results of these great spiritual forces, are the powers which make for civilization both local, national, and universal."[57] Because, as we have seen, civilization comes with the presence of Teutons, the practice of free speech by Teutonic subjects allows for the further spread of civilization, a positive value for both Teutonic nations and the world. There is, then, a certain systematicity to free speech when it is practiced by rightful subjects: civilization is both a precondition for subjects to have a right to free speech and an outcome of their free speech. Free speech, understood within this paradigm, reproduces the conditions of its own possibility.

But just as the rules for recognizing a subject who may rightfully engage in free speech imply a constitutive exclusion for Wilson or Bagehot, so also is there an outside to Burgess's free speech scheme. In discussing the constitutional provisions for free speech, Burgess argues that the framers "set aside, thus, the philosophy of the Orient, of Middle Age Europe . . . in regard for, and discovery of, truth in the foundation of politics, right, and law." Thanks to the systematicity of civility and speech rights, the free speech provisions in the U.S. Constitution can function for Burgess as a guarantee of a temporally and racially distinctive American identity constituted in opposition to the "Orient." Moreover, anyone who disagrees with Burgess's assessment of freedom of thought and expression as the "fundamental principle of American political philosophy" does not qualify for citizenship in this or any other "real republic." Instead, this person "belongs to the Orient."[58] The gap between East and

West that is unbridgeable by Bagehot's conception of government by discussion is also unbridgeable by the deliberative qualities of free speech in Burgess's thought, where the proper role of "American Indians, Asiatics, and Africans" is to "receive, learn, follow Aryan example."[59] Either one is perceived as conforming to the constitutional requirements of the subject position or one is excluded from its rights, in this case, to free speech and deliberation. Thus, in the late nineteenth and early twentieth centuries there is a discursive formation that structures argumentation regarding rights and free speech according to the racial parameters of Teutonic origins theory. In light of this formation, Wilson and Burgess, rather than being opposed figures as Graber suggests, in fact have a great deal in common.

The Political Conjuncture and Free Speech

Having shown the similarities in thought between Burgess and Wilson, I will now demonstrate the continuities between their thought and the wider ideological field of the early twentieth century. The discursive patterns present in legal reactions such as legislative proposals and outcomes and legal argumentation having to do with radical protests or the protection of speech rights of protestors in favor of the improvement of working conditions or the right to organize laborers converge with the lines of perception established within Teutonic origins theory. Thus, by locating questions of "speech" within the wider ideological field, we will see how Burgess's and Wilson's views are symptomatic of the political conjuncture in which they existed and how they aligned with the repressive side of some of the significant controversies of the day. There is an additional lesson here for political and legal scholars in the ways that radical politics during this era were perceived through a racial lens. This should warn against reading back into history interpretations of radicalism produced by the class-based paradigm we currently use to understand issues of economic justice, and instead enjoin us to comprehend how that period understood such issues. If radical protest was seen to be determined by population-related factors, as I contend, then advocacy of population management must count for us as an instance of repression of free speech since it made sense as such a strategy for those who employed it. And, if population management was an aspect of managing political opinion at the time, then Burgess's population purification measures would have aligned him in the eyes of his contemporaries as being on the repressive rather than the libertarian side of free speech issues.

The racial norms of Teutonic origins theory provided the intellectual resources through which major political crises of the first quarter of the twentieth century were understood. Teutonic origins theory, distinguishing America for its Aryan racial heritage, justified the perception of a danger to America's security in the immigration of eastern and southern Europeans. With the growth of industrial capitalism in this period, conflict between business and labor became heightened. The problem of rising radicalism, then, became associated with the influx of racially different immigrants. Although there was no inherent reason for the two separate issues of immigration and radicalism to be thought about together, they were. That is to say, the racial presuppositions of the U.S. intellectual formation at that time enabled the articulation of these issues to each other such that suppressing immigration and immigrants became a seemingly reasonable means to suppress a radicalism that had acquired racial connotations. Because racially inferior populations were perceived as lacking the capacity of speech or as being unable to exercise a right to free speech properly, immigration opponents came to focus on testing the capacity of speech—in terms of both literacy and holding correct political opinions—of those seeking entrance to the United States as a preferred means of discriminating between those whom America could safely allow into the country and those whom America could not allow entry. The process also functioned in reverse. That is, improperly radical political opinions were attributed to inferior racial elements within American territory. Not measuring up racially to "real" Americans, suppressing such elements did not violate, but in fact furthered, national interests. In sum, free speech as a political and legal issue was located at the nexus between immigration and radicalism. As we shall see, John Burgess, contrary to what Mark Graber would lead us to expect, took positions on immigration and radicalism—the leading issues with free speech implications in this era—that were repressive rather than libertarian.

The twentieth century opened in the wake of violent acts in the late nineteenth century suppressing radicals, like the conflict in the coalfields of Pennsylvania that led to the attack by private police forces upon the "Molly Maguires" in the late 1870s and the Haymarket affair of 1886.[60] The assassination of President McKinley by Leon Czolgosz, an American with a foreign-sounding name who claimed to be an anarchist, further fueled the association of immigration and radicalism. The historian Sidney

Fine describes the main political fallout of President McKinley's assassination as proposals for the exclusion of anarchist immigrants due to the widely held belief that anarchism was not indigenous to the United States (a solution overlooking the fact that the president's assassin was native born). In President Roosevelt's first address to Congress, he suggested that war should be waged against anarchists and their sympathizers and suggested that legislation should be passed to exclude and deport alien anarchists. The result was the immigration law of 1903, the first time since 1798 that newcomers were penalized for their opinions in the United States.[61]

The period under consideration here came to a close in the 1920s and was marked by a series of legislative acts restricting immigration and by the "Palmer raids" against the Industrial Workers of the World (IWW). The Emergency Immigration Act of 1921 and the permanent statute of 1924 discriminated especially against prospective immigrants from southern and eastern Europe. The National Origins Quota System was a further expression of an assumed link between race and radicalness.[62]

Opposition to the Industrial Workers of the World (IWW), culminating in the Palmer or "red" raids of 1919–20, illustrates how antipathy toward radicalism during the early twentieth century linked it with being foreign at a time when being foreign was in turned linked to the need to protect America's racial identity in order to preserve its security as a nation. Organized in 1905, the IWW engaged in famous "free speech fights" between 1909 and 1912 for the right to make public speeches and organize in various towns. These "free speech fights" played a significant role in bringing a right of free speech to public consciousness.[63] During World War I, the federal government focused a significant portion of its repressive activities on the IWW. In these efforts, the federal government used immigration and naturalization law as its preferred legislative and administrative weapon against the IWW.

Opponents of the IWW referred to it as a "foreign" or "alien" organization. In 1917 deportation legislation, Congress made the time period indefinite during which aliens would be subject to deportation for radical ideas. By doing so, it established that "an American made dissident was a 'far fetched proposition,'" by assuming that the radicalism could not have been acquired during the period of residency, no matter how long this period might have been. In other words, radicalism was seen to come from outside of America. Because it operated within a paradigm of thought that placed great emphasis on racially determined identity rather than on social environment as a causal factor, immigration law made sense as a possible weapon against radicalism. In fact, William Preston describes the Immigration Act of 1917 as being aimed specifically at the IWW.[64]

An example of the racial aspects of antiradicalism and the corresponding antipathy toward the IWW during the World War I period can be found in the historian Robert Murray's account of the red scare. Murray cites a statement by the General Intelligence Division of the Department of Justice that estimated that about 90 percent of all domestic radicals were aliens.[65] Demonstrating the part that racial motivation played in the red scare, Murray presents Attorney General Palmer's description of "radical aliens" who were rounded up in his raids on the IWW. The description depends on a visual racism that focuses on physical traits and then infers qualities like intelligence from these outward traits: "Out of the sly and crafty eyes of many of them leap cupidity, cruelty, insanity, and crime; from their lopsided faces, sloping brows, and misshapen features may be recognized the unmistakable criminal type."[66] Indeed, even the most extreme vigilante punishment of IWW members evoked the IWW's racialization: castration and lynching.[67]

The political and legal attention focused on the radicalism of the IWW as a foreign if not a racial threat was simply a specific instance of the general ideological conjuncture in which the problem of radicalism became a problem of foreigners, aliens, immigration, and naturalization that had been building for years. Therefore, radicalism received meaning within the same racial narratives that constructed the nature of the threat that immigration posed to America. Forms of thought, both polemical and scholarly, that forged the link between radicalism and race often turned on the pivot of "speech" as they fueled and rationalized legal policies on immigration, naturalization, and censorship.

For example, William Hornaday published a polemic against immigration and radicalism in 1918 under the auspices of the American Defense Society, an organization the historian John Higham describes as one of the principal preparedness organizations during the World War I period. In this book, Hornaday claims that an "idiotic" immigration policy was responsible for the menace of "Alien Socialism" by permitting a constant inflow of "alien races from all quarters of the globe."[68] Hoping to arouse America from a slumber in which it wallowed in a "riot of luxury and extravagance," while Germany sought after world power and conquest, Hornaday was liberal in his invocation of racial narratives and metaphors to incite his readers to action.[69] For example, socialist leaders adopt principles of "free love," according to Hornaday, which would cause such a degeneration of society that its few survivors would return to the condition of "skin clad savages," and "Lenine [*sic*] and Trotsky" resemble "two East African baboons who have invaded a drawing room."[70] In a context in which radicals like the IWW (whom Hornaday identified as the worst danger of all to America) cited the First Amendment's free speech guaranties for protection against oppression, Hornaday exclaimed that it was "high time that the 'free speech' fetich [*sic*], now grown more ugly and more dangerous in influence than any Congo-Negro idol, should be kicked off its pedestal and buried out of sight."[71] By linking race and radicalism, Hornaday identified immigration policy and the question of speech as the two sites policy should target while utilizing racial invective to mobilize appropriate national action on these fronts.

Prescott Hall, influential with the Immigration Restriction League (whose president was the Teutonic historian John Fiske), published a 1906 book that contributed to a series by the publisher on "American Public Problems" in which he assessed the deteriorating racial composition of the United States and related it to the rise of radical political parties. Hall acknowledged the influence on his book of Richard Mayo Smith, a Columbia University professor, member of the Institut international de statistique, and vice-president of the American Statistical Association, whose 1890 book *Emigration and Immigration* had argued that socialism and anarchism "are not plants of American growth nor of Anglo-Saxon origin," but rather are imported by "foreign agitators" who should not be "given a share in that government which they do not understand."[72] In his own study, entitled *Immigration*, Hall used statistics to describe the social consequences of the changed and diminished racial basis of U.S. immigration.

Hall employed the "great racial divisions" as his categories of comparison because the "racial effects of immigration are more far-reaching and potent than all others."[73] In Hall's analysis, immigration became a public problem because it threatened the nature of the public. While the country started with "the best stock in Europe," there had since been an increase in immigration from southern and eastern Europe, particularly since 1880.[74] What was worse for Hall was that lower types of immigrants seemed to deter the better types, causing a displacement of certain racial elements, such as Germans, who were then choosing to emigrate elsewhere.

Moreover, he associated social problems with racial typologies. According to Hall,

[A]narchy and socialism are the result of a certain degeneracy of race. . . . "The anarchist and ultra-socialist do not, as is commonly supposed, derive their chief support from the Teutonic element; their ranks are rather recruited from among these members of the Semitic and Slavonic races." The increase of the socialist vote in certain districts of the East Side of New York, through the growth of the Semitic, Polish and Hungarian population in those districts, would seem to confirm this view.[75]

Needless to say, for Hall, "the political effect of the Teutonic immigration of the last century . . . has been beneficial. . . . There have been few socialists or agitators among them, and these have had no large following."[76] Thus, Hall linked radicalism with racial identity, which in turn made immigration and naturalization law into a key site for policing popular beliefs.

Hall wrote his study when the literacy test was a hotly contested aspect of immigration policy. He described the "educational test" as a way of furnishing "an indirect method of excluding those who are undesirable, not merely because of their illiteracy, but for other reasons." Hall claimed to have established links between illiteracy and various other social problems such as crime, pauperism, and the disposition to congregate in slums of cities. Then, conceding that some illiterates might make good citizens and that illiteracy in itself could be conquered, Hall nevertheless maintained that "the hereditary tendencies of the peoples illiterate . . . cannot be overcome in a generation or two." Furthermore, "the most powerful factor in assimilation, both social and political, is the ability to read."[77] By making literacy both a symptom of racial characteristics and a vehicle for producing normal subjects, Hall not only situated the literacy test within a biopolitical matrix but gave speech-related capacities a sort of governmental systematicity that converged with the views of Burgess, Bagehot, and Wilson discussed above.

"Literacy," then, functioned as a racial signifier as well as a means for governing a large population. On this dual basis, Hall defended the literacy test against criticism. Against those who would claim that the literacy test would not discriminate racially with a high enough degree of accuracy due to the spread of education, Hall argued that it would work to the intended effect for many years, and that "with increasing immigration from Asia and Africa, this safeguard is needed in the immediate future."[78] As for the effectiveness of the test against crime and anarchy, problems that might be caused by well-educated individuals, Hall responded that the real problem was less a few intelligent criminals and anarchists, and much more "large numbers of men too ignorant to see through their arguments, and forming inflammable material which can be easily kindled into the flame of disorder." Literacy functioned both as a trope for racial identity in the case of immigration from Asia and Africa, and as a technology to facilitate the governance of the population by its potential for ameliorating other social problems. Thus, the significance of the controversy over the literacy test must be understood as biopolitical, like Bagehot's concept of government by discussion, Wilson's understanding of the character needed for American democracy, and Burgess's linkage of rights to a Teutonic racial basis.[79]

At the risk of a digression, we might note the prominence of statistical methodologies in these highly racist defenses of the literacy test and the restriction of immigration and naturalization. Indeed, Burgess writes in his autobiography that had it not been for the ethnological statistics he learned in his statistics course in Germany, he could not have written the (genocidal) portions of his major work on comparative constitutional law on the nation.[80] The concept of the "population" and statistics enjoyed a co-related rise to prominence as the state required knowledge of "the population" to preserve its well-being and protect it against degeneracy— and a key variable for the determination of degeneracy, as we can see from the studies above, is the racial composition of the population. Hence the imperative toward statistical knowledge in this period is inextricable from its racist and nationalist anxieties. These studies certainly help us make once again the old yet not nearly familiar enough point that statistical description does not equal objective knowledge. But there is a more paradoxical point to be made as well. While the rise of statistical thinking has been linked to the constitution of racial and national populations, statistics has also been linked to democratic aspirations since the well-intentioned state should be interested in how its policies affect all segments of the population. Hence the recurring quandary of the U.S. census—on the one hand financial aid and political representation are linked to its results, while on the other it, like any other survey, reproduces the very racial identities that have unfortunately structured this nation's history. Indeed, it is well known to politicians and social scientists that survey design influences both the short-term responses and the long-term beliefs of a study's respondents. We can view this problem as analogous to the paradox of rights and nation that is the main focus of this book—claiming rights within a national constitutional system reproduces the very identity formation that limits the recognition of rights for some while at the same time enabling the recognition of rights for others.[81]

Perhaps the most enduring legacy of this period from a jurisprudential standpoint was Justice Holmes's famous dissenting opinion in *Abrams v. U.S.* (1919), a case involving poor Russian immigrants who were convicted for circulating a leaflet in New York City protesting the U.S. invasion of Vladivostok after the Russian Revolution. When the law professor John Wigmore wrote a notable critique of Holmes's dissent, he mobilized the resources of the ideological field that the activists, scholars, and politicians I have been discussing helped produce to facilitate his legal argument and to support the Supreme Court's legal ruling. This is an ideological field for which Burgess was partly responsible as well.

Since the United States was not actually at war with Russia, to find a violation of the Espionage and Sedition Acts of 1917 and 1918 might be, to put it mildly, a difficult sell. Wigmore, however, constructed Russia as a threat to all "civilized countries," hence relying on Burgess's racialized moral geography to define the American nation's enemies.[82] Then, using this line of perception to justify the conviction of these protesters, Wigmore described protests against U.S. policies during World War I as having "nothing American in them," as being "engineered by alien agents," and as appealing to the "alien-born and alien-parented," making sure to point out that the circulars were printed in Yiddish (though they were also printed in English on the other side).[83] Echoing Burgess, anticipating Carl Schmitt's theory of sovereign decisionism discussed in chapter 1, and citing the Social Darwinist Herbert Spencer, Wigmore emphasized that the line between "Freedom of Speech" and "Freedom of Thuggery" must be informed by a distinction between normal situations and abnormal ones, with the latter being defined as when all interests must be subordinated to "the national right in the struggle for national life." Thus, in the case of a threat against a nation by an external enemy, he elaborated a scheme of free speech based on a military model in which all "conceivable reasoning views . . . get represented," but the bounds of the conceivable are defined by the purpose of saving the national life. This scheme, Wigmore claimed, was necessary because under modern conditions, when a national war was conducted by a democracy, success was dependent upon a general consensus among the citizenry. But just as I argued in chapter 1 that when sovereignty is located in the people, the space of sovereign decisionism cannot be contained within limited times or zones, so also did the abnormal bleed into the normal for Wigmore, who concluded that even during peacetime

Holmes's advocacy of "free trade in ideas" and his pragmatic view of the Constitution as an "experiment" could threaten "the entire constitutional fabric itself."[84]

Thus, the significance of the suppressive legislation of the period that gave rise to the most significant First Amendment jurisprudential developments must be understood within the racially organized ideological field I have elaborated. President Wilson justified the need for this legislation by invoking a racial miscegenation narrative, charging foreign-born opponents with "pouring the poison of disloyalty into the very arteries of our national life."[85] And Wigmore defended it against the famous dissenter by reiterating the elements of the field.

In this light, we can see how the wider intellectual and political context of the era linked a disposition toward politically radical doctrines to inferior racial types, and held changes in America's racial composition brought on by the changing composition of America's immigrants responsible for the era's sociopolitical turbulence caused by anarchism and socialism. By understanding racially inferior groups to be lacking speech-related capital like literacy, the policy advocacy of Hall, Wigmore, the American Defense Society, and others converges with the Teutonic histories of Bagehot, Wilson, and Burgess, which mapped spaces where racially inferior populations were described by their lack of speech and other, Teutonic, spaces that were governed by discussion. As we can see by the way that the regulation of speech was justified during the World War I period, Burgess's thought is substantially consistent with the arguments of many others who linked radicalism with racial inferiority and thereby advocated governance both of speech and of the population in order to promote American national security. Indeed, as we shall see in the next brief section, Burgess not only helped produce an ideological field in which suppression was justified since political dissidents were not considered American for racial reasons, and indeed were perceived as a threat to the security of a nation whose well-being and capacity for self government rested on the maintenance of its racial identity. He also explicitly endorsed repressive legislation. This evidence falsifies Graber's portrayal of Burgess as a libertarian in contrast to Wilson and others who endorsed speech-restrictive governance for the sake of social welfare during this period.

Although this may be seen as "clinching" an argument against Graber in a narrow way, there are larger issues that still remain. Not only must we explain Burgess's criticisms of the Wilson administration's suppressive legislation in light of the argument presented thus far, but we must make good on our hints that something more complex has been developing than an opposition of liberal legal rights to nationalist politics. After using the literacy test as a sign for racial correctness, Hall concedes that literacy can be used for the purposes of good government. And Wigmore values a certain exchange of ideas, acknowledges that the success of war depends on a consensus that would have to be produced by the dissemination of ideas, and has trouble distinguishing normal times of governance from those abnormal times when the nation's security must take precedence. In fact, both Burgess's criticisms of suppressive legislation and the more complex relationship among free speech, liberal government, and the biopolitical concerns of nationalism are connected, as we shall see below.

The Smoking Gun

Prior to World War I, one of the main ways that free speech questions were constitutionally posed was through immigration and naturalization law. The reason was not only ideological but institutional as well. The constitutional revolution of the Civil War amendments had not yet taken full effect—indeed, the Supreme Court did not hold that the First Amendment was "incorporated" within the Fourteenth Amendment, and hence an applicable restraint on state (as opposed to federal) laws, until 1925.[86] W. W. Willoughby's 1910 treatise on constitutional law cited a mere three cases in his discussion of the First Amendment's free speech guaranties—compared with over 250 pages of commentary in the 1988 edition of Laurence Tribe's treatise or over 430 pages of edited speech and press cases in the 1997 edition of Gerald Gunther and Kathleen Sullivan's casebook on constitutional law.[87] Two of these were cases that implicated the federal mails. The first of the three cases Willoughby discussed, however, was *U.S. ex rel. Turner v. Williams* (1904), which dealt with the exclusion and deportation of the alien John Turner for anarchistic beliefs.[88] Free speech, however, entered into national popular consciousness and became widely perceived and effective as a right through IWW free speech fights, which occurred at the state and local levels.[89] Thus, the two main free speech issues between the turn of the twentieth century and World War I were immigration controversies and radicalism controversies raised in significant measure through the IWW. These two areas intersected through the construction of radicalism as foreign and as a racial threat to America.

Immigration and radicalism were the two main political conflicts of the period that raised free speech questions. Burgess supported the repressive side of these conflicts by opposing protests in favor of labor interests and by supporting the limitation of immigration from southern and eastern Europe in the name of both racial purity and political normalcy. Therefore, with respect to the major controversies involving claims of "free speech" of his era, Burgess cannot be portrayed as a staunch advocate of speech rights as Graber intends.

In a 1907 address, Burgess argued that

> immigration of foreign race elements is . . . serious. So long as this immigration was confined to comers of the Teutonic races . . . everything went well. They are people with a conscience, with a basis of self-control and, therefore, prepared for the enjoyment of civil and political liberty. But now we are getting people of a different sort—Slavs, Czechs, Hungarians, South Italians. They do not know our language and do not intend to learn it. They are inclined to anarchy and crime. . . . They are, in everything which goes to make up folk character, the exact opposite of genuine Americans. It remains to be seen whether Uncle Sam can digest and assimilate such a morsel. One would infer from the last Naturalization Act . . . of June 29, 1906 that he concluded to spit it out.

For Burgess, the most important provisions of this act included the exclusion from citizenship of non–English speakers, anarchists, those who belonged to organizations that were anarchistic or taught about anarchism, or anyone who was not a monogamist. He concluded: "It is evident that Uncle Sam does not want such rabble for citizens." Burgess blamed these immigrants for the increase in governmental power that was infringing upon liberties. The basis for this blame was that labor strikes necessitated military force to suppress them, thereby damaging American institutions.[90]

This address proves that Burgess lent his voice to the forces that were repressing those who were claiming free speech as a right at that time. In this address Burgess endorses the Naturalization Act of 1906, which made citizenship contingent upon holding correct political opinions. He interprets immigration through the lens of Teutonic origins theory, associates inferior races of immigrants with radicalism and anarchism, and then, rather than conceptualizing labor protests as a species of free speech, he implicitly blames non-Teutonic immigrants for labor unrest requiring military suppression.

The First Amendment alchemist Zechariah Chafee discusses the Naturalization Act in his book *Free Speech in the United States* and gives it the dubious honor of being listed in his appendix on federal laws affecting free speech.[91] Within six years after the act passed, federal judges in the Pacific Northwest would turn it into a significant tool in their war against the IWW by denying naturalization to anyone who either was a member of the IWW, was engaged in pro-IWW activity, had been a member at any time during the five-year residency period, or relied on citizen IWW members as their character witnesses (or citizens who were even *married* to an IWW member).[92] As this address shows, Burgess was not supportive of the free speech side of the major controversies facing the United States at the time, and he participated in, and helped promote, the very ideological field that contributed to federal suppression efforts during World War I.

Thus, Burgess's support for the 1906 Naturalization Act is no different from Wilson's efforts to root out dissent; nor is Burgess any different from those who sought to suppress the IWW and who wanted to take those efforts further than Wilson did. By relating the issue of the immigrants' inferior racial stock to radicalism, Burgess mirrors Wilson's assessment of the threat posed by immigration, as well as the assessments of those who attempted to go further than Wilson in their antipathy toward foreigners. Both Burgess and Wilson shared the same free speech paradigm, one which, in turn, was situated within effectively the same moral geography. But if Burgess and Wilson shared so much, then what explains Burgess's advocacy of free speech during World War I, on which Graber places so much emphasis? The answer, I contend, rests with Burgess's adherence to Teutonic origins theory and the changes to the general racial formation in the United States as the nation went to war.

Burgess's World War I Advocacy of Free Speech

Although Graber omits Burgess's Teutonic supremacy from his discussion of Burgess as a libertarian, Burgess certainly did write the things Graber attributes to him—defenses of free speech in face of government policies of suppression at a time when opposition to the government incurred suspicion. Did Burgess completely change his stripes? To the contrary, with World War I, the racial formation shifted, but Burgess did not. His Teutonic-centered racism became anachronistic in a period of an Anglo-American alliance against Germany.

According to the historian John Higham, Madison Grant, the historian who has come to exemplify the era's most extreme racism (he was also vice-president of the Immigration Restriction League), brought out a hastily revised edition of his book *The Passing of the Great Race* in 1918 that eliminated references to early American settlers as Teutonic and that found most current inhabitants of Germany to be Alpines, rather than the race Grant favored—Nordics.[93] Higham argues that after 1915, "little more was heard in the United States about the origins of liberty in the forests of Germany." What occurred, according to Higham, was an Anglo-Saxon secession from Teutonic origins theory with the approach of World War I.[94] American national identity became purified around an Anglo-Saxon racial core detached from Teutonic origins.

Rather than adjusting to this shift as so many others did, Burgess fought it. As early as 1904, Burgess published an essay in *Political Science Quarterly* the purpose of which was to argue for the necessity of cooperation between the three Teutonic powers in spreading "Teutonic culture" into the other parts of the world. Unfortunately, world politics was a tangled web, so Burgess was forced to discuss the impediments standing in the way of "Teutonic cooperation" and how to solve them.[95] The main problem, as Burgess saw it, was the "Slavic peril" of Russia. Because of the differences between Russia and the "civilized states of the world," Russia was a natural enemy to the United States, but the people of the United States were not sufficiently conscious of this. Burgess argued that it was the "transcendent duty" of the United States to bring the Teutons of the world together for the purposes of world order and to impel the uncivilized toward a civilized status.[96]

Considering Burgess's plans for the world, World War I must have seemed to him a disaster. The Teutonic nations were fighting one another, and two of them were in alliance (for a time) with Slavic Russia, the main threat to world civilization. At the beginning of the war, Burgess publicized what he understood to be the causes of the outbreak in terms favorable to Germany. These writings were critical of his former student Theodore Roosevelt for having intervened in the Russo-Japanese war of 1904–5 in a way somewhat favorable to Japan, thus causing Russia to turn the "force of the Pan-Slavic program . . . back upon Europe." Writing on August 17, 1914, for the German American Literary Defense Committee, Burgess feared that the Britain-Russia-France alliance would give Russia "the mastery of the Continent of Europe," and he hoped that this could be prevented since its consequences would require a military defense of U.S. territory and commerce that could endanger prosperity as well as the existence of republican institutions.[97] In a pamphlet entitled *Germany's Just Cause* published around 1914, Burgess made many of these same points, as he feared that if an immediate cessation to the hostilities did not occur, the U.S. government might be influenced to "throw its weight in a direction which will be ultimately found to be injurious to our own best interests and to those of universal peace and civilization." Therefore, he supported Wilson's offers of mediation and encouraged the expression of "public opinion" to make Great Britain feel that its alliance was "unnatural."[98]

To sum up, before World War I, Burgess had advocated a union of Teutonic nations in the interests of world civilization and as a defense against Slavic Russia. With the outbreak of hostilities, Burgess not only saw his hopes for a racialized world civilization evaporate, but thought that "unnatural" cross-racial alliances were being forged with the chief racial threat to Teutonic hegemony—the Slavic-Asiatic Russians. This contradicted his conception of the national interest as defined by Teutonic origins theory and violated the principles of his moral geography.

Burgess's only chance to save civilization as he understood it was for public opinion to convince Great Britain that its alliance with Russia was "unnatural." Thus, there was an ethnical-ethical duty (to use Burgess's terminology, which seems appropriate here) to engage in practices of free speech to put the truth before the nation and Great Britain. Hence not only his defense of free speech but his publications in pamphlets like *Germany's Just Cause* (which was devoted to the "Fatherland") were all driven by the "social interest" of Teutonic supremacy and a Teutonic obligation to civilize the rest of the world. Unlike Madison Grant, who enjoyed great popularity during the 1920s, Burgess never went along with the Anglo-American secession from Teutonic origins theory and became largely irrelevant.[99]

To repeat, the conceptual opposition between a libertarian free speech absolutism and a concern for the social interest through which contemporary political theory operates, and which Graber uses to comprehend the differences between Burgess and Wilson, cannot describe Burgess's defense of free speech. Burgess's "libertarianism" is falsifiable with reference both to his scholarly writing, which only respects rights for the civilized, and to his endorsement of repressive legislation, which is based in the same mechanisms of justification that supported the suppression of disloyalty during World War I and its immediate aftermath. Burgess, like Wilson and the Progressives in Graber's depiction, wanted to promote the social interest of civilization, which he understood to be contradicted by World War I, and so he engaged in practices of free speech and defended free speech against governmental censorship.

We cannot call Burgess a "libertarian" defender of free speech—as that term is commonly understood—just for his advocacy of free speech in the war era. Rather, we should understand Burgess as seeking *to free the speech* that will promote the national interest as determined by his interpretation of Teutonic origins theory. When power is dispersed into multiple institutional sites, as it commonly is under liberal systems of governance, there must be some mobilizing force to achieve political goals. Free speech is one of those forces. It produces the public opinion that Burgess hoped would correct the violations committed by World War I to his moral geography. Burgess argues that democratic government requires a form of common consciousness, and I suggest that free speech can be productive of this commonality. This is consistent with William Hornaday's arguments on behalf of the American Defense Society during World War I. Not only does Hornaday advocate the censorship of radicals, but he also praises the press as the strongest defense of the American nation against socialism, revolution, and anarchy, and without the "clean-strain Americanism" it promotes, he argues that this country "would not be fit for a decent white man to live in."[100] Liberal democratic government requires free speech. I am not talking about Marcusean "repressive tolerance"—allowing dissenters to blow off steam and then reincorporating such dissenters back into the system. I am talking about the Foucauldian notion that power is productive and active and necessary for the achievement of aims. In other words, even though Burgess is more similar to Wilson than Graber recognizes, I want to preempt a temptation to construe his advocacy of free speech as therefore a façade.

Sovereignty and Liberty

Burgess's exposition of the U.S. constitutional system is insightful and makes overt dimensions of the system's logic that much contemporary scholarship treads upon lightly at best.[101] By examining Burgess's constitutional theory, we will see how the U.S. constitutional system puts into play a relationship between rights and national security that eludes the conventional opposition between rights and nationalism. Above, I suggested that something more complex was afoot as various thinkers of Burgess's era sought to use speech-related capacities like literacy or freedom of the press in a *regulatory* rather than a *censorial* manner—valuing, that is, "speech" as it relates to the project of governing a population rather than as an element limited to a yes-no logic. Burgess makes more obvious the rationality of the U.S. constitutional system as he synthesizes and makes more coherent these tendencies present in other thinkers of his era. In other words, because of the dominance of Teutonic origins theory of which Burgess was an expositor, the significance of Burgess in the institutional emergence of political science in the United States, and Burgess's ability to express the logic of the U.S. constitutional system, Burgess's thought represents a form of political reason and a technology of government that are important to grasp if we are to understand the era's political and legal events.[102]

Burgess and Wilson are more similar than Graber recognizes, despite the fact that Burgess criticized Wilson administration policies. It distorts Burgess's thought to apply the conventions of political and legal theory to his condemnation of those policies and come to the conclusion that Burgess was a libertarian defender of free speech. Closer attention to Burgess's constitutional theory would have guarded against this mistake. Burgess's thought is not well captured by the disposition of political and legal theory to oppose liberal rights to nationalism. In order to understand how Burgess can be both a supporter of First Amendment rights and the most racist form of nationalist, we need better theoretical tools and a shift in our manner of political and legal perception. In his histories of different forms of power, and the interest he took in different forms of political reason toward the end of his life, I suggest that Michel Foucault has begun to provide us with those tools.

There are three ways that Foucault assists our efforts of reconstruction here. First, Foucault's work justifies the importance of an adequate understanding of Burgess's thought. Foucault is well-known for focusing upon a power-knowledge nexus, particularly at the end of his life when he began to elaborate the forms of knowledge and reason "modern" states used for their governing practices. Burgess is methodologically significant for scholarship informed by Foucault because of his location at this nexus. Teutonic origins theory informs the logic of political activity during the late nineteenth and early twentieth centuries, and Burgess was a key member of this school of thought.[103]

Second, Foucault's work eschews the tendency so prominent in conventional political and legal analyses to oppose freedom to power. For most conventional theories, where there is power, freedom is absent. For liberal theorists in particular, to protect fundamental individual freedoms against the power of politics, there must be nonpolitical legal rights that limit power. Foucault's work on government, however, approaches power and freedom differently. He describes the exercise of governmental power as "a total structure of actions brought to bear upon possible actions . . . a way of acting upon an acting subject or acting subjects by virtue of their acting or being capable of action. A set of actions upon other actions."[104] For Foucault, government is not limited in its terms of reference to the "political," or to state structures. It applies more broadly to the way in which the conduct of individuals or groups might be directed. Thus, to govern is to "structure the possible field of action of others." By characterizing government in this way, however, one recognizes that power is exercised over and through free subjects. Consequently, for Foucault, "there is no face-to-face confrontation of power and freedom, which are mutually exclusive (freedom disappears everywhere power is exercised), but a much more complicated interplay."[105]

This reconfiguration of the relation between power and freedom is necessary for our comprehension of Burgess and the form of political reason he represents. Because Burgess distinguishes "barbaric liberty" from the kind of freedom the civilized Teutons exercise, and because he sees no contradiction between freedom and national sovereignty, Burgess's thought defies the conventional opposition of freedom to power, and thus it requires us to find more complex tools for political and legal analysis. Moreover, we have found this more complex relation between freedom and power in others besides Burgess who view speech-related capacities as useful to govern a national population. Thus, the analytical tools Foucault's historical work supplies rather than the concepts of conventional political philosophy or jurisprudence are necessary to grasp the logic of political and legal action of this period that is put into play by the U.S. constitutional system. Rather than freedom versus power, we must understand the *types, modes, forms,* or *practices* of freedom that a form of government enables or disenables.

Third, despite the appeal liberalism holds for Foucault as a kind of insistent critical questioning of government, he does put liberalism into relation with biopolitics in a way that is appropriate for our purposes here. Conventional theory translates the opposition of freedom to power into an opposition of liberal rights to nationalist politics. Foucault's historical account of liberalism, however, positions it as a questioning of government: Why must one govern? Liberalism represents the shift from mercantilism, state reason, or *Polizeistaat*, for which the state is the end to be achieved by government, or older, feudal notions of government for which control over territory is the end to be achieved. Now, the security of "society" or the welfare of the "population" is the end to be achieved. According to Foucault, liberal thought "starts not from the existence of the state . . . but rather from society." So the question becomes, what ends should government pursue with regard to society in order to justify its existence?[106] Thus, within what Foucault calls "governmentality"—the style of government he argues begins to develop gradually after the administrative states of the fifteenth and sixteenth centuries—there is a co-emergence of liberalism and "population" as a "datum, as a field of intervention, and as an objective of governmental techniques."[107] Using the tools Foucault gives us, we must go beyond Foucault to interrogate the relationship between liberal government and biopolitics in a sharper manner than he posed the question. And for this, Burgess provides an interesting case study for the way he puts liberty in relation to sovereignty. Thus, we shall focus on Burgess in order to use tools that Foucault has given us to explain the co-relation of liberal government and biopolitics in a particular site and with greater specificity than Foucault had a chance to do.

Burgess explicitly rejects the conventional terms of political theory through which Graber attempts to categorize Burgess's own thought. In his major work of comparative constitutional law, Burgess notes that in the conventional view, state sovereignty implies "the destruction of individual liberty and individual rights." Against this view, he argues that state sovereignty is "not only not inimical to individual liberty and individual rights, but it is their only solid foundation and guaranty."[108] For Burgess, the "state" is an organized unit of a portion of humanity. It is conceptually distinct from any particular organization, though it does not come into being in a regular form without a constitution. The state is also distinct and prior to the government. The relationship between the state and the nation is that the state is the nation organized politically. And for Burgess, as we have seen, the most modern states are national states.

So, to put this in the American context, behind the government lies the Constitution, and in back of the Constitution we find the original sovereign state, which "ordains the constitution of both government and liberty."[109] In the United States, the sovereign vests the courts of the central government with power to interpret the Constitution and to defend it against arbitrary actions of the executive and legislative branches.[110] Thus, for Burgess the state is less an institutional structure than a community organized for political and legal purposes. Ideally, this state would be a singular nation, and the state should strive to attain this ideal situation.[111]

Against the conventional view and in support of his conception of the relationship between sovereignty and individual rights, Burgess makes several arguments. He argues, first, that if there were a limit placed on state power, then that which places the limit would be sovereign rather than the state. In the world, however, there is no such sovereign organization over and above the national state. Thus, even if someone should invoke international law or laws of nature, it is the state that must interpret these for those within its jurisdiction. Second, Burgess argues that the unlimited sovereignty of the state is the "source and support" of individual liberty, because if the state were deprived of its power to determine the scope of individual liberty, each individual would have to make this decision for himself, and this would lead to conflict. As a consequence, only those with power would be free, while the rest would be in subjection. According to Burgess, the state "sets exact limits to the sphere in which it permits the individual to act freely." In light of Foucault's attention to the complicated interplay between freedom and power that characterizes modern government, we may rewrite that sentence to read: *By defining a sphere of liberty, the state enables individuals to act freely.* This is consistent with Burgess's own rejection of the conventional opposition of freedom and power, which he makes clear in pointing out that absolute monarchies of the fifteenth, sixteenth, and seventeenth centuries "gave liberty to the common man by subjecting the nobles to the law of the state." Therefore, Burgess argues that if state sovereignty were weakened, individual liberty would in fact become less secure, and the "barbarism of individualism" would appear.[112]

Why do people persist in posing a contradiction between state sovereignty and individual rights? Burgess believes it is because of a failure to distinguish the government from the state. It is possible that the government might violate individual rights, but it is the state's role, in Burgess's understanding, to restrain the government from violating such limitations. Thus, the state is the defender and definer of individual liberty as its very source. But as its source, to reiterate, it makes no sense to say that the state is limited by individual rights. Moreover, there is no liberty outside of state organization.[113]

The state is the definer of the sphere of individual liberty—the principles of rights, the character of wrongs. This state consciousness Burgess also calls "common consciousness." In national states, according to Burgess, the population will have a common language and a common understanding of rights and wrongs. This "common understanding is the strongest moral basis which government can possibly have."[114] "National harmony," for Burgess, is the social condition that precedes and makes possible "the existence of the democratic state." Thus individuals must rise in their mental development to the consciousness of the state.[115] To this end, one of the most important policies for the state is to perfect its nationality. In so doing, it is securing its sovereignty. How may it achieve this goal of national harmony? The state can pursue its goals by one of two strategies, government or liberty. For Burgess, when a people is emerging from barbarism, government will be the primary strategy of the state. With the growth of civilization, however, the state will widen the sphere of liberty to achieve its ends.[116]

Foucault's work on government, in which one who governs attempts to structure the actions of active subjects, and his discussion of the historical emergence of population as something with its own principles that the state must take into account lest it govern too much and to counterproductive ends, bring forward the notion that power can be exercised over and through free subjects; the existence of freedom does not indicate the absence of power. Similarly, Burgess argues that it is erroneous to believe that the state does nothing except through government. In fact, he contends that the state's most important results are achieved through liberty.[117] Using only slightly different terminology than Foucauldian scholarship on governmentality, Burgess also views power as exceeding state institutions and as requiring active subjects. In this vein, Burgess defends the First Amendment as a political technology for producing various benefits, the most important of which is a deeper dissemination of national subjectivity among persons within the state's jurisdiction.

Burgess contends, "If the state guarantees the liberty of conscience and of thought and expression, and permits the association of individuals for the purposes of religion and education, and protects such associations in the exercise of their rights, it does a vast deal *for* religion and education." Burgess also argues that the state should hold associations "to the fulfilment of their public purpose."[118] In Burgess's terms, there is nothing contradictory about these two statements. Since the national state as sovereign enables First Amendment rights to be exercised, it would be contradictory to allow these rights to be exercised in a way that threatened their very basis.

Burgess's work also helps us to link Foucault's research on disciplinary institutions to practices of liberal government in an explicit way that complements the latter's own work on sexuality.[119] Burgess values intermediate institutions as disciplinary sites that will produce subjects who have both internalized the state's normalizing gaze and also are empowered by its disciplinary technologies to act in certain ways. Burgess contends that public self-control rests on individual self-control, which is in turn based on personal morality. The best means for developing a strict morality and influence over the thoughts and acts of individuals, according to Burgess, is for the nation to encourage and cultivate voluntary associations. Churches are valuable, Burgess states, "not as theological institutions, but as powerful social organizations among men."[120] And the right of free association promotes the development and spread of "customary morality" as a mechanism of self-control for individuals.[121] We might translate Burgess's linkage of public self-control to individual self-control into a language of self-government: national self government cannot be had without subjects who govern their selves as nationals. And Burgess values voluntary associations as mechanisms for producing national subjects. He writes: "[T]he more that may be done through freedom, the better, because the employment of this means of accomplishing things signifies the participation of all." He explains: "These voluntary . . . associations make out of near-dwellers real neighbors, produce neighborly relations . . . and develop the capacity to view things from another's standpoint as well as from one's own." These associations cultivate mutual confidence and trust, which he claims is necessary to "become a free people."[122] They are productive of the common consciousness and the national harmony necessary for a democratic state.

Burgess therefore values the rights inscribed within the First Amendment in part because they enable a more thorough discipline of society, producing subjects who can be entrusted with the powers of government. Burgess values the First Amendment as a technology or mechanism for governance that helps produce a more deeply disseminated national subjectivity among those active subjects who avail themselves of this freedom. In other words, he values the First Amendment for promoting a national consciousness that, in turn, makes the basis of rights more secure.

Conclusion

John Graber describes the attempt to repress political dissent by Woodrow Wilson's administration and John Burgess's criticism of this policy as the difference between promoting the national interest and having a libertarian concern for individual rights. Political and legal theory typically perceives nationalism and individual rights as opposed and conflictual concerns. To pose the difference between Wilson and Burgess as the difference between nationalism and libertarianism, however, misrepresents the form of political and legal thought Burgess exemplifies.[123] Burgess's defenses of free speech do not make him into a "libertarian," as that term is generally understood. Burgess's racialized nationalism and his defense of the First Amendment shows that contrary to what conventional political and legal theory leads us to expect, questions of legal rights like freedom of speech have been joined to the problem of national identity within the U.S. constitutional system, a system that is premised upon the sovereignty of the American people. Burgess's argument that individual liberty does not conflict with the sovereignty of the national state is symptomatic of this system of rights.

To translate Burgess's formulation of the relationship of liberty and sovereignty into the terminology of the U.S. Constitution, its contemporary exposition by James Wilson, and a more recent one by Bruce Ackerman: if the sovereign American people, expressing its will through the Constitution, reserves the right of free speech to itself rather than allowing the government to make laws regarding speech, then protecting the right of free speech under these circumstances requires the ongoing preservation of the American people for the very existence of this right.[124] This is akin to Carl Schmitt's argument, addressed in chapter 1, that there can be no law of pure chaos, and hence that a stable empirical situation is a prerequisite for legal validity. Evaluating one's claim to the right of free speech in these circumstances therefore requires an evaluation of one's claim to be a part of the American people, since free speech is a right reserved to the people. Thus, Burgess could, on the one hand, defend a right to free speech, and on the other hand limit his recognition of this right to those he deemed "civilized," which he measured by Teutonic norms since the Teutonic race was his standard for who counted as a "genuine" American. He could do these things while remaining consistent because free speech is a right the sovereign American people reserves to itself. If the right of free speech exists within a system determined by national sovereignty, then national sovereignty is the condition of possibility for the continued existence of that right. As we can see from Burgess's white supremacist scholarship, the biopolitical sovereign decision Schmitt discusses and Giorgio Agamben elaborates cannot be contained within the exceptional zone of immigration and naturalization law or the exceptional time of war. It exists whenever the American people must be conjured, which means whenever the American people's rights are claimed. The biopolitical question will haunt rights as long as rights exist within a legal and political system that is authorized by the people, for the people.

Burgess's racism is relevant to his defense of a right of free speech, and it is extreme. Although Burgess had been long forgotten when Graber unearthed him, the racial discourse that posits being civilized as a condition for the right of free speech is as general as it is persistent—as we shall see in subsequent chapters. While few political or legal scholars mention Burgess anymore, many do refer to John Stuart Mill for the purpose of explaining what is meant by free speech and why it is valued. This scholarship rarely discusses Mill's racial presumptions, let alone their relationship to free speech. In addition to probing this relationship in the next chapter, I will also amplify, through a close reading of Mill, an insight that I share with others: however "natural" various forms of identities may appear, they are in fact artificial, though their status as artificial does not make them any less real in their effects. Identities are produced rather than natural, and they are produced by the very discursive interventions that refer to identity as causing other social phenomena—though they are never "finally" produced once and for all since the mechanism of production is discursive. Because identity has no natural, transhistorical essence, and is instead a function of discourses that employ identity-based categories, we will find categories of identity to be unstable when invoked to refer to "inherent" differences between humans. Since identity is not natural and must instead be produced and reproduced lest the identity no longer exist, wherever the question of the American people surfaces, we then have a moment of sovereign decision. Though these problems may be most obvious when the border police sort insider from outsider, they are insinuated unavoidably within our everyday legal practices. Burgess, then, is notable not for the ubiquity of his biopolitical concerns, only for the explicit and uncompromising nature of the racism he exhibited.

3

A Moral Geography of Liberty
John Stuart Mill and American Free Speech Discourse

The United States Constitution establishes rights on the authority of the sovereign of the national community—the American people whose will the Constitution represents. The Bill of Rights represents the rights of the people. Therefore, the practice of claiming constitutional rights like freedom of speech in the American context entails assumptions, counterassumptions, and struggles over the substance of the American people. These struggles help constitute the regulatory norms and boundaries of this imagined community. If the background assumption of an American rights-bearing community is necessary to establish the possibility for protecting American constitutional rights in an international context in the first place, this assumption also establishes the limits of these rights in the boundaries that distinguish America from other possible peoples and places.

In this chapter, I explore the discursive background of the American constitutional rights of freedom of speech and press by way of the conventional construction of the time and space coordinates associated with the emergence of a right to free speech. The American appropriation of this discursive formation locates America as a place where one legitimately claims rights to free speech. I will interpret John Stuart Mill's work on free speech as an exemplary and influential instance of this narrative, and I will refer to this discursive formation as the "Millian paradigm." When Americans assert a right of free speech, they often inhabit this discourse for their claims to make sense. The Millian paradigm offers a frame of inclusion and exclusion for identifying a people for whom freedom of speech is appropriate and those for whom it is not. Mill's system of enabled and disenabled identities has functioned in a symbolic politics of speech to produce a "West" and the "Rest." This moral geography is significant because it structures the claims to free speech rights, and is, in turn, constituted by the process of invoking a right to free speech.[1]

Mill and American Free Speech Protections

I define the Millian paradigm as a predominant, if not the dominant, discourse of freedom of speech in the United States. This discourse defines the system of speech to be a marketplace of competing ideas. Persons enter this system as reasoning subjects who, in exercising these capacities, distinguish good ideas from bad and make progress toward truth. The familiar statement "The best response to bad speech is more speech" becomes meaningful by being situated within this discourse. It tells individualists that this clash and conflict helps to develop individual capacities. It tells absolutists why they should value freedom of speech as a right. For liberals who use the absolutist position as a pole to situate their understanding of speech rights, this paradigm becomes a principle that can stand above the fray of bias or politics in order to aid in the adjudication of controversies. In other words, this discourse provides a vocabulary that allows one to talk about issues involving freedom of speech, allows one to value it as a right, and constrains the sorts of utterances that can be made about this right. It creates a problematic.[2]

Zechariah Chafee, who, as I discussed in the previous chapter, is an important influence upon what has come to be considered "modern" free speech doctrine in the United States, refers to Mill a number of times in his classic *Free Speech in the United States*. According to Chafee, "the philosophical speculations of John Stuart Mill" have contributed to "the making of the constitutional conception of free speech."[3] Consistent with the Millian paradigm, while also referring to Walter Bagehot, Chafee defines the "true" meaning of freedom of speech to be "the discovery and spread of truth on subjects of general concern," which is "only possible through unlimited discussion." Having said this much in favor of "unlimited discussion," however, Chafee then goes on to qualify this interest with other, more national purposes of government such as "order, the training of the young, protection against external aggression."[4] In this way, Chafee can be seen as embracing two sides of Mill—the side of Mill that values free speech for the development of the individual, and the side of Mill that values free speech for more social purposes such as its role in the discovery of truth. According to Chafee, the First Amendment protects two kinds of speech. It protects the individual interest in self-expression necessary to make life worth living, and the social interest in the attainment of truth so that "the country may not only adopt the wisest course of action but carry it out in the wisest way."[5] Thus, Chafee interprets the First Amendment's guaranties in a manner that is consistent with the national interest and the interests of the individual, as long as the latter are consistent with the individual identity of a national subject.

Chafee incorporates the "marketplace of ideas" aspect of Mill's thought as well. Mill supports individuals' contributing different ideas and contesting the ideas put forward by others so that truth can be distinguished from false opinions, or so that missing parts of the truth can be added to partial truths put forward in discussion. According to Mill, "[S]ince the general or prevailing opinion on any given subject is rarely or never the whole truth, it is only by the collision of adverse opinions that the remainder of the truth has any chance of being supplied."[6] Similarly, Chafee argues that truth "can be sifted from falsehood only if the government is vigorously and constantly cross-examined. . . . Legal proceedings prove that an opponent makes the best cross-examiner." In light of this model for producing social truth, Chafee argues that even during wartime "it is a disastrous mistake to limit criticism to those who favor the war." Critics should be protected to assure that the point of the war is clearly defined and that the war is not being diverted to improper ends.[7] Thus, both Mill and Chafee use what is now called the "marketplace of ideas" as a way of describing the ideal free speech process, a system of distinguishing good ideas from bad through criticism in order to make progress toward truth, and which is preserved by protecting the right of free speech.

While Mill, or the framers of the U.S. Constitution for that matter, may give a certain justification for free speech, they are not the source of the value of free speech on Chafee's understanding. According to Chafee,

[T]he free speech clauses must also be interpreted in the light of more remote history. The framers of those clauses did not invent the conception of freedom of speech as a result of their own experience of the last few years. The idea has been gradually molded in men's minds by centuries of conflict. It was the product of a people of whom the framers were merely the mouthpiece. Its significance was not fixed by their personality, but was the endless expression of a civilization.[8]

In addition to mentioning the role of Mill in his description of the making of the constitutional conception of free speech, Chafee borrows from Justice Holmes to summarize his position that "[t]he provisions of the Constitution are not mathematical formulas having their essence in their form; they are organic living institutions transplanted from English soil."[9] Chafee is arguing that free speech rights must be understood in the context of a given civilization, rather than in the abstract. Therefore, it is relevant that these rights are the product of a people whom the framers merely represented. Free speech lives as a concept because it is part of a social body that sustains it in its life. This organism, once nourished by English soil and now (trans)planted in America, must be understood, according to Chafee, as the proper frame of reference for speech rights. In this, one can hear an echo of John Adams, who justified American rights by describing rights cleaved to the bodies of ancestors who migrated from England, as well as of Teutonic and Social Darwinist historians John Burgess, Woodrow Wilson, and Walter Bagehot. Chafee makes other remarks that evoke this geohistorical narrative for justifying American rights more specifically. He cajoles his readers by arguing that "[t]hose who gave their lives for freedom would be the last to thank us for throwing aside so lightly the great traditions of our race."[10] Chafee also praises Charles Evans Hughes as the "champion of Anglo-Saxon liberties."[11]

Mill's free speech scheme, however, is double-edged. The Millian paradigm emphasizes progress toward truth as the main purpose of free speech, and places responsibility for such progress on the reasoning capacities of its subjects. On these grounds, speech that is unlikely to contribute toward truth, and persons unlikely to be able to push forward this progress, have no claim on speech rights. The U.S. Supreme Court case *Chaplinsky v. New Hampshire*, in language almost identical to that of Chafee's *Free Speech in the United States*, trades on the Millian paradigm's exclusionary aspects. In this case, Justice Murphy argued that certain categories of speech may be excluded from First Amendment protection. These "utterances are no essential part of any exposition of ideas, and are of such slight social value as a step to truth that any benefit that may be derived from them is clearly outweighed by the social interest in order and morality."[12]

The First Amendment's importance has increased substantially since World War I in the United States, especially since the late 1930s with the establishment of the "preferred position" doctrine. Footnote 4 of Justice

Stone's opinion in *United States v. Carolene Products* is taken to be the constitutional origin of this doctrine.[13] The preferred position doctrine defines certain provisions of the Bill of Rights to be more fundamental than others. During the middle of the twentieth century, legal intellectuals defended and interpreted this doctrine. According to these interpretations, America was represented as the "land of liberty," and a few rights were seen as fundamental to this liberty, so fundamental that they occupied a "preferred position" in constitutional adjudication, with the First Amendment coming to be the predominant right within this small subset of fundamental rights. Thus American liberty became closely associated with the First Amendment, and specifically with freedom of speech.

After World War II, many legal intellectuals followed in the trailblazing footsteps of Chafee and made claims that America was a nation that particularly enjoyed and respected liberty and that the First Amendment was fundamental to its greatness. For instance, Robert McKay argued that it "is not too strong to say that without freedom of speech and thought, all other provisions in the Constitution would lack foundation and might well not survive."[14] The preferred position doctrine creates for McKay a "mood," which "recalls to mind the simple but majestic fact that here is a society in which the important freedoms count for something." For McKay, "freedom of speech and conscience" is something particular to the Euro-American population that has existed in America since its beginning—the First Amendment and *United States v. Carolene Products*, note 4, are merely landmarks along a constant evolution. This "preference for freedom" can be traced to England, and it "le[ads] unmistakably toward the first amendment" and Justice Stone's famous footnote 4. Therefore, the preferred position is just a recent codification of this essential preference of a people for freedom, rather than its creation. Indeed, McKay argues that Justice Stone can claim credit for its "expression" but cannot claim "authorship" for the "idea that lies behind."[15] Thus, for McKay as for Chafee, "the first amendment has been accorded a preferred position in this larger sense at least since 1791." Freedom of speech is something integral to America, and America is defined as the embodiment of this principle. As such, America acts either as a norm others may strive toward if they seek to practice freedom of speech or as a standard to measure their efforts.

The work of McKay and others illustrates the way much of the intellectual production pertaining to the preferred position doctrine reflects Mill's essay "On Liberty," taking free speech to be the foundation for all other liberties.[16] Mill took the West in general, and England in particular, as the standard of liberty and "progress," while legal theorists like McKay do the same, only they insert America into the narrative as the nation with the special "preference for freedom." America can be a standard of world-historical progress through an association with "free speech" because of a certain model of free speech. This model posits a self with its reason protected by rights of freedom of thought, speech, and press from forces of power that might constrain or determine its conclusions. This model of free speech represents historical developments as guaranteed by reason and thus as examples for others to follow.

More contemporary legal scholarship also uses Mill's arguments defending liberty of speech to suggest a principled First Amendment jurisprudence, or refer to Mill's arguments as a standard against which First Amendment doctrine or the obligations of free speech may be better understood. R. George Wright defends a proposal that "Millian values" should be used to impose principles of inclusion and exclusion regarding what should count as "speech" in a constitutional sense and to distinguish what ought to be excluded from constitutionally protected speech.[17] While Wright utilizes Mill to create a legal basis for the exclusion of nude dancing from First Amendment protection, various other legal scholars also use Mill to comprehend U.S. First Amendment jurisprudence, to elaborate a more "liberal" position, or to suggest that a demise in civility is due, in part, to the influence of Mill on constitutional doctrine such that people do claim that things like nude dancing are protected by the Free Speech Clauses. Thus, it appears that Mill defines the discursive field within which American free speech controversy occurs.[18]

Method

When John Adams opposes "freedom of thinking, speaking and writing" to power, or when Mill presents his argument about liberty by starting with "Liberty of Thought: from which it is impossible to separate the cognate liberty of speaking and writing,"[19] one can see how freedom of speech is organized around what Jacques Derrida has described as the metaphysics of presence.[20] This means that the self and its consciousness exist prior to social interactions such as speech, as if something of the self's consciousness could elude social intercourse. Speech and writing, rather than being themselves constitutive of meaning, are presented as representatives of consciousness which, in applying its reason to brute data, is the creator of meaning. The proximity of one's voice to one's self allows one to convince oneself that one originates and controls the meaning of one's speech, according to this myth.[21] An opposing view understands the self as unable to make sense of its situation without relying upon social conventions and social discourses that precede it. This approach evades the attempt to pinpoint an origin to meaning within the self or a category of persons.

In contrast to these logocentric models of the self, I take a genealogical approach that stresses the ways in which different social formations demand different identities or relations of the self.[22] On this understanding, the model of free speech that is organized around the metaphysics of presence becomes a rather transparent justification of a particular present produced by a particular social formation. It points to a determined result of this formation—the normative self and related self-consciousness—as its legitimizing foundational condition.

In the genealogist's account, different discursive formations produce different preconditions and commitments that constrain the direction inquiries may take through their regulation of the significant and the insignificant. What one recognizes as reasonable can only emerge in relation to preconditions and preexisting rules for distinguishing the meaningful from the meaningless. To privilege practices of speech that appear reasonable, make progress toward truth, or deepen intelligibility, therefore, is to privilege speech practices that further entrench this discursive formation. Speech that refused to play by the rules of this formation would not further any of the goals conceivable from within this formation, hence it could not be identified as "progressive." And speech that refused to recognize the grammar of this formation would be, by definition, insignificant.

For example, First Amendment jurisprudence has taken for granted an American self-inscription within the Millian paradigm that puts forth this nation as reflecting the historical progress of reason. Against this background, it has created the category of obscenity as being the opposite of reason or the intellect and as lacking *social* value.[23] Properly speaking, it is not *speech*.[24] Therefore, practices of nudity that society values, such as the ballet, fall within First Amendment protection, while those that society does not, such as "nude dancing," have been found to be open to regulation.[25] In this way we can understand one of the senses in which the recognition of "writing" has been determined by ethnocentrism.[26]

The genealogist rearranges the research problematic. Instead of pursuing a greater understanding of the Western practice of free speech and then hypothesizing the interventions necessary to impart this practice to the underdeveloped non-West, the genealogist pursues a different question. The genealogist investigates the array of subjectivities and regimes of knowledge constitutive of "Western modernity" and "non-Western stagnation" by using the dominant free speech discourse both as a reflection of and as a practice that has helped to produce this particular world. If we understand the production of these identities, familiar discussions about "freedom of speech" appear in a new light. To this end, I turn my attention to Mill because his work on liberty of speech is still an important landmark that continues to orient debate about freedom of speech in America.

Mill's Multidimensional Moral Geography

Mill uses speech-related terms like *reading, literature, press,* and *discussion* in such a way that they acquire meaning in the context of a Eurocentric geography, a spatial imaginary that is created by the invocation of these loaded terms. This reciprocal relationship between the terminology and the geography creates an economy of meaning that is put into play the moment any particular aspect of it is invoked. Mill's frequent use of speech-related terms reflects his understandings about the West in general, and England in particular. In turn, his use of this terminology creates these identities by marking their borders. One might argue that Mill is concerned with stabilizing two entities, an "internal" frontier and an "external" border. This chapter focuses on the external border and the seepage into the West's presence that it fails to prevent.

Though rarely acknowledged in an explicit way by the political or legal literature, this economy of meaning is reinvoked and structures the arguments Mill makes throughout "On Liberty." We can therefore understand "On Liberty" to be performing a map of liberty. It inscribes a moral geography of civilization and barbarism that describes and delimits who merits liberty. This distinction, as we shall discover through an investigation of Mill's other essays, is constituted through Mill's use of speech-related terminology like "discussion." In turn, Mill's use of speech-related terms acquire their meaning only in the context of his Eurocentric moral geography.

Edward Said notes that an Orientalist politics requires a place to be identified as the "Orient." This process necessitates a large-scale intervention by Western social science that constitutes a certain "type" of being and articulates it to a specific geographic locale. Thus, a form of culture creates a map organizing the world.[27] Analogous to Said's tracking of a form of knowledge that creates both a justified colonizer and a place to be colonized, I demonstrate how a right of freedom of speech as a distinguishing characteristic of the West (or England or America as representatives of the West) depends upon a mapping of places of speech, and of nonspeech, which creates the foundations for the valorized speech rights (foundations that will, in turn, justify a lack of speech rights elsewhere).

These issues are important for legal studies because law and social space are interwoven. Not only is law produced in specific spaces, but "those spaces, in turn, are partly constituted by legal norms. Either way, law cannot be detached from the particular places in which it acquires meaning and saliency."[28] To talk about law's determinacy, and therefore the stability of free speech practices and the First Amendment, is to make a claim not only about the stability of history (as McKay and others do by describing free speech as something that essentially characterizes American identity over time), but also about the stability and naturalness of social space. To this end, I examine the temporal and spatial imaginaries that underwrite speech rights in the place of America as it takes itself to be the exemplar of Western civilization. While this chapter elaborates what is meant by Western civilization and how America is imagined when it appropriates the Millian paradigm to make sense of itself and its rights of free speech, the next chapter shows how the meaning of America as a national space changes when subjects are led to reimagine global space and America's place within it.

The Time and Place of Speech

Legal or political theorists who approach freedom of speech through the Millian paradigm, whether explicitly or implicitly, pay little attention to what Mill said about the non-West. Perhaps his remarks are considered unfortunate but irrelevant to the principles that he enunciates for the practice of liberty within the West. But Mill the imperialist and colonial administrator is linked to Mill the theorist of Western freedom. One of the points of intersection is what he had to say about speech-related phenomena.

In his essay "Representative Government," Mill describes the age in which he lives and of which he is writing as "days of discussion": "[I]n these days of discussion, and generally awakened interest in improvement, what formerly was the work of centuries, often only requires years."[29] In "Civilization," his present is a "reading age" (Civ, 69). In "The Spirit of the Age," Mill writes,

> The progress which we have made, is precisely that sort of progress which increase of discussion suffices to produce. . . . When all opinions are questioned, it is in time found out what are those that will not bear a close examination. Ancient doctrines are then put upon their proofs; and those which were originally errors, or have become so by change of circumstances, are thrown aside. Discussion does this. It is by discussion, also, that true opinions are discovered and diffused. (SA, 9–10)

Discussion and reading, for Mill, mark the boundary between one historical age and another and are a cause in this historical progression.

In a favorable review essay of Alexis de Tocqueville's *Democracy in America*, Mill performs a series of substitutions that give substance to the "present" defined by reading, discussion, and literature. He first identifies the object of Tocqueville's books as "the modern world," a term that is then exchanged for "tendencies of a progressive civilization," which is then exchanged for "the nations of civilized Europe" (T, II, 234–35). Thus, by the end of two pages, a temporal sequence also becomes a geographic and an ethical one. To reinforce this exchange and displacement, Mill states that certain forms of particularly bad government belong to "past ages, and can no more exist out of the pale of Asiatic barbarism" (T, II, 258). In this way he also associates the past with a geographic place which is also synonymous with a people, articulating time, place, and people. He replicates this relationship in "On Liberty" by associating non-Europeans with an age of nonmaturity. The identity Mill creates for non-Europeans justifies a refusal to engage with "different" peoples and cultures dialogically or as equals and legitimates a practice of authority—the sort that a rational parent exercises over an irrational or prerational child—as opposed to the right of speech.

Mill's boundaries around "progressive civilization" are explained later in the same essay when he argues that China is a homogeneous and stationary community, while giving a slight rebuke to Tocqueville for his use of the term "law of progress": "[T]he European family of nations is the only one which has ever shown any capability of spontaneous improvement, beyond a certain low level" (T, II, 282–83).[30] He then shifts from a geographical to a temporal and ethical boundary, emphasizing that to the "spirit of commerce and industry or to its consequences [i.e., "acquirements of the mind," see Civ, 53] we owe nearly all that *advantageously* distinguishes the present period from the middle ages" (T, II, 283, my emphasis). Historical progress, as we can see here, is not just a brute fact but a regulatory norm with ethical significance.

Mill uses the word *civilization* with some frequency, and his struggles to maintain its connection with its object—Europe—testify to its instability as a category. Mill concedes that civilization sometimes refers to human improvement in general, but he appropriates a more narrow sense of the word. Specifically, civilization stands for "that kind of improvement only which distinguishes a wealthy and populous nation from savages or barbarians" (Civ, 51). Civilization, on this understanding, "is the direct converse or contrary of rudeness or barbarism," or the life of a savage tribe (52). In its narrow sense, it refers to the ontology of a place—Europe generally, and Great Britain in particular. "All these elements exist in modern Europe, and especially Great Britain, in a more eminent degree, and state of more rapid progression, than in any other place or time" (53).

Civilization is a precondition of Mill's defense, in "On Liberty," of freedom of speech (OL, 15). As such, it doubles as a useful definition of the present that he also describes as "days of discussion" or a "reading age." Spatially, it constitutes an exclusionary boundary in Mill's moral geography by inscribing the place of a "civilized community" and other places of rudeness and barbarians (OL, 15). Temporally, the discourse of "civilization" not only denies to non-Europeans the ethical standing of an interlocutor but also begins to signify the otherness inescapably within the place of Europe.

Identifying the Civilized Self and Protecting Its Consciousness

Not only are savages outside of the capitalist economy, but they are the Other of civilization, because they also illustrate the opposite of the "powers and acquirements of the mind." This helps explain why "rude nations, or semi-civilized and enslaved nations" have made such a poor showing in war against the civilized (Civ, 55). "Discipline, that is, perfect cooperation, is an attribute of civilization" (Civ, 55). This form of knowledge is the power that the savage lacks. "Look at the savage," Mill tells us; "he has bodily strength," but it is "only civilized beings who can combine." The problem of the savage is that his "impulses cannot bend to his calculations." The savage and the slave both lack the self-control necessary for discipline or cooperation (Civ, 55). Their selves are not properly constituted.

If civilization distinguishes its self by its abilities of self-control, bending impulses to calculation, the power of knowledge or the mind, then these qualities are all understood as the inverse of the body (and the mind) of the savage. The civilized mind recognizes itself because it is not the body of the savage. Superior to the savage body is the self demanded by and trained to fit into farming, manufacturing, commercial and military practices. Mill wonders what could teach a savage to cooperate. One answer is the division of labor in manufacturing, "the great school of cooperation" (Civ, 56). If manufacturing produces the appropriately disciplined self, then these habits of discipline, he thinks, can be transferred to other areas where they may be needed.

Not only is the Western metaphysics of presence preserved along an external boundary through the control or military defeat, and thus the negation, of the savage body, but Mill also understands it to be threatened by the body that suffers or is in pain (Civ, 64–65). In this case, mere spatial imaginaries fail Mill, and he must supplement their geography with a temporal axis in order to address the otherness within the place of Europe.

> There is another circumstance to which we may trace much of the good and of the bad qualities which distinguish our civilization from the rudeness of former times. One of the effects of civilization . . . is, that the spectacle, and even the very idea of pain, is kept more and more out of sight of those classes who enjoy in their fullness the benefits of civilization. . . . The state of perpetual personal conflict . . . from which it was hardly possible for any person, in whatever rank of society, to be exempt, necessarily habituated every one to the spectacle of harshness, rudeness, and violence, to the struggle of one indomitable will against another, and to the alternate suffering and infliction of pain. . . . [But now, a]ll those necessary portions of the business of society which oblige any person to be the immediate agent or ocular witness of the infliction of pain, are delegated by common consent to peculiar and narrow classes: to the judge, the soldier, the surgeon, the butcher, and the executioner. (64–65)

In this remarkable passage, we have the issue of the maintenance of the civilized or "refined classes." The metaphysics of presence, in addition to the self-present subject, can also imply certainty through proximity by referring to either the "fact" of "experience," or "seeing it" with one's "own eyes," so to speak, both of which imply direct and unmediated knowledge. In this passage, Mill describes a past age of "perpetual conflict." This was an age not of reason but of its opposite, an age of force and its associated indecent body ("rudeness," "suffering," "pain") uncontrolled by middle-class norms of behavior. These things need to be kept at a distance in order to prevent the corruption of Europe's pure consciousness of reason associated with its civilized or refined body. Violence, as Mill explains, "is rather a thing *known of* than actually experienced" (emphasis added). This is a distant knowledge, for "even the very *idea* of pain" is kept from the most civilized classes (emphasis added). Mill thus protects the purity of the civilized self's consciousness.

Interestingly, Mill concedes that such violence cannot be confined to Europe's past but also occupies its present (though it is "almost at an end"). Therefore, in order to preserve Europe's "present," which partakes of the metaphysics of presence rather than of violence, a boundary must be created within Europe's present to guard its purity. The "judge, the soldier, the surgeon, the butcher, and the executioner" constitute an anomalous category to mediate between civilization and barbarism, to protect civilization from its own barbarity. They are the ones who are the "immediate agent[s] or ocular witness[es] of the infliction of pain," so that the practice does not "degrade" the "minds" of the community by intervening as a direct experience or even as an idea. The civilized community maintains its presence of mind by maintaining its distance, making violence and pain only something "known of."

Civilization, therefore, is constituted against both the savage of bodily strength but no self-control and the violence of Europe's past. In this way Mill makes doubly sure to maintain a strict boundary around the West's identity not only through geographic measures, but by denying co-temporality to its Other through its association with the past. European identity, civilized and described by discussion and reading, permeated by literature, is thus predicated upon the absolute negation of the savage (an identity and negation, however, that are deferred through the reappearance of violence within the present of Europe). The Western body is amenable to discussion because it is civilized or disciplined, and the West's institutions produce selves amenable to discussion's benefits or pushing knowledge forward. This capacity of discussion, however, is integrally linked with its juxtaposition to the savage body. All of these dimensions of Mill's argument—geography, time, the Western mind and body—labor to give a basis to the West as fundamentally a place of discussion.

The Presence and Absence of Bodies of Speech

The contradiction between speech-related phenomena and barbarians or savages can be illustrated by Mill's statements with regard to India. For Mill, "publicity"—public scrutiny—is "ample power, and security enough for the liberty of the nation" (RG, 226). He argues, "publicity and discussion . . . are a natural accompaniment of any, even nominal, representation" (RG, 201). The triumph of democracy [depends] upon the natural laws of the progress of wealth, upon the diffusion of reading, and the increase of the facilities of human intercourse" (Civ, 60).[31]

Of course, discussion and its concomitant publicity make an assumption: "A certain amount of conscience, and of disinterested public spirit, may fairly be calculated on in the citizens of any community ripe for representative government" (RG, 243–44). Some people, however, may be "more or less unfit for liberty."

> A rude people . . . may be unable to practice the forbearances which it demands: their passions may be too violent, or their personal pride too exacting, to forgo private conflict. . . . In such a case, a civilized government, to be really advantageous to them, will require to be in a considerable degree despotic: to be one over which they do not themselves exercise control, and which imposes a great amount of forcible restraint upon their actions. (RG, 149)

For Mill, institutions need to relate to the "stage of advancement" of the people (RG, 172), and a "despotism" is necessary to "tame the savage" (175), because the "first lesson of civilization [is] that of obedience" (202). Therefore, "subjection to a foreign government . . . is often of the greatest advantage to a people, carrying them rapidly through several stages of progress, and clearing away the obstacles to improvement which might have lasted indefinitely if the subject population had been left unassisted to its native tendencies and chances" (207). The "mind" needs to "be disciplined into the habits required by civilized society" (174); otherwise the basis for discussion properly understood does not exist.

India, according to Mill, is a "peculiar country," and in certain respects "totally different" from England, which, as we have learned above, is a leading example of civility. What is "totally different" from civilization exists in a different place and time, justifying a refusal to engage with it dialogically on a basis of equality. Perhaps their empirical voices make noise, but Indians fail to achieve "speech" and therefore receive no authorization for a right of discussion. Thus, rather than engaging in dialogue with India, as Mill testified before the House of Lords, India must be studied, and "the study of India must be as much a profession in itself as law or medicine." India must be studied and ruled, not engaged as a speaking subject. Mill asserts that "the great security for good government—public discussion—does not exist for India, as it exists for this country [i.e., England] and its other dependencies" (WI, 49). Thus, "the public of India afford no assistance in their own government. They are not ripe for doing so by means of representative government" (49). The dividing line between England and India, again, is also expressed in term of civilization: "I do not think that India has yet attained such a degree of civilization and improvement as to be ripe for anything like a representative system" (51).

Some of England's other "dependencies" are not in the same position as India. For, as Mill argues, some dependencies "are composed of people of similar civilization to the ruling country; capable of, and ripe for, representative government: such as the British possessions in America and Australia. Others, like India, are still at a great distance from that state" (RG, 402). While this passage does much work toward the creation of India as a place, geography cannot totalize Mill's field of explanation of why India is not yet ripe for discussion or representative government; or rather, he needs to amend a strictly Eurocentric map with a more differentiated one. The principal distinction, finally stated, is this: "It is now a fixed principle of the policy of Great Britain, professed in theory and faithfully adhered to in practice, that her colonies of European race, equally with the parent country, possess the fullest measure of internal self-government" (WI, 403). Thus, as he testifies before the House of Lords, in "Canada and Australia there are local representative bodies perfectly competent to exercise that antagonistic discussion, which seems to me an essential element of good government everywhere; but for India you cannot have any local body which shall produce that result" (45). Therefore, the "only means of ensuring the necessary discussion and collision of opinions is provided within the governing body itself" (49); that is, by those who have made India an object of knowledge and have "studied India as it were professionally" (49).

In this way, we can see how the capacity for discussion is grafted to the civilized, English body. Because the very concept of discussion is constitutive of Western identity and is created through the rejection of the savage body, discussion simply makes no sense in the East, unless carried out by the English (or other civilized people). Indeed, as Mill states forcefully in "On Liberty," discussion is meant to prevent England and the West from degenerating and becoming like the East. As Mill puts it, "We have a warning example in China" (OL, 88). One could also say that the speech practices of the English national body will be oriented toward maintaining its distinction from China as long as China, for instance, continues to be a warning example in this way.

The Moral Geography of "On Liberty"

The moral geography practiced by Mill in "On Liberty" is hardly marginal to his central concerns about speech-related phenomena and their fundamental relation to liberty in general. Rather, just as the boundary between the civilized West and the savage or barbarian is the condition of possibility for discussion, so his remarks to begin "On Liberty" which inscribe this map and its boundaries cannot be taken as peripheral to what he has to say in the rest of the essay. They must be understood as the very condition of possibility for his main argument.

In his "Introductory" to "On Liberty," Mill's main argument is that "the sole end for which mankind are warranted . . . in interfering with the liberty of action of any of their number is self-protection. That the only purpose for which power can be rightfully exercised over any member of a civilized community, against his will, is to prevent harm to others" (OL, 15). For the genealogist, of course, such a principle only defers the ultimate question, which now becomes: What identity formation and its privileged self ought to be protected? Mill responds to the genealogist's question with a crucial clarification. This clarification was already hinted at through his use of the qualification "civilized" to define the community to which his argument applies.

It is, perhaps, hardly necessary to say that this doctrine is meant to apply only to human beings in the maturity of their faculties. We are not speaking of children, or of young persons below the age which the law may fix as that of manhood or womanhood. . . . *For the same reason, we may leave out of consideration those backward states of society in which the race itself may be considered as in its nonage. . . . Despotism is a legitimate mode of government in dealing with barbarians,* provided the end be their improvement. . . . *Liberty, as a principle, has no application to any state of things anterior to the time when mankind have become capable of being improved by free and equal discussion* . . . (a period long since reached in all nations with whom we need here concern ourselves). (OL, 15–16, emphases added)

In this way, Mill has mapped the civilized community for whom liberty pertains onto Europe and England, which is then determined as a place through its juxtaposition with the East through the "warning example" provided by China (OL, 87–88). It is also determined temporally and racially through the reference to other races as "backward." These backward states of society are mapped as regions where despotism is appropriate, thereby creating a multidimensional moral geography articulating people, place, and time. Rather than understand this moral geography as peripheral to the main concerns of "On Liberty," I have argued that a proper understanding of the conditions of possibility for "discussion" renders this map critical to the subject position that authorizes a particular voice to assume the protection of "freedom of speech." Furthermore, the reciprocal semiotic power of "discussion" acts as a marker of a specific identity formation. In this formation, "discussion" and other speech-related phenomena attempt to stabilize the "West" as especially self-present, and its position a measure of true accomplishment and therefore of justified value rather than "accidental" force. And when America's civilized status is invoked, as it continues to be as we shall see in later chapters, to justify its right to free speech, the attributes of the discursive field Mill exemplifies are put into play, their life reanimated and extended. As we shall also see, this field continues to function with similar regulatory effects as some are authorized to produce constitutionally protected speech while others are denied such legal standing, depending on how the structure of civility is imposed upon them and how they negotiate its landscape.

The Hinge between Mill's Orientalist and Domestic Politics

In "On Liberty," Mill states:

> The greater part of the world has, properly speaking, *no history*, because the despotism of Custom is complete. *This is the case over the whole East.* ... Those nations must once have had originality; they did not start out of the ground populous, *lettered*, and versed in many of the arts of life; they made themselves all this, and were then the greatest and most powerful *nations* of the world. What are they now? *The subjects or dependents of tribes.* ... A people, it appears, may be *progressive* for a certain length of time, and then stop: when does it stop? When it ceases to possess individuality. (OL, 87–88, emphasis added)

In this passage Mill once again argues that speech-related phenomena, this time "letters," are a sign of progress. He concedes that this is part of the East's past, when they were "progressive." Writing about the present, however, "On Liberty" attempts to ensure the contemporary protection of discussion in the West as the means of maintaining its difference from the East. As we have seen in Mill's remarks to the House of Lords, India is unfit for discussion, and the only discussion that occurs there is through the English ruling body. I have already argued that discussion, which leads to progress for Mill, marks the boundary between civilization and the savage or barbarian. Here, Mill takes the next step by arguing that today the East has, properly speaking, no history.

Speech-related phenomena guarantee the presence of and access to reason. The West, defined by its association with discussion—indeed, constituted by it—has become the standard of historical progress, while the East, lacking discussion, is without history. Now, the West exemplifies history. Its confidence of this fact is guaranteed by discussion, just as there is certainty that the East lacks history because it lacks discussion. The only way, therefore, for the East to join history is under the auspices of the West—if it will ever become Westernized. This is a standard with mirage-like qualities because there can be no "West" without an "East"; this is a development the East will never achieve. For such a development to be conceivable, however, it could only occur at the hands of the West.

Once again, Mill's honesty is disarming. Referring to China, he argues that "if they are to be farther improved, it must be by foreigners" (OL, 89). Similarly, good government in India is associated with English presence and is something England gives to India, and then persuades the people of India that this has been done (WI, 39). India has no moral agency in the matter at all due to its inscription within the East. Similarly, in Mill's "A Few Words on Non-Intervention," barbarians, that is, the peoples of the non-West, are excluded from the argument, but the problem is that this "fundamental distinction" between civilized nations and barbarians is not apprehended by those who "write in strains of indignant morality on the subject" (NI, 406).

According to Mill, to "suppose that the . . . same rules of international morality, can obtain between one civilized nation and another, and between civilized nations and barbarians, is a grave error" (NI, 406). The reason for this fundamental difference relates to the difference between the civilized and the barbarian with respect to the presence of mind.

> In the first place, the rules of ordinary international morality imply reciprocity. But barbarians will not reciprocate. They cannot be depended on for observing any rules. *Their minds are not capable of so great an effort, nor their will sufficiently under the influence of distant motives.* In the next place, nations which are still barbarous have not got beyond that period during which it is likely to be for their benefit that they should be conquered and held in subjection by foreigners. Independence and nationality, so essential to the due growth and development of a people further advanced in improvement, are generally impediments to theirs. The sacred duties which civilized nations owe to the independence and nationality of each other, are not binding towards those to whom nationality and independence are either a certain evil, or at best a questionable good. (NI, 406, emphasis added)

At root, the problem is this: *international* morality cannot apply to barbarians who are not *nations*, because they have no rights as *nations*. Thus, Mill argues:

> To characterize any conduct whatever towards a barbarous people as a violation of the law of nations, only shows that he who so speaks has never considered the subject. A violation of great principles of morality it may easily be; but barbarians have no rights as a *nation*, except a right to such treatment as may, at the earliest possible period, fit them for becoming one. (NI, 406)

The treatment in question for barbarians, he tells us in "On Liberty" and "Representative Government," is "despotism."

What contributes to the conditions of modern nationalism, and thus toward entry into the community that can claim a right to international morality? Discussion. As Mill argues in "Representative Government":

> It is by political discussion that the manual labourer . . . is taught that re-
> mote causes and events which take place far off, have a sensible effect even
> on his personal interests; and it is from political discussion, and collective
> political action, that one whose daily occupations concentrate his interests
> in a small circle round himself, learns to feel for and with his fellow-citi-
> zens, and becomes consciously a member of a great community. (RG,
> 276)[32]

In "Representative Government" Mill's treatment of the manual la-
borer, whose vote Mill takes great care to dilute if not exclude, becomes linked with his treatment of the barbarian through the importance that he gives to discussion, with each narrative informing the other. The barbarian could not be part of international morality because the barbarian lacks speech-related capacities to guarantee its presence of mind. This is signified by an inability to allow the will to be guided by "distant mo-
tives," suggesting that the savage is ruled by immediate appetites—func-
tions of an uncontrolled body rather than the guidance of regulatory reason. In "Representative Government," the manual laborer will begin to perceive and understand "remote causes and events" through discus-
sion. The manual laborer is thereby brought within the fold of national consciousness. The manual laborer is also being brought within the fold of history.[33] Both of these moves are linked with the normalizing effects of discussion, and both are denied barbarians. Just as Mill excludes from the vote those who cannot read, write, or do arithmetic—such persons could have no "real political opinion;" this is a suffrage accessible (and thus limited) to "all who are in the *normal* condition of a human being" (RG, 279, 281, emphasis added)—the barbarian is excluded as "not ripe" for representative government (WI, 49, 51). Discussion marks an ethical division, as illustrated by the barbarian's lack of a claim on international justice or self-government and the grant of moral standing through citizenship, with its associated voice and vote, to the English manual la-
borer. We might also note that discussion becomes a distributive and

regulatory process through Mill's scheme for weighting the vote according to increases in education.

The Continuing Relevance of the Millian Paradigm

Michael Shapiro has argued that conversations always occur within a "preconstituted meaning system"—a "protoconversation"—that provides a spatiotemporal location for the conversation, an economy of meaning for the said and the unsaid.[34] In light of these remarks, we can regard Mill as a "protoconversation" that has been appropriated by Americans in order to inscribe the place of America within a universe of social possibilities. Locating America in this way as a precondition for specific conversations about free speech (a) enables the possibility of protecting free speech; (b) regulates its practice, including the subjectivity one must assume as a matter of practice; and (c) limits the recognition of potentially legitimate claims of right. At the same time, practices of speech help locate the place of America.

As I explain in subsequent chapters, the values of this moral geography inform the very process of creating American subjects who can produce socially valued speech, and whose speech is therefore protected under the Constitution. For example, in chapter 6 we will see how the question of whether sexual expression is protected by the First Amendment is adjudicated according to the parameters of this protoconversation. So, as an illustration of the argument we shall see there, we can take Chief Justice Burger's decision in *Bethel School District v. Fraser* that penalties imposed by a high school upon a boy for his speech do not violate the First Amendment. Matthew Fraser, the boy, gave a speech laden with "sexual metaphor" to a student assembly. Burger understands the purpose of the American public school system is to prepare pupils for "citizenship in the Republic." This process involves the inculcation of "fundamental values of habits and manners of civility." Schools, Burger continues, "must teach . . . the shared values of a civilized social order." Therefore, as "instruments of the state," schools "may determine that the essential lessons of civil, mature conduct cannot be conveyed in a school that tolerates lewd, indecent, or offensive speech and conduct such as that indulged in by this confused boy."[35] Thus, although public speech has the strongest claim to First Amendment protection, and a public school is an arm of the state, which is in turn obliged to protect the liberties inscribed within the Bill of Rights like the First Amendment's guaranty of free speech, Burger justifies the school's punishment of young Matthew by drawing upon the same narrative that underwrote the colonial project in order to conclude that regulating Fraser's speech does not violate the First Amendment.

Fraser does not fit the image of a civilized American subject. Mill associates the savage with the lack of maturity that describes European children and argues that international morality or the rights of nations do not apply to barbarians since they are not yet national subjects. Moreover, there is a history of associating excessive or deviant sexuality with the savage.[36] Since Burger associates American national identity with civility and positions Fraser as a boy who is not behaving according to the norms of civilized conduct, he is able to register Fraser as being not an American subject who is authorized to claim his right to free speech, but rather that which is to be regulated in the name of a civilized national order. Indeed, Burger argues that the proper role of the school is to turn unruly savages like Fraser into civilized American citizens, much as Mill argues that the only rights barbarians can claim from the civilized is the despotic treatment that will allow them to become national subjects. Thus, Burger describes the school as justifiably disciplining a student rather than violating speech rights, since Matthew Fraser in this instance is not a subject with a legitimate claim upon First Amendment rights. He is not yet an American subject; hence he cannot claim the rights accorded to American subjects.

Many other discussions of free speech also use metaphors like Burger's "civilized" that refer to Mill's multidimensional geography and derive their meaning from it. In this way, they indicate the identity of the subject who can be understood to practice free speech. Justice Louis Brandeis claims that the greatest menace to freedom comes from an "inert people."[37] Wright recapitulates Mill's statement that subjects must show a "capacity for being improved" as a "prerequisite to the regime of free speech." In so doing, Wright refers to the passage in which Mill qualifies his argument in "On Liberty" according to his racialized scheme of civilization versus barbarians.[38] Metaphors like "inert," "traditionalist," "underdeveloped," and references to the West as "rational," "progressive," or "modern" all impose historical and normative dimensions on their geographic referents (and normative referents on their geohistorical dimensions).[39] These metaphors use a relation of racialized difference to distinguish the subject who can exercise free speech from those who are excluded, showing how Mill's moral geography provides a continuing context for American free speech discourse.

I would not claim that the narrative exemplified here by Mill has maintained a constant or stable significance throughout American history, though one can find many examples of its tendencies. Although some of the most important political thinkers in the late nineteenth and early twentieth centuries America used a rights paradigm that was even more severely racialized than Mill's arguments about liberty (see chapter 2), such narratives became less significant to the extent that America located its identity in opposition to Soviet communism. As we shall see in the next chapter, however, with the waning of the cold war mapping of geopolitical identities, Mill's global imaginary has become newly significant for understanding America's place in the world. Indeed, Samuel Huntington's infamous *Foreign Affairs* article, "The Clash of Civilizations?" is an excellent example of a leading foreign policy analyst trying to persuade his readers to look at the world through the prism of, in his own words, "The West versus the Rest."[40]

This identity formation surfaces in recent thinking about freedom of speech within both the legal doctrine produced by courts and the broader legal culture as produced by scholars and in polemics. As we shall see in chapter 6, Judge Posner finds it persuasive to evoke images of the "Saudi" and "Islamic clergy" as negative points of reference in order to win American support for his conception of what is entailed by freedom of speech.[41] The constitutional scholar Samuel Beer has defended American "government by discussion," which is defined as embodying the rational modern spirit as opposed to the particularist practices of Eastern, traditionalist societies.[42] And the polemicist Jonathan Rauch, whom I will discuss in chapter 4, contributes to legal culture by reevoking the moral geography I have used Mill to exemplify.

Rauch uses this moral geography as the lens through which he views the American controversy over hate speech codes and multicultural curricula. He describes the calls for these policies as the most far-reaching challenge to the "modern West" and Western liberal science since the days of the great battles between religion and science.[43] He also associates the advocacy of these policies with the sort of fundamentalism that he finds exemplified in the death sentence Ayatollah Khomeini pronounced on Salman Rushdie.[44] Thus, this controversy over questions of knowledge, culture, and free speech brings to the surface anxieties about the location of America and its boundaries; haunting anxieties that Rauch attempts to manage through the spatial and temporal controls provided by the moral geography I have used Mill to exemplify here. The year 1989 bears the weight of the crumbling of the "Iron Curtain" and the Rushdie affair. Rauch calls February 1989 a "defining moment" for *Western* intellectuals.[45] And so perhaps it was.

Conclusion

Mill's very use of the term "discussion" is born out of the distinction between civilization and barbarism. I have treated his use of this concept and other metaphors for speech-related phenomena as a hinge for joining his two sides—Mill the Orientalist, imperialist, and colonial administrator and Mill the great theorist of Western liberty who is so important for American free speech discourse. Mill answered the question "To whom do rights refer?" with an argument about civilization. This argument served as an important precondition—one that established the basis for a justified claim of right and was itself mapped according to a multidimensional moral geography in which the "West" and the "Rest" were bounded according to racialized axes. Mill's Orientalist politics, rather than being an issue of peripheral importance for his arguments pertaining to liberty in the West, in fact established the conditions of their possibility as a vehicle for defining the identity formation of the West and the preconditions for justified claims of right.

As a perceptive analyst, however, Mill recognized that practices he took to be symbolic of barbarism could not be kept at the distance his spatial imaginary strove to keep them. These practices existed in the place of Europe, and Mill attempted to protect Europe's presence of mind by limiting these practices to its past. But this, too, was unsuccessful. The final success of attempts to control such impurities and project them outward in order to save a privileged identity must always be deferred, as it was for Mill. This is what Geoffrey Bennington means when he argues that the Other always maintains a haunting presence.[46]

For Mill, the English working class achieved the ethical status of national citizen to the extent that they could be distinguished from barbarians. But insofar as they resembled barbarians through their lack of speech-related capital, either they were excluded from rights, or their voices were reduced in value through Mill's weighted voting scheme.[47] Any basis that is used to justify rights can be used in the next instant as the basis that is used to deny them. This is a paradox of rights.

4

The Landscape of Rights Claiming

The Shift to a Post–Cold War American National Formation

> Nothing Existed. He was in a void, and if he were to survive he
> would have to construct everything from scratch, he would have to
> invent the ground beneath his feet before he could take a step. . . .
> Things had to be made.
>
> —Salman Rushdie, *The Satanic Verses*

Introduction

Salman Rushdie's fabulous fiction, in which dreams blend with reality, allows his readers to understand their world better by making the naturalness of space an achievement. At the same time, he draws his readers' attention to the penalties assigned to identities that are out of place. We are frequently blind to the question of space, as if it were a neutral stage with invisible foundations. Yet space is constantly reachieved through the retracing of narrative paths. Although narratives create their invokers as historical subjects, they also contribute the resources for these subjects to act in new circumstances, circumstances that oblige strategic redirections.

This chapter examines how "America" is a national space that helps to constitute the possibility of claiming rights like freedom of speech, and yet is itself also constituted in part through legal practices. The focus of this chapter is how different national formations have differing consequences for rights claiming. Contrary to those who assume a constant American identity over time or characteristics that become more developed by evolution over time, I show the different identities America makes for itself through the different ways that it gives meaning to the world and America's place in it. I argue that America's inscription of itself and the world within a cold war imaginary after World War II created a system of possibilities and constraints within which one had to operate to claim rights during this period. I do this by analyzing the discursive regularities of claiming and contesting civil rights at that time. In the remainder of the chapter, I examine the way that the controversy over Ayatollah Khomeini's death threat on Salman Rushdie became a vehicle for America to begin making sense of itself and the world after the cold war. I argue that the controversy over *The Satanic Verses* and free speech became a mechanism for America to shift its understanding of itself and the world away from the ideological considerations of the cold war to a more racialized geography of the "West versus the Rest." As the meaning of social space shifts, those identities that are valued or penalized also shifts. Thus, if "free speech" is understood as a right unique to the "West," then the identity of being a Westerner helps one to be perceived as protected legitimately by this right. It is significant that Rushdie, despite the complexity of his personal history and the hybridity of the languages spoken in *The Satanic Verses*, was often represented as a Westerner, and his book as not intended for the non-West, in order for his right of free speech to be defended.

Because the entity "America" always raises the question of boundaries, of signs of difference, I will argue that this question is not a peripheral issue acquiring importance only at the margins of otherwise unproblematic practices. Rather, the boundary inscribed by the "Rushdie affair" is evoked and reproduced by subsequent controversies that raise issues of free speech. These free speech controversies simultaneously police the boundary of, and go to the heart of, "America" by continuing along a Millian trail that has been reforged as America has come to grasp the significance of Rushdie for its post–cold war identity.

To reiterate, this chapter emphasizes two points in connection with the Rushdie affair. First, this controversy, as it was significant in the United States, registers the shift in America's meaning—and, therefore, its moral geography—from a cold war to a post–cold war identity. Although I condense long-term processes within my analysis of a particular instance, this instance is especially important because 1989 was both the year that Ayatollah Khomeini pronounced his judgment of death upon Rushdie and the year that the Berlin Wall came down in Germany, symbolically ending a major battle and geographic boundary of the cold war. Second, I treat the meaning of America's boundaries (are they anticommunist or racial?) as an issue that is important for the way that domestic issues, such as struggles over the meaning and limits of speech rights, are engaged. In other words, the way that America imagines itself within global space affects American law and politics. I make these two points by contrasting the rhetoric of rights claiming during the cold war with the landscape of meaning that began to emerge in 1989 that contextualized perceptions of Rushdie's rights as an author.

The study of law and attention to social space might seem to be antithetical. Most scholarship presents modern law as embracing principles that, all things being equal, must be respected in all cases. It is not rooted in any particular place.[1] The rules of modern law, it is said, purport to be universally applicable because they are given at a certain level of abstraction and formality. The question of rights in a liberal legal system, and of freedom of speech in particular, illustrates this opposition of modern law to considerations of social space. As discussed in chapter 1, liberal rights are frequently represented as "trumps" that defend an individual's personal discretion. The failure to protect a right to free speech according to universal principles—a failure of law to rise above not only politics but social context—is perceived to be a grave shortcoming by those liberal theorists who consider universality to be a central attribute of modern law. The title of one book and its implied denunciation summarize this shortcoming: *Free Speech for Me but Not for Thee.*[2] On this view, the success of liberal rights is related to abstraction; hence this view's negation of considerations of social space.

In contrast to the understanding of legal rights as socially atomizing forces, the law and society movement engages law in its social context. "Law" must be understood as existing in a mutually constitutive relationship with "society."[3] Social identities are internal to law, while legal representations are social forms through which meaning is created. If law and society are mutually constitutive, then to study the sociospatial context that helps to produce the meaning of law or legal rights in any given instance is to study the geographical conditions of possibility for positive legal meaning. Put another way, stability of the geographical meaning of social life is an important force that helps to maintain legal determinacy. In sum, there is an interweaving of law and social space such that the study of law and geography can be understood as one of the several dimensions of law and society research that take seriously "the more general sociotheoretic problem of meaning and interpretation."[4] From this perspective, modern law does not succeed in rising above the questions of place and identity as some of its defenders might assert. Nor, for that matter, does it succeed in creating the social atomism that some of its Marxist and communitarian critics might fear, as we shall see at greater length in chapter 6. Instead, law and geography work reciprocally to produce subjects with ethical standing and boundaries that limit the rights claims that can be made legitimately.[5]

Although the meaning of social space gives a context for normative action, we should be attentive to the ethical ambivalence implicated in the word *territory*. As William Connolly reminds us, the derivation of *territory* is ambivalent. On the one hand, it derives from *terra*, meaning "land, earth, soil, nourishment, sustenance." On the other hand, *territory* derives from "terrere," meaning "to frighten, to terrorize, to exclude." And *territorium* is a "place from which people are warned." To occupy territory, then, is "both to receive sustenance and to exercise violence."[6] For instance, the Australian context of Paul Carter's formulation of the naming process as a "spatial moment and a cultural expectation" also reminds us of the violence necessary to maintain one cultural expectation as opposed to others: the very real violence that accompanied the enforcement of a particular spatial imaginary.[7]

Geo-graphy—writing or inscribing territorial space—is a practice that reflects both ethics and its lack. To study the possibilities for justice, the constitutive violences, and the residual injustices of territorial practices is to perceive a "moral geography."[8] In other words, it is to recognize how the inscription of historical space brings certain practices within an ethical perception and gives certain agents the standing and cultural capital to make claims upon a right to justice. Furthermore, it is to recognize how the inscription of historical space creates limits and boundaries that, in delineating ethical standing in a determinate place necessarily determine peoples and places that are meaningfully Other than this place. Last, it is to understand that any organization of space has its horizons that occlude the ethical perception and deny standing to other possible agents or claims. These cannot be located on the map and are correspondingly given no significance. For instance, as I discussed in the previous chapter, John Stuart Mill defends colonial practices of England and France against those who criticize them on the basis of rules of inter*national* morality. Mill's argument against such critics can be comprehended as an instance of denying "barbarians" standing on the grounds that "barbarians" are not "nations"; hence the rules of international morality are beside the point.[9]

This chapter takes up Peter Goodrich's challenge to chart ourselves through multiple modes of legal transmission.[10] In this spirit, I will pay particular attention to legal struggles as they circulate outside the state's courts, for the most part. The text also shifts from the art of Rushdie's *The Satanic Verses*, or Martin Luther King Jr.'s speeches, to the prose of an academic. The juxtaposition of this fantastic art reminds us of the radical neutralization that occurs as the nation-state's law flattens and contains space. By staging this confrontation between nationally held truths and self-conscious dreams and fantastical fictions, I hope to make the fictional and imaginary characteristics of institutionalized truths more apparent and thereby open to questioning as well as to more emancipatory hopes and dreams.[11] Similarly, the contrast between the context of the civil rights movement and the Rushdie affair shows how radically what we take for firm ground beneath our feet can shift. The result of this shift—the reemergence of a conception of global space that rests upon the racial division between the West, as a "modern civilization" and the barbarism of the Rest—also reminds us of the highly significant way that Rushdie's sensitive observations of space and identity were (determinately) neutralized in his transmission along the paths of American sovereignty.[12]

The Cold War, Civil Rights, and the Dream of a Nonracial National Imaginary

In chapter 3, I argued that the territory to be negotiated in American free speech practices has been importantly influenced by a paradigm of thought that John Stuart Mill is frequently taken to represent. Although Mill has been very influential in American free speech jurisprudence, such jurisprudence, and the legal culture surrounding free speech in America, have also been influenced by the cold war. The "clear and present danger" test to determine the limits of toleration in a capitalist society became closely associated with communist speech and the dangers it presented to national security.[13] With the waning of the cold war, however, there was an opening for Mill's moral geography to become newly significant, and this significance may be exemplified by the framework within which the Rushdie affair was situated as it circulated within the United States.

Though the cold war may have been the dominant schema for the post–World War II American national formation, I acknowledge that there were other crosscurrents that remained subterranean until more recently.[14] The third world was created as the categorical residue left over from the geopolitical rivalry between the United States and the Soviet

Union over which power would win the right to define "modernity." Furthermore, in the wake of the great northward urban migration of American blacks in the twentieth century and the civil rights movement, the Republicans inaugurated methods of campaigning based upon a "Southern strategy" and "law and order." This resulted in white flight not only from urban space but from partisan space as well. By the late 1980s, the Evil Empire rhetoric of the Reagan administration had become increasingly empty if not inapplicable, while Willie Horton became a household name that promised a far greater potential for mobilization.[15]

The importance of the cold war has been underemphasized as a context for desegregation and civil rights. But, as the legal scholar Mary Dudziak argues, the cold war and concern for the image of the United States in international politics motivated the American government to support civil rights claims.[16] I would add that the cold war provided an important landscape to this ongoing dispute that tended to *regulate* it. That is, the cold war as a terrain of rights claiming did not *determine* a specific position on civil rights, but its imposing presence as a fundamentally defining characteristic of American national identity in the mid-twentieth century demanded that it be addressed and negotiated by those who engaged in this rights struggle.

Because rights gather meaning within the context of social relations, claiming rights in a given context requires negotiating this context and its available subject positions. As I have argued in chapters 1 and 2, for those within the jurisdiction of the U.S. Constitution, this means making a claim upon American identity in order to gain the standing necessary to make a justifiable claim of right, and thereby interpellating a community that then recognizes this rights claim as legitimate. The content of this American identity on which such interpellative practices were engaged during the post–World War II era, as we shall now see, was supplied by an anticommunist nationalism and its correlative cold war global imaginary.

In the brief for the United States as amicus curiae in *Brown v. Board of Education*, the government states its interests in the case by rehearsing issues of international importance, while also constructing the term "American" in an inclusive way such that the rights of blacks would be justifiably protected according to their identity as Americans. The government cites President Truman, who argued, "We shall not . . . finally achieve the ideals for which this Nation was founded so long as any *American* suffers discrimination." The "constitutional right invoked in these cases," the government continues, "is the basic right, secured to all *Americans*, to equal treatment before the law." It adds: "Under the Constitution every agency of government ... must treat each of our people as an *American*, and not as a member of a particular group classified on the basis of race or some other constitutional irrelevancy."[17]

After constructing a racially inclusive American people to justify the rights being claimed in the case, the government addresses the international context of the issue. Quoting at length from the Truman administration's civil rights report, *To Secure these Rights*, the government argues that

> [T]he shamefulness and absurdity of Washington's treatment of Negro Americans is highlighted by the presence of many dark-skinned foreign visitors. Capit[o]l custom not only humiliates colored citizens, but is a source of considerable embarrassment to these visitors. . . . Foreign officials are often mistaken for American Negroes and refused food, lodging and entertainment. However, once it is established that they are not Americans, they are accommodated.[18]

The government argues that racial discrimination has an "adverse effect" upon the international relations of the United States. More to the point, the government states: "Racial discrimination furnishes grist for the Communist propaganda mills."[19]

The government acknowledges how the denial of civil rights domestically has hurt its international interests:

> During the past six years, the damage to our foreign relations attributable to this source has become progressively greater. The United States is under constant attack in the foreign press . . . and in such international bodies as the United Nations because of various practices of discrimination against minority groups in this country. As might be expected, Soviet spokesmen regularly exploit this situation in propaganda against the United States . . . which reaches all corners of the world. . . . The hostile reaction among normally friendly peoples, many of whom are particularly sensitive in regard to the status of non-European races, is growing in alarming proportions. In such countries the view is expressed more and more vocally that the United States is hypocritical in claiming to be champion of democracy while permitting practices of racial discrimination here in this country.[20]

The government concludes that although progress is being made, the "continuance of racial discrimination in the United States remains a source of constant embarrassment to this Government in day-to-day conduct of its foreign relations; and it jeopardizes the effective maintenance of our moral leadership of the free and democratic nations of the world."[21] The U.S. government, therefore, defines its interests, which are constituted in the context of its cold war identity, as supporting the claims for civil rights.

When the *Brown* decision declared the segregation of public schools unconstitutional, the Voice of America translated Chief Justice Warren's opinion into thirty-four languages to broadcast overseas. Domestically, however, many news outlets were silent on the Supreme Court's decision, and the Universal newsreel did not mention the decision either, because it was too controversial.[22] These facts illustrate how the civil rights issue was pressed into the service of cold war interests by the United States government.

The cold war regulates rights claiming at mid-twentieth century. This is evident in the discourse of those claiming rights like Dr. Martin Luther King Jr. Making one of his first political speeches as the new leader of the Montgomery bus boycott in 1955, King begins by saying: "We are here in a general sense, because first and foremost—we are *American* citizens—and we are determined to apply our citizenship—to the fullest of its means." He continues: "Just the other day . . . one of the finest citizens in Montgomery—not one of the finest Negro citizens—but one of the finest citizens in Montgomery—was taken from a bus—and carried to jail and arrested—because she refused to give up—to give her seat to a white person."[23] This beginning to the speech gives the protesters standing for their claim of right by asserting their identity as Americans. In so doing, King challenges the white supremacist definition of rights previously prevailing in Montgomery. He does this by constructing a new fundamental basis of rights in this space. According to this new baseline—a nonracial American identity—whites and blacks have an equal claim on these rights.[24]

King also negotiates America's cold war imaginary as an important dimension of American identity at the time. He argues: "If we were incarcerated behind the iron curtains of a *communistic* nation—we couldn't do this. If we were trapped in the dungeon of a totalitarian regime—we couldn't do this. But the great glory of *American* democracy is *the right to protest* for right." Then, distinguishing the protesters of segregation from those who would enforce it, King states: "There will be no crosses burned at any bus stops in Montgomery. . . . There will be no white persons pulled out of their homes and taken out on some distant road and murdered. *There will be nobody among us who will stand up and defy the Constitution of this nation.*" By invoking the First Amendment and obedience to the Constitution, King situates civil rights protesters as Americans. Then, King supports his argument by referring to the recently decided *Brown* case: "If we are wrong—the Supreme Court of this nation is wrong. . . . If we are wrong—God Almighty is wrong!"[25] Thus, we can see how King's rhetoric skillfully negotiates the discursive landscape forming the background of rights claiming in that context. Most effective is the way that King situates the actions of the protesters as part of American tradition by focusing on the First Amendment, which he argues distinguishes the United States from communist nations. Then, using the Constitution, he pivots and defines white supremacists as threatening the law of America's existence, as being un-American. With the issues of standing established in favor of the civil rights movement, he then proceeds to establish the rightfulness of his legal claims by citing the Supreme Court's rule of law in *Brown*, a citation that aspires to produce as an effect its motivating, yet uncertain, presupposition that *Brown*, rather than Montgomery's practices of segregation, is truly the law of the land.

King works to refigure American identity on a nonracial basis by using a two-pronged approach, invoking the cold war and citing the fundamental laws of the nation. These discursive patterns are present in other King speeches as well. On the third anniversary of the *Brown* decision, King gave the keynote address during the Prayer Pilgrimage for Freedom on May 17, 1957, in front of the Lincoln Memorial. In this speech, King refers to the Supreme Court's decision in his opening sentence, calling it a "reaffirmation of the good old American doctrine of freedom and equality for all people."[26] In a speech dedicated to securing the right to vote for blacks, King refers to "our basic rights," "our citizenship rights," and "our nation's history."[27] In this way, King encompasses blacks within the national people whose rights are protected on an equal basis by law. He also negotiates the cold war basis of the nation's identity. King uses the cold war to increase the urgency of securing voting rights. He argues that "the civil rights issue is not an ephemeral, evanescent domestic issue that can be kicked about by reactionary guardians of the status quo; it is rather a moral issue which may well determine the destiny of our nation in the ideological struggle with communism."[28] Thus, King utilizes the strategies of both legal citation and anticommunism to produce grounds that will enable the rights of the American people to be extended legitimately to blacks.

In another speech delivered December 11, 1961, before the AFL-CIO, King acknowledges how those struggling for civil rights are denounced as communists in order to deny the legitimacy of their claims. Referring to assorted reactionary forces that "threaten everything decent and fair in American life," King argues that their target is "labor, liberals, and the Negro people, not scattered 'reds' or even Chief Justice Warren, [or] former presidents." While attempting to mobilize people for the hardships ahead in the civil rights struggle, King acknowledges that some will be called "reds and Communists merely because they believe in economic justice and the brotherhood of man. But we shall overcome."[29] These attempts to deflate the charge of communism and to distance the civil rights movement from it illustrate how the boundary separating American from un-American is drawn according to the logic of anticommunism.

King's speech before the AFL-CIO also demonstrates the sophistication with which he forged a national basis to justify the claims of civil rights. The contribution of the nonviolent method of protest toward the end of constituting a community that will bind itself to the obligation of respecting these rights becomes especially clear on this particular occasion. He states that the labor movement and the Negro freedom movement together will "extend the frontiers of democracy for the whole nation." He argues that "[w]e want to rely upon the good will of those who oppose us. Indeed, we have brought forward the method of nonviolence to give an example of unilateral good will in an effort to evoke it in those who have not yet felt it in their hearts."[30]

Elsewhere, King emphasizes that he is not interested in defeating whites. What emerges is the keen insight on King's part that he must forge the social relations that will form the basis of legitimacy for the recognition of rights. Whites must understand blacks as fellow members of the community, rather than understanding themselves as making a grudging concession to a victorious opponent (and blacks, King makes clear, must also understand themselves as part of the community with fellow whites, and not victors over a particular group of people). In a commencement address, King explains this position, arguing, "We must make sure that we make the psychological adjustment required to live in that new society. This is true of white people, and this is true of Negro people." While whites need to shed the vestiges of white supremacy, Negroes must not substitute one tyranny for another.[31]

If the basis of the community is racial, then King and the civil rights movement will undoubtedly fail to achieve their goals. Rather, it is necessary to construct a sociopolitical formation that will sustain these rights claims, and at this point in King's career in the civil rights movement, this basis is the nation and not race.[32] Therefore, the goal is to protect the rights of blacks without defeating whites or making the basis of that recognition of right a racial basis at a fundamental level. Thus, he ends his speech before the AFL-CIO by aspiring to the day "when all of God's children, black men and white men, Jews and Gentiles, Protestants and Catholics, will be able to join hands all over this *nation* and sing in the words of the old Negro spiritual: 'Free At Last, Free At Last. Thank God Almighty, We Are Free At Last.'"[33]

King's effort to found the nonracial nation as the basis for rights claims was potentially aided by the cold war, and King attempted to use this potential. At one level, the cold war was based upon an ideological struggle to define modernity. As I suggested above, this can be interpreted as grafting an ideological struggle upon a basis of racial normality. At the level of an ideological struggle, however, the question was ostensibly one of beliefs and faiths, rather than one of typologies of populations, as racial thinking is. The cold war, therefore, can be understood as a struggle between different conceptions of freedom and democracy. From a U.S.-based perspective, neither the Soviet Union nor China could call itself democratic without certain legal protections of various rights. And from a Soviet perspective, the United States could not call itself democratic with extreme levels of inequality so obviously in evidence. King masterfully inserted the question of civil rights within this competition over which nation, representing the respective cold war ideologies, best exemplified the progress of modernity. The effort to found a nonracially based nation to support these rights claims, and the strategy of using nonviolent methods to forge community rather than to orchestrate defeat, were both dimensions of the civil rights struggle that meshed with the structural necessity of engaging the play within the cold war system.

Finally, King's practices illustrate how law functions as a constitutive social force.[34] King's work reimagines the American nation as nonracial. Such a legal/political/social entity does not exist in reality, like an object waiting to be found. It needs to be called into being. King's nonviolent protests call into existence the forms of consciousness needed to support such an identity formation. King's uses of the law, also, constitute such a national public.

Martin Luther King Jr. frequently discusses the law—necessarily so since he was trying to change laws and support new legislation and court decisions. Significantly, King often returns to foundational legal texts that created America, like the Declaration of Independence and the Constitution, in order to participate in this ongoing process of creation.[35] In a commencement address entitled "The American Dream," King cites the Declaration of Independence: "'We hold these truths to be self-evident, that all men are created equal, that they are endowed by their Creator with certain unalienable rights, that among these are life, liberty, and the pursuit of happiness.' This is the dream." King's analysis of this passage evokes a nonracial American identity to support the claims of rights by blacks: "One of the first things we notice in this dream is an amazing universalism. It does not say some men, but it says all men. It does not say white men, but it says all men, which includes black men. It does not say all Gentiles, but it says all men, which includes Jews. It does not say all Protestants, but it says all men, which includes Catholics." After describing how American practices have not lived up to this dream, King argues that if "we are to implement the American dream we must get rid of the notion once and for all that there are superior and inferior races."[36]

In his address on the third anniversary of *Brown*, he describes *Brown* as a "deathblow to the old Plessy doctrine of 'separate-but-equal.' It came as a reaffirmation of the good old American doctrine of freedom and equality for all people."[37] In contrast, when the Supreme Court reaffirmed a federal court decision that the segregated bus system of Montgomery was unconstitutional, the local judge forced to dissolve his pro-segregation decrees denounced the decision as based on neither "law nor reason," but an "evil construction."[38] In this way, King must be understood as doing rhetorical—and thus legal—battle with supporters of interposition, nullification, and those who signed a "Southern Manifesto."

Not only does law constitute forms of subjectivity, but human interpretive practices constitute a text as law.[39] Therefore, we should understand King as attempting to call into existence the interpretive authority that will recognize *Brown* as law. He does this by asking Americans to understand themselves as a nation that does not discriminate racially but that recognizes rights according to a national basis. The hoped for consequence of King's success in causing Americans to be interpellated in this way is that *Brown* would be recognized as law, rather than the segregation practices white supremacists sought to defend through interposition and nullification. His strategy, on several occasions, to call this America into being is to refer to the Declaration of Independence—one of the legal documents that first imagined America. King is making the case that racial hierarchies are inconsistent with the fundamental laws of the nation and that his legal interpretation is superior to that of the white supremacists who understand challenges to segregation to be not law but examples of an "evil construction."

The American identity that will provide a legitimate basis for the civil rights claims and for legitimizing the Supreme Court's and King's interpretation of the law, while withholding legitimacy from the pro-segregation legal interpretation, does not exist "out there." It is a "dream." King refers to the "Founding Fathers of our nation [who] dreamed this noble dream" in his commencement address entitled "The American Dream."[40] In his famous "I have a Dream" speech, King stands in the shadow of Lincoln, cites the Emancipation Proclamation in language reminiscent of Lincoln, and reminds his audience that when "the architects of our republic wrote the magnificent words of the Constitution and the Declaration of Independence, they were signing a promissory note to which every American was to fall heir. This note was the promise that all men, yes black men as well as white men, would be guaranteed the unalienable rights of life, liberty, and the pursuit of happiness."[41] After acknowledging how America has defaulted on its promise to this point, he abandons the imagery of wealth sitting behind the doors of a vault waiting to be put into circulation, an image that modern economics itself has long since rejected. He replaces it with "a dream deeply rooted in the American dream that one day this nation will rise up and live out the true meaning of its creed—we hold these truths to be self-evident, that all men are created equal."[42]

There is no "America" or "law" waiting to be discovered. It needs to be invented. It needs to be called into existence through fantasy, dreams, and faith. King also recognizes this fact, which forms the basis of his rejection of that genre of radical thinking in which the ends justify the means. Such thinking makes sense only if there is an object that is the "end" that lies waiting to be discovered. But if one acknowledges social contingency, then one must realize that "America" and "American law" exist only in the various moments in which these things are imagined and people act upon these beliefs. Thus, King argues with respect to those who believe in nonviolence, in contrast to ends-justify-the-means radicalism, that "we realize that the end is preexistent in the means."[43]

King then paints a picture that is fantastic for its incongruence with reality, a reality to which King remains "proud to be maladjusted and to which I call upon all men of good will to be maladjusted":[44]

I have a dream that one day on the red hills of Georgia, sons of former slaves and slave-owners will be able to sit down together at the table of brotherhood.

I have a dream that one day, even the state of Mississippi, a state sweltering with the heat of injustice, sweltering with the heat of oppression, will be transformed into an oasis of freedom and justice.

I have a dream my four little children will one day live in a nation where they will not be judged by the color of their skin but by the content of their character. I have a dream today!

I have a dream that one day, down in Alabama, with its vicious racists, with its governor having his lips dripping with the words of interposition and nullification, that one day, right there in Alabama, little black boys and black girls will be able to join hands with little white boys and white girls as sisters and brothers. I have a dream today![45]

After describing his dream for a postracist America, King remarks, "This is our hope. This is the faith that I go back to the South with." He adds: "[A]nd if America is to be a great nation, this must become true."[46] In other words, the truth is not "out there." The nonracist America required to support the claims of civil rights does not exist; it can only be dreamed about. But should a community share this dream and act based on the faith in its possibility and its existence, then it will *become true*. And King's use of both nonviolent protest and legal argument are efforts to bring this dream into existence—to *constitute* the American public that can provide the conditions of legitimacy for these claims of right.[47]

Reflecting this effort at producing a performative utterance, King then shifts his rhetoric from the first person singular to the inclusive and plural "we" after sharing his dream.[48]

With this faith we will be able to transform the jangling discords of our nation into a beautiful symphony of brotherhood.

With this faith we will be able to work together, to pray together, to struggle together, to go to jail together, to stand up for freedom together, knowing that we will be free one day. This will be the day when all of

> God's children will be able to sing with new meaning—"my country 'tis of thee; sweet land of liberty."

By enveloping his audience within his transformative faith through the use of "we," King attempts to call out to his audience so they can respond by testifying to its validity and begin the process of making King's dream a reality.

While both the U.S. government and Martin Luther King Jr. use the cold war as a justification for recognizing the claims of the civil rights movement, opponents of civil rights also would use the cold war and accusations of "communism" as a means of delegitimating such rights claims. King's speech to the AFL-CIO, in which he addresses such charges, manifests this tendency. Taylor Branch's history of the civil rights movement also illustrates the prevalence of these efforts to delegitimate the civil rights movement. Branch describes a letter to the editor of the local paper during the Montgomery bus boycott speculating that there must be a communist hand behind such strife. FBI chief J. Edgar Hoover, of course, would often suspect a communist shadow lurking behind civil rights agitation.[49] Additionally, there was suspicion that the urban disorders of the late 1960s were influenced if not directly caused by communists.[50] In fact, the House Committee on Un-American Activities specifically investigated such a possibility.[51]

The global context of American national identity is different now that memories of the cold war are fast fading. The year 1989 not only marked Khomeini's fatwa on Rushdie, but it was also the year the Berlin wall came down. The late 1980s and the early 1990s witnessed the disappearance of the Soviet threat, but with its evaporation, all that was left was the third world. In these changed circumstances, Samuel Huntington encouraged the use of a new global imaginary, one that pressed old and familiar narratives to new use, while bending and reinflecting their categories to present conditions.[52] Into this social context *The Satanic Verses* fell, hoping to invent its ground—perhaps a third space—but finding, instead, that other authorities had laid claim to the territory.[53] There's a sign.

Rushdie as a Sign of the Times

Salman Rushdie functioned and continues to function as a liminal figure for America when it represents itself as the "West." Structural anthropology, and those like John Fiske who have made use of its methods in their interpretations of popular culture, give theoretical importance to anomalous figures, categories, and "liminality."[54] These are figures that are neither nature nor culture but both, their meaning is "excessive," and they function mythologically for cultures by helping them to negotiate the boundaries between the extremes of a binary opposition. Cowboys like John Wayne are understood as too wild to fit into "culture," too cultured to fit into "nature," and yet it is they who save "culture" from the "Indians" ("nature"). In liminality, for Victor Turner, the ritual subject becomes "ambiguous, neither here nor there, betwixt and between all fixed points of classification." Turner argues that it is through liminality that community emerges.[55]

Rushdie is a sign: an articulated, impure, hybrid figure whose ultimate meaning is perpetually deferred. The controversy surrounding *The Satanic Verses*, and Rushdie as a sign, however, became a major occasion for America to rewrite its boundaries. America has deterritorialized its cold war identity while rewriting its global imaginary and reterritorializing itself within this new imaginary. And with this rewriting, the meaning of its boundaries has changed.

Born in India, Rushdie went to England in his early teens to attend school, and with the exception of a short period of time spent in Pakistan, he has lived in London since and is a British citizen. In one interview he says, "[P]eople will ask me—will ask anyone like me—'are you Indian? Pakistani? English?' What is being expressed is a discomfort with a plural identity. And what I am saying to you—and saying in the novel—is that we have got to come to terms with this. We are increasingly becoming a world of migrants, made up of bits and fragments from here, there. We are here. And we have never really left anywhere we have been."[56]

In the same interview he describes *The Satanic Verses* as writing himself—"The English part, the Indian part. The part of me that lives in London, and the part of me that longs for Bombay."[57] On another occasion, he expresses the same sentiment: "Like millions of people, I am a bastard child of history. Perhaps we all are, black and brown and white, leaking into one another, as a character of mine once said, *like flavours when you cook*."[58] Or again, elsewhere, "I have always to some extent felt unhoused."[59] Often, in pictures or cartoons of him, Rushdie's face is portrayed half in the light and half in shadows. Under the picture of him that accompanies a 1990 *Newsweek* interview, even his name is written in such a way, R-U-S in white; H-D-I-E in black.[60]

In a book that seeks to understand recent events in cultural politics, including multiculturalism and hate speech controversies, Jonathan Rauch inserts Rushdie into his narrative in a position structurally analogous to that of Jesus, another anomalous figure who mediates between heaven and earth and who comes from the "East" and yet whose contemporary followers take him as representing or saving the "West." On the book's dedication page, Rauch writes, "In Memoriam / Salman Rushdie / June 1947–February 1989 / Et expecto resurrectionem mortuorum." The book's last chapter is entitled "Et Expecto Resurrectionem," and Rauch encourages his readers in its last sentence to "pray—no, fight—for [Rushdie's] resurrection."[61]

Rauch argues for a system of play and constraint—though he is rather unself-conscious about justifying his constraints—to enable "speech" while protecting "knowledge" in a way that will live up to the West's heritage in valuing science. For Rauch, "speech" is good, but multiculturalism must be excluded from universities as knowledge-producing institutions. So if Rushdie is to be defended by Rauch, his multiculturalism must be sifted in order to defend *The Satanic Verses* as "speech." Rushdie must be made to speak as a Westerner. And indeed, Rauch introduces the Rushdie affair in the following way: "Then came a defining moment. . . . In February 1989, fundamentalist Muslims rose up against the *British* writer Salman Rushdie."[62]

Post–Cold War Moral Geography

In the beginning of *The Satanic Verses*, Gibreel Farishta and Saladin Chamcha fall like a sign, an essentially hybrid and impure origin or articulated category of signifier and signified, and it was Chamcha who falls while reciting lines from the eighteenth-century poet James Thomson.[63] Ironically, when the "founders" invented the ground beneath their feet as America and named their Other "Indians," they also were reciting the lines of James Thomson.[64] Thomson's poetry created a geography of liberty by telling his readers where liberty was out of place owing to indolence or luxury (as in southern European nations) and where liberty was at home (namely, in England). He was one among many writers of the Whig moral geography, and was himself a consumer of the Whig historians whom the framers studied.[65] As we have seen in chapter 1, the founders wrote themselves into the narrative of liberty provided by Thomson and the Whig historians, and extended it to this new place of America. John Adams, in his "Dissertation on the Canon and the Feudal Law," states, "Let us see delineated before us the true map of man."[66] Adams imposes this map upon other possible geographies, which he clears in the process, taking no cognizance of their existence save as landmarks within his own. He narrates the colonial process of territorializing America: "Recollect their amazing fortitude, their bitter sufferings . . . the severe labors of *clearing their grounds* . . . amidst dangers from wild beasts and *savage* men." The narrative that gave meaning to American rights, however, also created new frontiers and limits to justice. The Declaration of Independence, which claimed American rights, also referred to "frontiers" and the "merciless Indian savages."

Thus, the founders were not simply in "space." They extended and reinflected familiar narratives and previously existing categories in new and different ways—America was not created out of nothing. Similarly, just when Rushdie's Chamcha was imagining the need to invent the ground beneath his feet before he could take a step,

> there was no need now to worry about such matters, because here in front of him was the inevitable: the tall, bony figure of Death . . . Death . . . wearing olive-green Wellington boots.
>
> "What do you imagine yourselves to be doing here?" Death wanted to know. "This is private property. There's a sign." [The territory had already been spoken for.]
>
> A few moments later, Death bent over him—to kiss me, he panicked silently. To suck the breath from my body. He made . . . futile movements of protest.[67]

Just as the ground had been claimed prior to Chamcha and Farishta's landing, so also was the space claimed into which *The Satanic Verses* landed by the moral geography I used Mill to illustrate in the previous chapter. Rauch crucially identifies Rushdie as British, significantly erasing any trace of hybridity from either him or his work in order to use him to justify the Western system of play and constraint regarding issues of speech and knowledge. Rauch understands the controversy over *The Satanic Verses* as presenting a challenge to *Western* intellectuals, and he refers his argument, if not just to Americans, then to the "*modern* West."[68]

Rauch's framing of the controversy recurs with great regularity in other coverage. The *New Yorker* describes *The Satanic Verses* as "a book that was written in a tradition different from that of his persecutors, and [that] was not intended for them." The piece continues, "Mr. Rushdie had every reason to think himself safe writing in England, enclosed by the Western world." A *New Republic* article describes Prime Minister Thatcher's protection of Rushdie as "the protection of Western civilization against . . . anti-Western forces."[69]

Also invoking the Millian paradigm to reconfigure America within the modern West, the *National Review* condemns Iran by describing its "fundamentalists" as "still stuck in the thirteenth [century], in a stalled time machine that has not registered the Enlightenment and never heard of John Stuart Mill." Modernity is again associated with reason, as the article continues to argue that there "is no easy way back to *sanity* in this vast and *ancient* country." It also goes on to describe the "West's united condemnation of the Ayatollah," which could very easily be perceived as factually incorrect if one forgets that the "West" is not a thing but a fantasy, albeit a fantasy with very real consequences. In a *US News and World Report* article we again get the "modern West"; Islam is represented as not just a religion but a place; and Rushdie becomes a "Muslim gone West." For Paul Berman, writing in the *New Republic*, "the affair did serve a useful purpose, which was to focus everyone's attention on what it is that people mean when they speak of that vague entity, half geographical, half spiritual—the 'West.'" "To be 'Western,'" Berman writes, "was to stand with the free thinking individual, no matter the expense or danger."[70]

Of course, Rushdie as a sign can be constructed differently, but the meaning of this sign in this context must still be regulated according to an Orientalist economy of meaning.[71] Therefore, while Patrick Buchanan attempts to metamorphose Rushdie into a non-Westerner, this sign is still ultimately pressed into the service of inspiring a superior "West." Although Buchanan initially describes Rushdie as a "Western" figure, he then reinflects the sign as "not even an American," finally unmasking Rushdie as an "Indian-born British subject, a man of the trendy left, who until recently was known for *savage* commentary on the very governments from which he now seeks support and safety." Drawing out the differences in America's pre- and post-1989 global imaginaries, Buchanan compares Rushdie unfavorably with the "enormous talent" of Alexander Solzhenitsyn. Finally, he comes to the bottom line: Buchanan opposes the treatment of Rushdie as a "Western icon" and argues that the way "Rushdie exercised his literary freedom was irresponsible and contemptuous."[72] Indian savages are seemingly incapable of exercising their freedoms responsibly, and perhaps that is why they are out of place in the West just as speech rights are out of place in the East.

In this way, the controversy over *The Satanic Verses* serves as an occasion for America to reinvent itself as part of an Orientalist-inspired "West," whether or not the publication in question contributing to the controversy is defending Rushdie. Leslie Gelb, moreover, demonstrates how this territorialization is also a *moral* geography. For Gelb, the controversy over *Satanic Verses* is an "affront to *Western* ideals of free speech and *justice*." The author's life and "our [i.e., American] liberty are slowly and certainly [unless Western governments stand up to Iran] 'sinking into the abyss.'" Only "political power," Gelb argues without the necessary irony, "can save Rushdie's life and *our* heritage."[73] Free speech and *justice* are *Western* ideals. They are part of a strictly bounded entity's "heritage." If there is a recognition that these endlessly repeated spatial boundaries still cannot contain an ambiguous field, polemicists would resort to an extra dimension by conceding that the West's heritage did contain the practices projected upon the East, but then distanced the West's identity from these practices temporally. Reminiscent of the way Mill distances the West's identity from practices that he understood to be uncivilized, the *New Republic* editorializes, "Europe was once" that way.[74]

The network of social relations occurring within this moral geography demands a Western subject position for the recognition of speech rights. Accordingly, *Commentary*'s Midge Decter forces Rushdie into a Western subject position: "For while he may have been born a Sunni Muslim, the author of *The Satanic Verses* is by now little more, or if you will, nothing less, than a thoroughly Western man of letters." The *New Republic* also stuffs Rushdie into the subject position of Westerner in order to defend his work as free speech. Though initially described as "Anglo-Indian Muslim," in the next sentence he is reduced to "one of those Western intellectuals [who misplace their support in third world causes]."[75]

The importance of Rushdie's Western identity became more clear when Rushdie pronounced his faith in Islam (which he later renounced). Though one should be careful about eliding religion, place, and people, Islam was constructed as a geographic locale throughout this controversy (Rushdie's novel, according to Roger Rosenblatt in *US News and World Report*, arrived "in Islam from the West," for instance).[76] Furthermore, the *New Republic* called Rushdie's "none of your business" response to a *British* playwright's regret over the conversion "impudent," sarcastically stating that his persecution was "all of *our* business; his conversion is none of *our* business."[77] Here, an American "our" envelops British national identity through the spatial bridge provided by the "West" and retreads the racial track of John Adams's memory of ancestors crossing the Atlantic with rights cleaved to their bodies.

In the wake of Rushdie's announcement, the *New Republic* found it necessary to wonder if Rushdie would now apologize to "the book dealers."[78] The *New Republic* accused him of betraying his book's readers, the book itself, the "principles" of the book, and its defense. With his proclamation of faith in Islam, the *New Republic* editorialized that the Rushdie affair "has not lost its villain, only its hero."[79] Now excluded from a Western subject position, apparently Rushdie became indefensible according to the peculiarities of the *Western* ideal of free speech.

The Significance of Boundaries

The controversy over *The Satanic Verses* became an occasion to reinflect the American national formation and lend its boundaries new meaning, boundaries that affected the foundations on which rights were and continue to be recognized and claimed, as well as the American national community's understandings of the obligations of justice. Boundaries, I contend, are not peripheral issues; they go to the heart of America.[80] The Rushdie affair has colored American perceptions of right, and *The Satanic Verses* controversy itself has become part of the landscape to evaluate rights claims in America. The Rushdie example and the examples that follow indicate a more general change: the shift in American national space from the cold war to the post–cold war. Practices of rights, therefore, no longer imagine America as a nation that represents an anticommunist ideology. America is now a nation that understands itself as representing the civilized West.

Illustrating how the Rushdie affair has itself become part of the landscape of rights claiming, Martin Peretz, in an article entitled "Embroiled Salman," ends by putting blacks outside of the American imaginary when he metaphorically aligns African Americans with the "anti-Western forces" that threaten Rushdie's life: "I cannot see how conversions by blacks to a religion that sees itself so at odds with America and its norms will speed their journey toward equality," he writes.[81] A letter to the editor of the *New York Times* by the editor of the University of Pennsylvania's campus paper invokes the Rushdie affair as a paradigm for understanding campus politics involving oppressed peoples and what he calls "offensive speech." Another letter to the editor describes the furor over an art student's exhibit at the Art Institute of Chicago. The problem was the way that the exhibit encouraged spectators to interpellate themselves with respect to the American flag. This writer uses the Rushdie affair as a way to valorize America despite the pressure put on the artist, Dred Scott Tyler. He is lucky, the writer seems to be saying—at least he was not threatened with death. In an article on the same topic, the artist is quoted invoking Rushdie to defend himself.[82] Letters to the editor and editorials addressing Jesse Helms's attempts to cut funding to the arts patriotically refer to the Rushdie affair to define American free speech obligations.[83]

In an essay published in the May 1995 *Harpers*, Jonathan Rauch presses Mill's multidimensional moral geography back into use against his favorite opponents, multiculturalists and those who defend speech codes and antiharassment measures in the workplace—who attempt, mistakenly in his view, to "eradicate prejudice" from public expression. He uses a temporal trope to take the ground out from under the feet of the "modern anti-racist and anti-sexist and anti-homophobic campaigners" by likening the current "crusade" to "earlier crusades."[84] In addition to the temporal trope of modernity, Rauch utilizes the spirits of Western civilization to define the enemies of America as well. He invokes the Rushdie affair to instigate this particular form of American self-recognition. Noting Rushdie's statements on behalf of "freedom of expression" in opposition to the "ayatollahs" who "sentenced him to death and put a price on his head," Rauch suggests the similarity between this death sentence and hate speech codes and hate crime laws in order to disqualify support for the latter. He takes particular aim at Toni Morrison, who has called oppressive language "verbal violence." The America that emerges from Rauch's arguments is one in which value increases as proximity to a feminized or racially colored voice decreases (recall that Rauch represents Rushdie as a Westerner in his book). Morrison's public identity as a black woman undoubtedly facilitates the reconstruction of an American national formation around a center anchored by Rushdie and against the ayatollahs. Rauch makes his case bluntly: "Salman Rushdie is right and Toni Morrison is wrong, and minorities belong at his side, not hers."[85] Although Rauch attempts to defend "pluralism" against the "war on prejudice" in America, pluralism must have its limits if "America" is to be maintained as a distinctive social unit. By locating America's identity in the West for the purpose of defining its social norms and its boundaries in contrast to other social formations,

Rauch's American imaginary is likely to hold few opportunities for those who either are inscribed or self-identify as racial minorities.

The May 12, 1995 edition of the ABC news magazine *20/20* also illustrates the persistence of the Rushdie affair as a way to understand issues of identity and free speech.[86] The story broadcast by *20/20* that evening was entitled "The Speech Police." It was about a male student, Craig Rogers, at California State University who made a claim that a lecturer, Joanne Morrow, sexually harassed him by presenting a lecture on female sexuality in a psychology course.

Rogers's complaint can be interpreted as a charge that the professor violated the norms of the decent public sphere by discussing female sexuality in a "personal manner" and not in a "clinical, professional manner." According to the reporter, John Stossel, Rogers defended himself against the charge that he was extreme in his recognition of these norms; he said he was "no prude" owing to his experience with "gang members who use coarse and sexual language." Apparently, Rogers could tolerate sexual expression as long as there was no threat to the relations of identity that inscribe the civilized and the savage. As a presentation that challenged relations of decency, gender, and sexuality, however, the professor's speech lost its value as knowledge, and Rogers condemned the presentation in no uncertain terms: "This wasn't education. . . . I wasn't here to hear raunchy talk." He condemned the threat to his decent, masculine public identity: "I had no power. I had no control. I was being aroused and didn't want it." He attempted to reassert his public identity through a resort to the law by suing the state for $2.5 million for sexual harassment.

The *20/20* reporter's sympathies, and those of host Barbara Walters, were obviously not with Rogers, and they situated his claims with those of racial minorities who support hate speech codes. Walters introduced the segment as addressing "one of our most-prized rights as Americans . . . freedom of speech." After describing the controversy, the reporter contextualized it within the larger conflict between the ideal of universities to advance knowledge by free speech, and the rules "prohibiting certain kinds of racial, sexual and what [campuses] call 'hateful' speech. One result is that now some people seem to be competing to see who can be most offended." The examples of harassment used by the reporter to support his presentation of the context included an incident of racial conflict at the University of Pennsylvania over the use of the term "water buffalo" in a shouting match, the use of a racial stereotype by a University of California fraternity, and a University of New Hampshire classroom incident that brought together race, sex, and gender. Stossel suggested that speech codes violate the First Amendment by stating that courts have rejected the attempt to regulate words in this context. Conceding that it is easy not to take racial minorities, and other oppressed groups, seriously, he then acknowledged that "when it's a white man who says he's oppressed, that makes people think again."

Stossel returned to the focus of the segment and engaged in an argument with Rogers's lawyer over whether Rogers had legal grounds or not for his suit. Asking the lawyer whether it would "be illegal if [the professor] told an ethnic joke?" and getting an affirmative response, the show shifted to a voiceover with Stossel rebutting the lawyer by stating, "Really? Extend that logic and you get Ayatollah Khomeini's decree." Then, a segment from *ABC News*, October 11, 1993, was shown, with Peter Jennings reporting: "Khomeini said today it was the duty of Muslims around the world to kill Salman Rushdie." The show returned to the Stossel voiceover: "The Ayatollah said Salman Rushdie's book was so hurtful to Muslims that he had to be killed, and one of his translators has been murdered." After giving other examples of censorship, Stossel returned to the screen: "Of course, Craig Rogers sees no connection between Joanne Morrow and Salman Rushdie." Rogers: "Well, thank God, in America he can say those things if he were here, and . . . that would be okay." Stossel: "But you're saying, in America, she can't say what she wants to say." Rogers: "Well, she can't say anything that's going to hurt me." The segment ended with Stossel defending the position that supports the remedy of more speech for bad speech to Hugh Downs.[87]

This episode presents a very interesting contrast with cold war America. During the cold war, as we have seen, those who claimed rights had to negotiate the cold war national formation, and the most effective charge that delegitimized such claims was the charge of "communism." In this 1995 news segment, a "white" man's claim that he was harassed was disqualified by association with the claims of racial subordinates. The United States has become a nation that understands itself as representing a racial division of the West versus the Rest. As I argued with respect to the cold war, this new meaning of American national space does not determine the outcome in controversies over rights. The national space is the shared terrain of the controversy, which is now America's identity as an exemplar of the civilized West. The shift in the American national imaginary changes the landscape of disputing, and different forms of identity become resources or burdens. There is a change in the way that rights are practiced and challenged, but the element of contestability persists. This is why I suggest that it is more productive to think of the social context of rights controversies as regulating the process, and not determining it.

Conclusion

I have argued that practices of rights occur within specific historical and spatial contexts. Furthermore, controversy over rights can be one force that helps to produce collective understandings of social space. I have shown how the controversy over *The Satanic Verses* became immanent within American free speech practices, whether one was referring to a student art exhibit, national funding for the arts, or campus politics. In each of these examples, Rushdie was a sign that functioned as a terrain of struggle and yet bore the traces, as the philosopher of language V. N. Vološinov might have argued, of previous engagements.[88] Different agents attempted to infuse Rushdie with an accent that would ground a national identity to sustain their claims of right, and to use him as a sign that would mark the limits of this space.

I should note, however, that despite the perpetual openness of Rushdie to remobilization, this possibility makes sense only in these instances within an economy of meaning in which significance is regulated according to an opposition between the West and the non-West. Of course, no sooner is this frame imposed than the territory becomes destabilized by other haunting presences that cannot be contained according to a spatial logic. Thus, other dimensions such as temporality, which are no less racialized, are employed in furious attempts to stabilize an identity formation. This is what Geoffrey Bennington and Rushdie's Mimi Mamoulian mean when they argue that the Other always maintains a haunting presence.[89] The Rushdie affair has taught us that the ground currently giving a person the authorship and authority to have his or her voice rise to the level of speech by right is the modern West, and its representative, America. The problem is that, no matter who we are, we are constantly saying to ourselves, "Watch out, Chamcha, look out for your shadow. That black fellow creeping up behind."[90] Although such a landscape may have presented a certain opening for the defense of Rushdie's right to free speech, it is a landscape that forecloses (or at least makes more difficult) other possible rights claims.

Postscript: *The Reality of Fantastic Art*

One of the most bitter ironies of the controversy over *The Satanic Verses* must be the fact that the issues raised by the controversy bore striking resemblance to many of Rushdie's perceptive insights about which he wrote in the book. One of the similarities that is relevant here is the relation between voices, bodies, spaces, and power. The character Chamcha, a man from India living in England, finds success by using his abilities to assume a variety of vocal characteristics.[91] This success, however, is bought at the price of making his body invisible within the space of England. Rushdie describes the success experienced by Chamcha and his colleague, Mimi Mamoulian, in the following way:

> Because [Chamcha] did truly have that gift . . . he was the Man of a Thousand Voices and a Voice. . . . On the radio he could convince an audience that he was Russian, Chinese, [or whatever]. . . . With his female equivalent, Mimi Mamoulian, he ruled the airwaves in Britain. . . . Her range was astonishing; she could do any age, anywhere in the world. . . . Saladin and Mimi were legends of a sort, but crippled legends, dark stars. The gravitational field of their abilities drew work towards them, but they remained invisible, shedding bodies to put on voices. She [Mimi] had become her voice, she was worth a mint. . . . She bought property. "Neurotic behavior," she would confess unashamedly. "Excessive need for rooting. . . ." [She described her property this way:] "All haunted," she explained. ". . . Nobody gives up land without a fight."
>
> His big break . . . had started small: children's television, a thing called *The Aliens Show*. . .. The stars of the show . . . Maxim and Mamma Alien . . . were played by Saladin Chamcha and Mimi Mamoulian. . . . [T]he actors . . . were processed through machines, obliged to spend four hours every day being buried under the latest in prosthetic make-up.

Although agents never enjoy an "absolute" freedom of choice with regard to their personal identities and voices, some circumstances are more oppressive than others and leave much less room for maneuver. As actors, Chamcha and Mamoulian must perform according to the constraints of the imaginary domain created by *The Aliens Show*. Their participation in this fantasy gives them means to pursue other fantasies that a critic might declare just as unrealistic as the one they are paid to perform. Chamcha aspires to efface the traces of his Indianness by conforming his voice and body to the social norms of civilized Englishness. Mamoulian aspires to create the territory where she can belong, where she can feel rooted because her identity is not out of place. She wants to feel at home.

As I suggested above, some spaces are more suffocating or oppressive due to the demands they put on their subjects, particularly identities that are perceived to be out of place. Elsewhere in the novel, Saladin Chamcha, feeling the frustration that comes from the prison house of dreams that confined him, "lay face downwards on a narrow bed and wept. 'Damn all Indians,' he cried. . . .

"It was at this moment that the police arrived to arrest him." It was the "men from immigration." He tried to protest, to no avail, "you've got to believe me, I'm a British. . ."

"[Rosa] did, finally, hear his voice rise in a last, despairing shout: 'Don't any of you watch TV? Don't you see? I'm Maxim. Maxim Alien.'

"'So you are,' said the [immigration] officer [taking him away]. 'And I am Kermit the frog.'"[92]

A black Englishman is as fantastic and unbelievable as a spectacular, yet safe, fall from an airplane. It was Gibreel Farishta's voice that cut through the commotion. He had come downstairs to see what was the matter, wearing a smoking jacket. "A more reputable looking gentleman you couldn't wish to see," writes Rushdie. Gibreel asks, "What do these men want?" and "every man there was seized by the desire to answer his question in literal, detailed terms." Without his fine clothes or his "lovely, white, English wife," Chamcha had lost the signifiers that could situate his body within this space.[93] Without these signs, the state forces that police the articulation of bodies to spaces decided he made no sense where he was and unhoused him. Similarly, when Rushdie announced renewed faith in Islam, it no longer made sense for the *New Republic* to defend him as an author.

5

Whose First Amendment Is It, Anyway?

What are the conditions of possibility for claiming a right to free speech in the United States? As we have seen, the U.S. Constitution's First Amendment describes the freedoms of speech, press, and assembly as the rights of *the people*. This makes a prior constitution of the American people, and the identification of the one claiming a First Amendment right with this American people, conditions making possible a successful rights claim. On the one hand, because law exists in relation to a given empirical situation, there must be a common understanding of this situation for a definition of its law to make sense. On the other hand, claims about what the law is or requires are often mechanisms by which this common understanding of the situation is produced or enforced. As we have seen in chapter 1, the British Americans based their claims to rights upon their identity as Englishmen while they produced the American nation by making rights claims (as they did through the Declaration of Independence, for instance). This example of eighteenth-century America, however, brings forward another point. Because meaning or identity is deferred, the gap of uncertainty between law and society that generates the need to *claim* in the first place can also produce new possibilities. Forms of law in one circumstance can become animated with contents different from those that governed an earlier time and place. As we have seen in chapter 4, Martin Luther King Jr. cited the Declaration of Independence in the context of America's anticommunism to expand conceptions of what it means to be an American in order to ground his claims that black Americans have rights like other Americans. And controversy over Salman Rushdie's rights as an author reconfigured the landscape of rights claiming, helping to dissolve this cold war imaginary and installing America within the context of Western civilization. This installation identifying the

American people as members of Western civilization became solidified through the controversy over political correctness (PC) that became an unavoidably dominant aspect of U.S. political and legal culture in the early to mid-1990s as the nation adjusted to its post–cold war identity and global imaginary.[1]

One of the more significant legal outcomes of the PC controversy was that hate speech codes came to be perceived as violating the First Amendment's guaranty of free speech. Critical legal studies (cls) has long argued on the one hand that law works to reproduce relations of power, and on the other that law is indeterminate. But if law is so malleable to judicial and other forms of interpretation, then why do legal outcomes display the consistency that cls criticizes as reinforcing domination (and that allows lawyers, judges, and professors to say confidently what the law in any area is)?[2] Building upon the insight that the relationship between law and society is mutually constitutive, I shall explain how the legal conclusion that hate speech codes necessarily violate the First Amendment became determined.

The campaign against PC puts a legal question (the constitutionality of hate speech codes) in relation to an identity question (the legitimacy of multiculturalism).[3] The National Association of Scholars (NAS), a key anti-PC organization of college professors, opposes hate speech codes in the name of diverse opinion and tolerance in its statement of principles. If diversity were its sole end, then we might expect the NAS to endorse proposals seeking to broaden university life beyond Eurocentrism through multicultural curricula. The NAS, however, *opposes* multicultural curricula. While it would be easy to criticize the NAS for taking contradictory positions, it is more productive to take the articulation of these two NAS positions as symptomatic of the sociolegal conjuncture during the early to mid-1990s and to diagnose this alignment in order to understand how the legal conclusion that hate speech codes necessarily violate the First Amendment was produced. The key to this diagnosis is to recognize that legal stability is related to stability in an empirical situation, and the significant empirical context for rights like freedom of speech in the United States is the people—what it means to be *American*. Opponents of multicultural curricula are reproducing and extending the post–cold war reconstruction of what it means to be an American discussed in the previous chapter. This reconstruction, in turn, structures questions of standing— whose rights are perceived to be at stake and who is not perceived to have a legitimate rights claim—according to the norms of Western civilization.

By identifying the people according to the norms of being civilized, the anti-PC campaign legitimizes the perception that hate speech codes violate the rights of (those who count as) speakers while delegitimizing the rights claims of those identified as racial minorities or feminine. Indeed, echoing the Millian paradigm in its statement of principles, the NAS values not only diverse opinion but "civility" as well.[4]

In this chapter, I will demonstrate that in the abstract, the legality of hate speech codes is indeterminate. Other scholars have demonstrated this point by arguing that a legal conclusion on the constitutionality of hate speech codes depends on whether the analysis begins from the Fourteenth Amendment's Equal Protection Clause, which prohibits discrimination by the state, or from the First Amendment, which prohibits governments from violating freedom of speech.[5] I shall argue, however, that the diversity of values First Amendment jurisprudence acknowledges and seeks to promote makes the constitutionality of hate speech codes ambiguous even if one frames the issue according to standards derived solely from this body of law.[6] While a cls analysis might stop at the point of demonstrating indeterminacy, I shall go on to reconstruct the logic that led legal interpretations to perceive hate speech codes as violating the First Amendment with some consistency. I shall show how the anti-PC polemics constructed America as part of Western civilization. This construction of America made valid the legal conclusion that hate speech codes violate the First Amendment. The legal conclusion by courts that hate speech codes are unconstitutional, then, was disseminated popularly to delegitimize multiculturalism and that which was categorized as "PC." In this way, the rhythm of this chapter follows the analysis of chapter 1, as an identity formation is used to support legal claims, and then legal interpretations are used to produce national identities.

Hate Speech Codes and First Amendment Values: The Right of Academic Freedom and the Geography of the University

In *Grayned v. City of Rockford*, a Supreme Court case dealing with a rally on a sidewalk outside of a public school where an antinoise ordinance regulated such protests during school hours, Justice Thurgood Marshall argues in the Opinion of the Court that "the nature of a place, the pattern of its normal activities, dictate the kinds of regulations of time, place, and manner that are reasonable. Although a silent vigil may not unduly interfere with a public library . . . , making a speech in the reading room almost certainly would. That same speech would be perfectly appropriate in a park. *The crucial question is whether the manner of expression is basically incompatible with the normal activity of a particular place at a particular time.*[7] As Marshall notes, how the nature of a place is defined affects the sorts of regulations that are perceived to be legitimate. Much of the debate over hate speech codes centers on the function of the university in society and what rules are appropriate given the nature of this place. Are universities like workplaces, in which case the legal standards developed in the area of employment discrimination and the Fourteenth Amendment's Equal Protection Clause should guide policy without substantial First Amendment problems? Or are universities places where speech should be freest? If so, then the First Amendment principles applicable to public fora should guide policy.[8]

Often, when people argue that universities are places where speech should be freest, they are assuming that the value university hate speech codes threaten is "academic freedom," which is protected under the First Amendment. Academic freedom, however, may be conceptualized in different ways, and some conceptualizations of academic freedom may have little to say about hate speech codes. Academic freedom, as the political philosopher Amy Gutmann describes, may be conceived as either an individual freedom or a corporate freedom creating a federalist relationship between the university and the state so that the university has a right to self-governance over its affairs.[9]

As an individual right, academic freedom requires some adjustment to address the question of hate speech codes. Because academic freedom is usually thought of as the freedom of scholars from the state, academic freedom says little, on this understanding, about hate speech codes promulgated by colleges or universities (rather than the state) to govern student behavior. If we push the concept, however, it may support an argument for increased participation by students in the governance of the university so that they can be said to have consented to the rule. As long as the rule conforms to my arguments below about value pluralism within the university, such a rule should not stifle the academic freedom of the student-scholar to pursue intellectual endeavors. This interpretation of academic freedom, however, provides strong grounds to oppose hate speech codes if they can be said to impede such intellectual endeavors.

A faculty code promulgated by the university might be perceived as an infringement of the individual right to academic freedom, although should a faculty member dispute the issue, he or she would be in the odd position—from the perspective of academic freedom—of asking the state through its courts to restore academic freedom violated by the university. A faculty code, written in a manner consistent with my arguments below regarding value pluralism in the university, ought not to violate the individual right of academic freedom unless it is so content or viewpoint based that it interferes unduly with teaching or research. For example, Title VII of the 1964 Civil Rights Act (regulating workplace discrimination) is already effectual for universities and should not be considered a violation of an individual's academic freedom.[10] Indeed, it supports the individual right of academic freedom by enabling one to teach and research without fear of discrimination based on race or gender.

The polemicist Jonathan Rauch, describing a system of liberal science in the course of arguments against both multiculturalism and hate speech codes, states that one of the principles of this system is the nonrecognition of personal authority in the practice of science. Knowledge is unrelated to the identity of either the source of the proposition or the interlocutor, and so he refers to "Everyman, a reasonable anybody," to describe the knowledge-checking process.[11] This rule bears some resemblance to the ideal of an individualist academic freedom because it builds upon the liberal distinction between the pursuit of truth and the establishment of authority, the latter viewed as a limit to free inquiry. Yet even if one believes in this distinction between academic debate and authority, it does not constitute a persuasive argument against hate speech codes. Hate speech can be understood as an attempt to impose a subordinating identity upon a person. Such an identity has nothing to do with the academic arguments that the student or scholar is making, and instead hopes to bias perceptions of the person and the worth of what this person has to say or write. This bias can lessen unfairly the value of one's participation in the knowledge-producing and knowledge-checking process. If a hate speech code prevents such direct harassment from imposing an inferior social identity upon a person, then it can be said to further Rauch's goals of an impersonal debate, and it can be understood to contribute to the individual's academic freedom to be treated on a par with other participants in the university community.

If academic freedom is understood as a corporate freedom, then to declare hate speech codes unconstitutional is a *violation* of academic freedom—particularly if faculty play a role in university governance and vote democratically to impose a code upon themselves. In this case, a hate speech code is an expression of their freedom to govern themselves, and intrusion from another governmental body violates this freedom. An institution, for example, might define its mission as one that provides zero tolerance for discrimination, and a hate speech code might reflect this sense of mission. In this case, for the state to enjoin the enforcement of a university hate speech code is to violate academic freedom.[12]

Owing to the ambiguity over what is meant by "academic freedom" and the relation of these conceptualizations to hate speech codes, it is far from clear that hate speech codes necessarily violate the First Amendment when academic freedom is taken to represent the First Amendment value hate speech codes are said to put in jeopardy. Moreover, when "academic freedom" is invoked, we imagine the university functioning as a public forum. In light of the various functions and values that university life attempts to fulfill, however, the *university* is too blunt as a unit of analysis. Universities do provide public fora, but this does not exhaust the types of practices institutionalized within a university. Recognizing the diversity of practices within the space of the university makes the claim that hate speech codes necessarily violate the First Amendment even more specious.

For instance, universities are places of employment, and to this extent, the legal scholar Mary Ellen Gale is correct to insist upon the relevance to university governance of Title VII of the 1964 Civil Rights Act and the legal standards that have evolved under this legislation, especially those relevant to the problem of harassment. Faculty have offices; faculty, staff, and students work in laboratories; and administrators staff university bureaucracies. The workplace is not a public forum—even if one works for the state or federal government—and management can govern the office in order to promote the purposes of this office rather than freedom of expression without running afoul of the First Amendment.[13]

Universities also provide housing, and discrimination in public housing is prohibited under Title VIII of the 1968 Civil Rights Act. When the Supreme Court addresses picketing of private residences, it upholds content-neutral ordinances that regulate protests targeting individuals in their own homes. If a protest makes persons captives of the protest message in their own homes, then they cannot choose whether to consume the message of the protest or not. Although it is tempting to focus on the First Amendment rights of the protesters outside of the residence, one might consider the ordinance, and the Supreme Court's judging such an ordinance to be constitutional, as protecting the First Amendment rights of the private residents by assisting their ability to choose that which they wish to listen to or view. Moreover, although one is expected to endure some unwanted speech when in public, one's residence is where one retires to seek peace, rest, and rejuvenation from the jostling of everyday life and to prepare to reenter public space. If even a picket that would be protected speech under the First Amendment when performed in a public park can be regulated when organized to target an individual in his or her home, then it should not be difficult to regulate hate speech in the context of a dormitory under previously established First Amendment standards.[14]

The classroom is not a public forum either. If one were to insist on reciting poetry in a physics class, the physics professor would be within his or her rights to ask the disruptive student to leave the class and to continue with the recitation on the nearest quadrangle or street corner. As Cass Sunstein notes, subject matter restrictions "are part of education. Irrelevant discussion is banned. Students cannot discuss the presidential election, or Marx and Mill, if the subject is math." Sunstein goes on to say that teachers can also require students to treat each other with a minimum of respect, and can certainly suspend a student for using consistently abusive or profane language in the classroom, "even if that language would receive firm constitutional protection on the street corner."[15] The classroom is where, to use legal scholar Robert Post's terminology, interests in management predominate, and some restrictions may be necessary for certain educational goals to be achieved.[16] Colleges also provide libraries where boisterous or disruptive behavior can be regulated.[17] And in these libraries, some books will not be bought or will be removed according to the discretion of the library's administration without violating the First Amendment.[18] Because speech can be regulated even based on its content in classrooms and libraries, it is a mistake to assume that all regulations of speech on a university campus are necessarily unconstitutional. A hate speech code could certainly be written that would target harassment in libraries and classrooms without diverging from already existing First Amendment precedents.

University practices also involve the hiring, promoting, and tenuring of faculty. These are decisions, as Sunstein argues, that are entirely based upon the content of speech. In fact, Sunstein recognizes that these are decisions that are frequently based upon viewpoint as well.[19] Indeed, economics programs often understand Max Weber and Karl Marx to be more relevant to the study of social and political issues than economics, although Weber and Marx certainly considered themselves to be writing on economic matters. Religious creation myths are out of place in biology programs, although they may be of interest to other departments.[20] Thus, hiring and promotion of faculty are conventionally done based on reasons linked with the content of speech and politically powerful viewpoints in order to create an economics or sociology or biology program, but this does not usually raise First Amendment problems. As we can see from this example as well, speech is frequently regulated in the university setting, contrary to some of the hyperbole surrounding the hate speech controversy.

Colleges also provide campus space—malls, "quads," and paths to and from class. Perhaps the most difficult hate speech issue to adjudicate is when harassment occurs in these campus spaces, especially as students take familiar and consistent paths to and from class, work, the student union, or the cafeteria. Although this issue presents difficult and subtle questions, there are familiar judicial standards to aid its resolution within the corpus of First Amendment doctrine. Harassment is commonly regulated, and can certainly be addressed in a way that is consistent with a due sensitivity to all rights involved in accordance with constitutional standards on "fighting words." Here, a harassment regulation that focused on targeted, intentional, face-to-face vilification aimed at specific members of an audience can increase the penalty for harassment based on gender, race, or homophobia without violating the First Amendment.[21] These cases are difficult to address in the abstract, but judicial practices in the area of torts suggest that such issues can be dealt with as they arise and judicial competence in these areas can improve with experience.[22] Indeed, the Supreme Court has been gaining just this sort of experience in its adjudication of ordinances and injunctions addressing the harassment of women and health workers in and around clinics where abortions are provided. These analyses are heavily fact based, and constitutionality depends on the nature of the regulation and how the regulation interacts with the geography of the clinic, its entrances, and the surrounding neighborhood.[23] The upshot of the abortion clinic cases—a line of cases that have admittedly emerged after the major legal developments surrounding the hate speech controversy—for our analysis here is that without a specific regulation and a specific fact situation, we cannot say that hate speech codes necessarily violate the First Amendment. The overall significance of cases addressing speakers with unwilling audiences is that if the unwilling listener cannot avoid the message through reasonable strategies and is forced to endure (is made captive to) an unwanted speech act, then such speech performances can be regulated without violating the First Amendment. Indeed, as I have suggested above, such regulations can be seen as promoting the First Amendment interests of the captive audience, in which case the issue changes from a failure to protect First Amendment interests to a question of whose First Amendment interests to protect in given circumstances.[24]

Of course, a college campus also functions as a public forum, where the college community is exposed to famous public figures, speakers with not-ready-for-prime-time views, student protests, and the perennial ministers telling the students that they will go to hell and who are being baited by those either crazy enough or new enough to college life to try to debate them.[25] When the college campus functions as a public forum, regulations on who may speak and what they may say are most constitutionally suspect. A content-neutral time-place-or-manner regulation is about as heavy a regulation of speech that could be allowed without violating the First Amendment. And if it were enforced through a permit system, it might even assist First Amendment values by providing a mechanism for taking turns when several groups want to mount the rostrum (it is hard to get a message out when one is fighting over the rostrum).[26] As long as fair warning is given so that offended listeners can either know to avoid the quad on a particular day at a particular time or can organize a counter-protest against some especially vile speaker, it would be unconstitutional for the college to regulate this vile speaker with the purpose of censoring him or her. Thus, to claim that a university is either like a workplace or a public forum is too blunt an instrument with which to carry out an analysis of policymaking regarding hate speech. Universities fulfill a variety of functions, and proponents of a hate speech code—or opponents of a proposed code—must be attentive to the plurality of values that universities institutionalize in their analyses.

Although some proponents of hate speech codes suggest that they may make room for more speech than they chill by eradicating hostile environments in which minorities are effectively silenced, liberal polemics proliferated in the early to mid 1990s counseling that the best response for bad speech is more speech.[27] Although the argument about silencing is an empirical question that cannot be rejected out of hand by opponents of such rules, I will proceed differently here.[28] Even if we grant the usefulness of the marketplace of ideas metaphor, upon which those who believe the best response for bad speech is more speech rely, this does not in itself weaken the case for hate speech codes. To say that the argument that the best response for bad speech is more speech sinks the case for hate speech codes makes the same error that arguments focusing on the special nature of the university make. Such arguments neglect the varied functions that the university fulfills. The nature of the university as a space, however, is also defined relationally. That is, we must consider the nature of the university in its relationship with society at large in order to understand the forms of speech and the types of regulations that ought to be permitted. In other words, where is the marketplace of ideas or the public forum that will be governed by the principle that the best response for bad speech is more speech?

At the core of the First Amendment lies political speech. The speaking subject is constituted in First Amendment law as an American citizen, and one's speech is oriented to the telos of the American nation-state as the center of politics.[29] Speech is conceptualized as being oriented toward the public sphere, and the "strong" public sphere is the American political system.[30] On these premises, one's effectiveness in this system is based in part on one's knowledge of the political process, understanding of the principles of liberal democracy and the issues affecting the polity, an ability to persuade others of the worthiness of one's opinions, and an ability to learn about new issues as they arise. One's exercise of the right to vote and ability to contribute to campaigns effectively, are affected by one's education, as are the multitude of other ways in which one exercises one's identity as a citizen in American society. In an article published prior to the controversy over hate speech codes, Amy Gutmann, for example, treats free speech and equality of educational opportunity as two sides of the same coin: one's citizenship rights.[31] In other words, there is no necessary contradiction between securing an equal right to education and securing one's First Amendment rights.

Universities not only provide public fora but also in the spaces that are not public fora help to prepare individuals to exercise their First Amendment rights in the public forum effectively and to contribute in a meaningful way to the marketplace of ideas or the political sphere. To deny students this preparation is to weaken their ability to exercise their First Amendment rights. Therefore, to the extent that hate speech codes can be said to protect one's rights to an equal university education, such codes can be said to contribute to one's First Amendment rights. If harassment interferes with one's ability to acquire an education, the steps that are taken to restrain such harassment are steps that will enable the object of such harassment to acquire the means to exercise better his or her First

Amendment rights in the public forum. In fact, the Supreme Court has recognized, even in the public forum, the force of the "heckler's veto" and the necessity of protecting the speaker against measures calculated to silence him or her by those interested in interfering with the speaker's exercise of his or her First Amendment rights.[32] In effect, the real First Amendment question is who is the relevant author or speaker being silenced, and who is a mere "heckler" or is part of a "hostile audience" that must be silenced to protect the First Amendment rights of the legitimate speaker? Whose First Amendment is it, anyway?

Constructing the "People"

The relation of hate speech codes to the First Amendment is ambiguous or "indeterminate." In other words, I have not been arguing for or against the constitutionality of such codes. I have been arguing that questions regarding the constitutionality of hate speech codes—to say nothing of whether they would or would not be a good policy on any given campus—cannot be answered a priori, or in the abstract, because one could dream up a scenario in which codes might be considered unconstitutional just as easily as one could dream up a scenario in which hate speech codes might be considered constitutional from a First Amendment perspective.[33] Yet during the early 1990s, there was a growing perception that hate speech codes necessarily violated the First Amendment. In order to understand why this presumption could appear valid in light of the indeterminacy of the legal question at an abstract level, one must reconstruct the context that compelled the conclusion that hate speech codes were unconstitutional. In fact, not only did this context generate the understanding that such rules were unconstitutional, but commentaries like those published in the *New Republic* and the *Progressive* described them as constituting the greatest threat that the First Amendment then faced.[34] The reconstellation of America and its global imaginary according to a landscape defined by Western civilization on the one hand and the savage or barbarian non-West on the other produced an identity for the American people whose rights are reserved to them by the Bill of Rights, which permitted the conclusion that hate speech codes violated the First Amendment.

First Amendment doctrine is more complex than references to the "university" in the hate speech controversy acknowledge. Yet the university was continually invoked. What must be uncovered, then, is what the university represented for those using it as the relevant context for arguing that hate speech codes necessarily violated the First Amendment. By referring to the university, opponents of hate speech codes were able to link two questions—the question of hate speech codes and the question of multiculturalism—that had no necessary reason for being thought about together. Opponents of hate speech codes used the university to articulate hate speech codes and multiculturalism—the effort to challenge Eurocentrism in curricular design and generally to make campuses more accommodating of the increased diversity U.S. universities had experienced since the mid-twentieth century—under the same issue heading of "PC" in order to argue that America's very being was being threatened. And indeed it was —America's racial being was being challenged.

Congressman Henry Hyde and his legislative counsel George Fishman, in a law review article defending the Collegiate Speech Protection Act, describe the conflict over hate speech codes. They argue that there seems to be "a more malevolent motivation behind many speech codes; the urge to eliminate . . . 'the more widespread prejudice that has ruled *American universities* since their founding: That the intellectual tradition of *Western Europe* occupies the central place in the history of *civilization*.'"[35] Hyde and Fishman's invocation of "university" links their argument against hate speech codes to the analytically separate controversy over multiculturalism, thereby making the controversy over hate speech codes just one front in a larger battle—the battle against PC.

This logic of linking the controversy over hate speech codes to the debate over multiculturalism in order to situate hate speech codes as one dimension of PC echoes the *Newsweek* article Hyde and Fishman quote in their argument. The article is part of a special section (the cover stories) on campus "thought police" and "politically correct" forces, and its first paragraph begins by discussing hate speech codes and the First Amendment. The second paragraph includes the passage Hyde and Fishman cite, describing how American universities have been governed since their founding by Western Europe's centrality to the history of civilization, and the third unites the ideas of hate speech codes and university curricula by defining them as two sides of the same "creed," which is instantly recognized as "PC—politically correct." Hyde and Fishman reiterate this logic by arguing that one may "justifiably fear that speech codes will become highly effective weapons in the arsenal of champions of political correctness." Hate speech codes, then, are taken as a symptom of a larger problem—the problem of PC, and the university represents the site of this battle, a battle over what it means to be American.[36]

Brigitte Berger, in an issue of *Partisan Review* dedicated to the problem of "political correctness," fears that the rise of multiculturalism will result in undermining the autonomy of the modern university and a "retribalization of American society" that would repeal the principles on which America is founded. As these two results combine, she argues that a third consequence, "a massive delegitimation of the modern university—and by extension of Western civilization"—would result since the "fate of the modern university and the fate of Western civilization are inextricably intertwined." Nothing less than Mill's multidimensional moral geography is at stake in Berger's view, since she describes universities as institutions that exemplify and reproduce the "modern West," and without their "civilatory mission," a mission that succeeds only in the defeat of multiculturalism in her view, America risks slipping backward to savagery and barbarism. Indeed, then president of Yale University Benno Schmidt Jr., in a speech before the National Press Club, refers specifically to John Stuart Mill in a passage describing how the goal of the university is to "liberate the mind from thinking that is *inert, habitual,* dulled by *convention.*" While Mill imagined the civilized West liberating the stagnant East through a civilizing process, Schmidt evokes a civilizing process internal to the nation, but with the university acting as the liberatory force for civilizing and modernizing the inert.[37]

The controversy over multiculturalism, then, was a fight over what it means to be American, and opponents of multiculturalism understood these stakes well. Historian Arthur Schlesinger Jr.'s book opposing multiculturalism was entitled *The Disuniting of America.* The book collecting polemics from *Partisan Review* taking issue with PC was entitled *Our Country, Our Culture.* And an article in *Time* magazine was entitled "The Fraying of America." The battle over multiculturalism was a battle over America's identity, and the enemy was a racial Other that threatened America's identity as part of Western civilization. Reiterating the racial landscape of the West versus the Rest used to make sense of the controversy over *The Satanic Verses, US News and World Report* columnist John Leo called supporters of multiculturalism "the academy's new ayatollahs." And Dinesh D'Souza described advocates of multiculturalism as "the new *barbarians* who have captured the humanities, law, and social science departments of so many of *our* universities." *Newsweek* reported,

"Opponents of PC see themselves as a beleaguered minority among *barbarians*," and described PC as "so seemingly at odds with what most *Americans* believe." Thus, American national identity was hitched to the racial narrative of the civilized West.[38]

By calling their enemy "politically correct," the opponents of hate speech codes and multiculturalism were able to capitalize on the Stalinist resonances of "correctness." Yet, as we can see from the title of their publications, the anti-PC front was hardly a group of wishy-washy, tolerate-everything relativists, since they were interested in defending "our country" and the core identity around which they claimed it had been "united." At issue was what is debatable and what is foundational and therefore beyond question, and the opponents of PC were asking for the protection of the subject position from which (what they considered) a debatable perspective could emerge. Securing America's fundamental identity bears legal consequences in this matter. If America's foundation is the racial identity of Western civilization, then derogating racialized minorities is constitutionally protected speech rather than illegitimate heckling, because the white supremacist speaker can claim to be American and thus to have the rights reserved to this people (while racialized minorities will have difficulty making an equivalent claim). In this way, we can understand the positions of the NAS opposing hate speech codes in the name of "tolerance," advocating the value of "civility," and opposing multiculturalism. This is not an abstract advocacy of tolerance since it opposes diversity in the area of curriculum construction, and its advocacy of tolerance is limited by the norm of civility. This is a contextual tolerance asking that freedom for a certain type of speech be protected.[39]

The struggles over knowledge and education are struggles over the bases on which to found and reproduce the American people. This is a question of significant gravity, since the American people is the legal sovereign whose will the Constitution represents. This is the subject position that produces law through its interpretive practices and thus authorizes certain claims of right. These stakes are also recognized by those opposing multiculturalism. Reacting as if he had just read Carl Schmitt on the relation of law to an empirical situation or John Burgess on the relationship of liberty to sovereignty, George Will links American identity to Western civilization and then recognizes the significance of the multicultural challenge for the nature of American law. Condemning those who threaten to "delegitimiz[e] Western civilization," Will worries:

[T]he transmission of the culture that unites, even defines America—
transmission through knowledge of literature and history—is faltering.
The result is collective amnesia and deculturation. That prefigures social
disintegration, which is the political goal of the victim revolution that is
sweeping campuses.[40]

For Will, the loss of an America built upon the racial norms of Western
civilization is a total loss, for he is incapable of imagining America in any
other way. He does not see the multicultural challenge as a movement
from one America to another America; he understands the options of the
present moment as comprising the America he knows, loves, and wants to
defend and the abyss, because the alternative is not recognizably American
according to the norms by which he identifies America.

Will then links the defense of this American identity to the law of
America's existence in his response to opponents of conservative Carol
Iannone's nomination to the National Council on the Humanities:

In this low-visibility, high-intensity war, Lynne Cheney is secretary of domestic defense. The foreign adversaries her husband, Dick, must keep at
bay are less dangerous, in the long run, than the domestic forces with
which she must deal. Those forces are fighting against the conservation of
the common culture that is the nation's social cement. She, even more
than a Supreme Court Justice, deals with constitutional things. The real
constitution, which truly constitutes America, is the national mind as
shaped by the intellectual legacy that gave rise to the Constitution and all
the habits, mores, customs and ideas that sustain it.[41]

As Will indicates in this passage, the question in the struggle over PC is
that of the American subject. Indeed, as chairman for the National Endowment for the Humanities, Lynne Cheney understood her governmental role in exactly the terms Will describes it. Cheney argues, since "Western civilization forms the basis of our society's law and institutions, it
might seem obvious that education should ground the upcoming generation in the Western tradition." Invoking a discourse of birthright where
national birth gives right, Cheney also refers to "this nation's *inheri-
tance*."[42] And as both Will and Cheney recognize, constituting the American subject founds *American law*.

Although I have emphasized race as the most prominent aspect of the
controversy over PC, the opposition to PC also gendered their enemies to

delegitimate their claims. For example, an article by Wilcomb Washburn in the *National Review* describes the controversies over free speech and multiculturalism at Dartmouth using gendered terminology: "If *her* [i.e., Dartmouth] principal concern is to guard against 'vexatious oral exchange' and to protect individuals or groups from criticism that might offend them, then *she* had best drop her claim to being an intellectual institution dedicated to the pursuit of truth, and *change her name to the Dartmouth Finishing School.*"[43] Just as the racial constitution of the American subject is linked to legal legitimacy, disturbing normalized gender hierarchies not only affects the pursuit of truth, as Washburn argues, but disturbs legal stability as the *New Republic* reports. Arguing against a hostile work environment test for sex discrimination, the *New Republic* editorializes that this would make the law unintelligible because

> the legality of speech would depend . . . on whether a "reasonable *woman*" would have found that it created an "intimidating, hostile, or offensive" environment. This turns the First Amendment on its head. The Supreme Court has traditionally protected offensive speech because "one *man's* vulgarity is another *man's* lyric." Under the new rules, speech can be banned whenever one *man's* lyric becomes a reasonable *woman's* vulgarity. The fact that men and women often find different things funny . . . makes the "reasonable woman" standard even more *perverse.*[44]

Although adjudication could proceed with stability as long as disputes arose only between one man's lyric and another's vulgarity, a public sphere not based entirely upon masculinist norms yields a legal disorder because men and women are different (they find different things funny). Illustrating a theme to be taken up in the next chapter that sexuality is significantly public, the *New Republic* finds that a displacement of the traditional common law standard of the "reasonable man" infuses the law with a deviant sexuality—makes the law perverse. Identity forms a ground for law.

Legal Decisions Issued from the Courts of Law

Landscaping America as part of Western civilization by making the controversy over hate speech codes just one front in a larger battle against PC had legal consequences. John Taylor, in an article entitled "Are you Politically Correct?" quoted a Yale dean who argued that the "West's tradition of civil liberties has produced 'a tolerance and respect for diversity unknown in most cultures.'"[45] By modifying "civil liberties" with the "West," this article illustrates the widespread tendency to consider the West as the sole standard by which to measure other efforts to protect rights. But this tendency also governs the practice of rights within the "West," as those claiming rights are disciplined or disenfranchised according to the norms of what counts as properly Western. Arthur Schlesinger Jr. makes this fact clear in the title of his critique of PC: "Multiculturalism vs. the Bill of Rights."[46] The first President George Bush also promoted this legal interpretation in his 1991 commencement address at the University of Michigan, Ann Arbor—one of the two key public university sites for the legal controversy over hate speech codes (the other was the University of Wisconsin). Lambasting PC, Bush called those making up this force "political extremists" who were "abusing the privilege of free speech."[47] PCers, for Bush, do not have a *right* to free speech; they abuse this *privilege*.

The anti-PC campaign's construction of America affected the Supreme Court decision that greatly influenced the perception that hate speech codes could not be written without violating the First Amendment. In 1989, a federal court decision, *Doe v. University of Michigan*, declared the University of Michigan's hate speech code unconstitutional on First Amendment grounds, but it did not close the door on the possibility that a hate speech code could be written without violating the First Amendment. It merely claimed that the code before the court was unconstitutional on the grounds of vagueness and overbreadth. For example, the University Policy regulated speech that was protected though offensive in addition to regulating harassment. The court's decision, however, proceeded to review constitutional and statutory bases in both state and federal law that prohibit discrimination in employment, education, and governmental benefits on the grounds of race, sex, ethnicity, or religion, as well as criminal penalties, civil penalties, civil remedies, and common law claims (e.g., the tort of intentional infliction of emotional distress) available to be built on by university policies or victim claims. According to the court, if the "Policy had the effect of only regulating in these areas, it is unlikely that any constitutional problem would have arisen," and noted specifically that the "First Amendment presents no obstacle to the establishment of internal University sanctions as to any of these categories of conduct over and above any remedies already supplied by state or federal law."[48] By the time, however, that the Supreme Court addressed St. Paul, Minnesota's Bias Motivated Crime Ordinance in 1992—either the peak or close to the peak of the "PC" controversy—the door had been closing on those who still wanted to contend that it was possible to write a hate speech code that was constitutional.[49]

In *R.A.V. v. St. Paul*, a white minor was charged with violating St. Paul's hate crime ordinance for burning a cross on a black family's lawn. On review, the U.S. Supreme Court unanimously declared the ordinance unconstitutional. The unanimity in judgment, however, masked a deep division in legal reasoning between the majority opinion written by Justice Scalia for five Justices and the concurring opinions representing four other Justices. The legal division was over the doctrinal architecture of the First Amendment that had been established over the decades of the twentieth century, but what hung in the balance was whether it might ever be possible to regulate identity-based verbal or symbolic harassment—such as racial or gender-based harassment—without violating the First Amendment.[50] Scalia's conclusion was that this would not be possible, a conclusion that would rule out a priori the possibility of a constitutional hate speech code on First Amendment grounds.

Although the controversy over hate speech codes was not directly before him, Scalia was clearly influenced by the polemics over PC and clearly interested in participating in the controversy over hate speech codes. In so doing, however, he ignored fifty years of doctrine that stood in his way while producing a laundry list of exceptions to his new rules so that long-established laws would not fall along with the St. Paul ordinance, like the federal law criminalizing making a threat on the life of the president. The symptomatic confusion in Scalia's opinion, from which the rest of his problems follow, is over whether burning a cross in a black family's yard is a "fighting word" or an example of speech and debate. The architecture of the First Amendment is based on the idea that speech, except for a few narrowly defined exceptions, receives full protection. These exceptions are things like libel, obscenity, child pornography, commercial advertising, speech causing a "clear and present danger" to national security or civil disorder, and "fighting words"—words that either are injurious by their very utterance or lead to a violent response and target their victim specifically.[51] Thus, words falling into one of these categories do not count, constitutionally speaking, as *speech*.[52] This First Amendment architecture reflects the preferred position of speech in the post–New Deal constitutional order. Scalia threatens this legal edifice by bringing a subcategory of fighting words—racial hate speech—within full First Amendment protection in his argument that it is unconstitutional to single out for regulation this subset of fighting words (hence the problems he causes for other areas of law, since by implication it would be unconstitutional to single out a sub-category of threats, like threats on the life of the president, as a unique legal wrong with specific penalties attached).

Scalia begins by paying lip service to the norm that the U.S. Supreme Court will be bound by the most authoritative interpretation of a state law by that state. In this case, this means that Scalia concedes that the St. Paul ordinance only reaches "fighting words," since this is how the Minnesota state supreme court construed the ordinance. This should mean that Scalia has conceded that the language covered by the ordinance is not con-stitutionally protected speech. If Scalia's opinion were consistent with this insight, then he would agree with the other Justices that the constitutional infirmity of the St. Paul ordinance is that it does not limit a violation of the ordinance to speech that specifically targets its victim and he would agree with their conclusion that the ordinance is overbroad. Yet once his argument picks up speed, Scalia contends that the ordinance goes beyond constitutionally suspect "content discrimination" and approaches "view-point discrimination," which is virtually sure to be found unconstitu-tional.[53] Scalia argues, "St. Paul has no such authority to license one side of a *debate* to fight freestyle, while requiring the other to follow Marquis of Queensberry rules."[54] He believes that the ordinance discriminates on one side of an ideological debate against another—a First Amendment sin.

The problem is that if the act in question is an instance of fighting words, which Scalia concedes, then it is not speech. If it is not speech, then the act cannot be a viewpoint in a debate, and Scalia cannot rule that the ordinance is an instance of viewpoint discrimination. Scalia cannot have it both ways. If we are talking about fighting words, then there are no viewpoints; if there is a debate with viewpoints, then we are not talk-ing about fighting words. Scalia, however, needs to be able to call racial hate speech "debate," because if the ordinance only reaches fighting words, then it will be possible to write a hate speech code that does not violate the First Amendment, as long as the policymakers avoid the over-breadth problems the concurring opinions find with the St. Paul ordi-nance. If hate speech is debate, then it will never be possible to regulate it without violating the First Amendment and Scalia will have successfully ruled on the controversy over hate speech codes. The problem with call-ing hate speech "debate" in this case, however, is that the Minnesota state supreme court authoritatively interpreted the ordinance as reaching only constitutionally unprotected fighting words, and on the facts of this case, it would be difficult to call the conveyance of a threat—the meaning, after all, of burning a cross on a black family's yard—an instance of debate.

According to Justice Stevens, "Whether words are fighting words is determined in part by their context." Taking Stevens's contextual approach to heart, what is the context that makes the white supremacist act of burning a cross into an example of debate, as Scalia implies for the sake of his argument that regulating racial hate speech is unconstitutional on the grounds of viewpoint discrimination? The answer lies in Scalia's incorporation of the national imaginary produced by the anti-PC campaign into his legal decision. He sets the stage for his argument by referring to the principles of "our society, like other free but *civilized* societies." Calling Scalia's far-reaching opinion "regrettable," Justice Blackmun writes, "I fear that the Court has been distracted from its proper mission by the temptation to decide the issue over 'politically correct speech' and 'cultural diversity,' neither of which is presented here." As a result, according to Justice White, "by characterizing fighting words as a form of 'debate' . . . the majority legitimates hate speech as a form of public discussion."[55] Scalia's use of the anti-PC campaign's construction of the American people as members of Western civilization leads to the determination that racial hate is constitutionally protected speech rather than falling outside of the First Amendment's protections and into the category of fighting words as a regulable social problem. The First Amendment protects *this* public's discussion and debate as the law becomes animated by its (civilized) people. Because of the racial significance of the discourse opposing the identity of the civilized and the savage, by identifying the American people in this way, Scalia incorporates white supremacist America and delegitimizes the rights claims of nonwhite minorities by denying them legal standing. The solidification of the anti-PC campaign's construction of the American people stabilized and made determinate the legal conclusion that governments cannot regulate hate speech without violating the First Amendment.

Legal Dissemination and Its Effects on Social Identification

As far as we were concerned this was a violation of our rights as citizens of the United States. The Constitution should protect us from violence, terrorism, and prejudice. All we wanted was for this criminal to be shown that he and his friends had done something wrong—that they had threatened us and should be punished for it. But the media used R.A.V. to push their own agenda about the First Amendment. They tried to turn the criminal into the hero—focusing on his rights to the exclusion of ours. It really made me mad. And when the Supreme Court decision was announced . . . [i]t almost seemed to be saying, "Well, it's okay to burn crosses on black people's lawns."

—Russ Jones, husband in the family targeted by the burning cross in *R.A.V. v. St. Paul* (1992)

When the Supreme Court agreed to hear the *R.A.V.* case, the *New Republic* (*TNR*) published an editorial urging the Court to declare the ordinance unconstitutional as a violation of the First Amendment. The editorial's title, "Breaking the Codes," expressly perceived the significance of the *R.A.V.* case for the controversy over hate speech codes. *TNR*, however, conceded that the U.S. Constitution does not protect speech that is likely to incite violence. The difference between a hate speech exception to the First Amendment and a "clear and present danger" exception is that there is "a rational and discrete standard upon which the Court makes this [the national security exemption based on clear and present danger standards] exception." In contrast, *TNR* argued that it "is not legitimate to limit expression solely because it arouses 'anger, alarm, or resentment in others,' as the St. Paul ordinance does. This, after all, gives 'others' a kind of veto power over the act of speech."[56] *TNR* allowed for the legitimacy of one speech regulation, but not another. In one case, there was a "rational" standard to determine the law—the clear and present danger standard used to evaluate laws to protect national security during the period when the nation's security was understood to be most seriously threatened by "communism." Now that the cold war was over, perhaps the greatest danger to America founded upon norms of Western civilization was that of racialized "others," to use *TNR*'s convenient terminology. And such others, in contrast to anticommunists during the cold war, must not wield veto power over speech.

With the stakes of the legal controversy well defined, *TNR* rejoiced in the outcome of the Supreme Court's decision in *R.A.V.* the next year and engaged in the process of disseminating the significance of the ruling. *TNR* referred to its earlier arguments in order to make clear the wider importance of Scalia's opinion for hate speech codes: "[T]he Court has exposed the unconstitutionality of many state bias laws and virtually all campus hate speech codes." The significance of this was not understated by *TNR*: "In a stroke, [the Court] has repelled the most serious threat to open debate that the current generation of students has experienced." Thus, it was "hard to imagine any campus speech code in its current form should survive Justice Scalia's reasoning."[57] In this way, *TNR* not only publicized the Supreme Court's legal decision but helped to construct the meaning of the ruling in such a way that hate speech codes became legally forbidden.

John Leo, writing for *US News and World Report*, described Scalia's majority opinion as one that "sweeps away all the speech codes at public colleges and universities," in addition to putting hate crimes legislation in question. He added that "some lawyers" thought a "warning shot" had been fired in the direction of sexual harassment law as well and concluded that "this decision is a significant victory for free speech." Leo described the concurring Justices as "dissenters," raising the question of what had been agreed to and what had not.[58] The Court was unanimous in concluding that the St. Paul ordinance was unconstitutional. The deeper disagreement lay in the different national formations that the five-vote majority and the four-vote concurrence relied upon to sustain their respective legal conclusions. The four-vote concurrence dissented from the Court's reliance upon, and the support the Court gave to, the American national identity that was being created in opposition to multiculturalism through the PC controversy. Indeed, Justice Blackmun was explicit in finding this aspect of Scalia's *R.A.V.* opinion "regrettable." The focus upon Scalia's opinion and its dissemination through the national media for its intersection with the PC controversy, however, assured that this meaning, however "regrettable," was the one that the Court's decision took on.

The *Progressive*, taking note that threats to freedom of speech were multiplying through hate speech codes, expressed relief that "[f]ortunately, even today's ultraconservative Supreme Court seems to retain sufficient respect for traditional First Amendment principles to rule against such legislation." The *Progressive* argued that if lower courts were diligent about applying the Court's decision, "they will go a long way toward slowing down, if not halting and reversing, the pernicious process of chipping away at First Amendment freedoms." One of the examples of this pernicious process that the *Progressive* mentioned specifically was the University of Wisconsin's new version of its hate speech code, produced after a federal district court declared an earlier version to be unconstitutional on First Amendment grounds in *UWM Post v. Board of Regents of the University of Wisconsin* (1991).[59]

The Supreme Court's decision in *R.A.V* was treated as a relevant precedent by policymakers at the University of Wisconsin, leading them to rescind a proposed hate speech code revised in the wake of the *UWM Post*
decision striking down the university's earlier efforts. With the support of
the Wisconsin Student Association and the faculty senate, the UW Regents
passed the revised hate speech code in May 1992. On July 10, 1992, the
code was endorsed by the Wisconsin State Senate's Higher Education
Committee, and it faced a vote by the State Assembly's Colleges and Universities Committee. In the wake of the *R.A.V.* decision, however, the Assembly committee asked the Regents to review the rule. On September 11
the Regents reconsidered and voted to rescind the code. These decisions
were taken as the controversy over PC was rising in a crescendo on this
campus and were guided legally by the Court's *R.A.V.* decision and a state
supreme court decision, *Mitchell v. State*, declaring Wisconsin's hate crime
legislation unconstitutional (which was reversed the next year by the U.S.
Supreme Court).[60]

On April 27, 1992, the *Badger Herald*, the more conservative of the two
student papers on the Madison campus, issued one of its many editorials
against the code and tied the code to the PC controversy by titling its editorial "UWS, Our PC enemy" (illustrating my argument about how opposition to hate speech codes was engendered by invoking a PC enemy).[61]
The day after the *R.A.V.* decision, the *Wisconsin State Journal* immediately
drew the legal implications of the decision for the University of Wisconsin
hate speech code. The *Journal* reported that "[o]pponents of the UW 'hate
speech' rule said the measure likely violates the First Amendment under
the reasoning in the high court opinion, which threw out a similar law in
St. Paul, Minn. They called for UW to withdraw the rule." The paper discussed the Scalia opinion, while acknowledging that a minority agreed
with the result but not the reasoning of his opinion. In addition to the
Scalia opinion, the article quoted two opponents of the code and one
statement in opposition to the code attributed to "Opponents of the UW
'hate speech' rule," but only one supporter of the code. This left the impression that if the university rule actually went into effect, it would be
found unconstitutional because of the Supreme Court's opinion in *R.A.V.*.
As one state senator described the issue: "I think the UW rule is clearly
gone."[62]

On September 11, 1992, in the wake of the *R.A.V.* and *Mitchell v. State*
decisions, the *Badger Herald* could now invoke the law against the "PC
enemy," by arguing that the proposed rule, up for a Regents vote later that

day, "flies in the face of recent state and federal court rulings and will likely be an expensive and wasteful legal failure for the UW, just as the first speech code was two short years ago." The Regents decided to reconsider the rule due to concern over its constitutionality. As the *Badger Herald* reported after the rule was rescinded, "Recent Wisconsin and U.S. Supreme Court rulings cast further doubt on the constitutionality of the redrafted version of the code," according to Regents president George Steil. The *New York Times* confirmed this interpretation that the *R.A.V.* decision had cemented the perception that the hate speech code violated the First Amendment. The *Times* paraphrased Steil justifying the decision to revoke the code based on "recent court decisions that raised the question of whether the rule violated students' rights of free speech under the First Amendment," while explicitly situating the question in the context of the Supreme Court's *R.A.V.* decision in the rest of the article. Even a regent quoted by the *Times* who opposed repealing the rule acknowledged the significance of the *R.A.V.* decision to the repeal, claiming that recent court decisions were being used as a smokescreen by those "looking for an excuse" to repeal the rule.[63] As we can see, the Supreme Court's law had important consequences at the University of Wisconsin. The validation the Court gave to one community, its "nomos," and the law that was generated through its narrative practices came to govern, and was represented in press reports as governing, the legal practices at the University of Wisconsin.[64] The dissemination of *R.A.V.* eradicated pluralism in legal interpretation and determined the judgment that Wisconsin's revised hate speech code violated the First Amendment.

About a year later, in December of 1993, the *Wall Street Journal* asked rhetorically, "Is the party over for the PC movement . . . on college campuses?" According to the paper, the evidence for the demise of PC was a "swelling student backlash," and "a rash of unfavorable court decisions . . . beginning to sweep aside or challenge the movement's most controversial icons: campus speech codes, and anti-harassment policies that sometimes impinge on free speech rights." In a report on PC the following spring, the *Wisconsin State Journal* described the sequence of enacting a hate speech code, having it declared unconstitutional, and then abandoning the project of regulating hate speech in the face of the *R.A.V.* decision as the "most prominent 'political correctness' battle fought at the University of Wisconsin."[65] By using the illegality of hate speech codes to represent PC and to claim its demise, the citational practices of the *Wall Street Journal* and the *Wisconsin State Journal* became legal acts that produced social identity—in this case, signaling the illegitimacy of PC and thus resolidifying the racialized American identity produced in the controversy over multiculturalism. Not only does a national formation generate perceptions of law, as I illustrate in my discussion of Scalia's *R.A.V.* opinion, but law is a basis used to claim a national identity as I show here. Law and society are mutually imbricated and mutually constitutive.

Conclusion

The relationship of the First Amendment to hate speech codes, a relationship that is indeterminate in the abstract, was determined by the popular linkage of hate speech codes to the PC controversy. The anti-PC campaign hitched the legal question of the constitutionality of hate speech codes to the struggle over what it means to be American in the battle over multiculturalism. The effort to defeat multiculturalism was based on a defense of America's identity as an exemplar of Western civilization, an identity formed through the racial opposition of the civilized to the savage. The result was that the controversy over PC constructed American identity, which in turn determined when American rights were being violated. This was demonstrated by Scalia's *R.A.V* opinion and the legal force this opinion acquired for hate speech codes both nationally in the popular media and at one of the key sites for the policy question of hate speech codes, the University of Wisconsin. As we have learned from John Stuart Mill, the obligations that the civilized owe one another cease at the boundary dividing the civilized from the savage. Thus, America's racially reformed post–cold war identity meant that those identified as racially subordinate within this system of meaning would be disabled from making legitimate claims upon American rights.

Moreover, the hate speech controversy—a legal controversy—bore constitutive consequences for American identity as the defeat of hate speech regulations in the courts was taken to represent the demise of PC and the project attributed to it of multiculturalism. As a result, the dominant legal interpretation against the validity of hate speech codes relied upon the construction of American identity in the PC controversy to determine its perception of rights, while the rules of law thus generated fueled the anti-PC position by giving it legal legitimacy. Law and society functioned in a mutually imbricated and mutually constitutive manner.

The controversy over hate speech codes and PC reiterates the changed legal grounds of post–cold war America described in the previous chapter. We have seen the constriction of legal instruments to address discriminatory harassment as PC strengthened its hold on the American imaginary. Unfortunately, an America constituted by the norms of Western civilization against the racially inferior savage or barbarian may hold less room for maneuver for racial minorities than the cold war competition between the Soviet Union and the United States provided and that Martin Luther King Jr. utilized so effectively to gain a foothold for black claims to equal rights.

While researching this controversy, I interviewed a black male undergraduate at the University of Wisconsin, whom I shall call "Marvin." Marvin's insightful comments bring out the agonistic elements of this sociolegal event. When I asked Marvin about the University of Wisconsin code, he responded, "I would support it passively." A regulation against hate speech would signify an incorporation of multicultural interests within national concerns, and the hope among those with multicultural sentiments is that such a legal intervention might help to call such a national formation into existence by working as a sort of legal performative. Yet such codes are torn between ineffectuality or an overbroad regulation of speech. Demonstrating the tension between these two poles, Marvin reminded me about a black professor whom we both knew who was asked whether he was an athletic coach by a white woman when he arrived to spend a year as a visiting professor at the university. As Marvin put it, "How do you enact a code against *that*?" This is an instance that exemplifies the racial norms inscribing inferior signs of mental worth upon black bodies. Since it is not an explicit form of harassment that a code could target while respecting a right of free speech, it would escape regulation. Because, however, the opposition to hate speech codes at the national level also engages with the constitutive aspects of the law by articulating opposition to hate speech codes to a monochromatic American imaginary through the synthesizing effects of PC, Marvin recognizes that neither side of the hate speech controversy offers much solace. While recognizing that black inferiority is communicated by more subtle means than a hate speech code could ever regulate, Marvin cannot oppose a hate speech code without the macrolevel national politics of PC incorporating such opposition and giving it effect as a rejection of a multicultural America and as an endorsement of an America based upon the norms of Western civilization.

It is certainly possible to support hate speech codes from within a paradigm of liberalism.[66] It is also possible to find specific regulations of hate speech unconstitutional without becoming a party to the opposition to PC.[67] The macrolevel effects of the widespread dissemination of the legal issue of hate speech codes as one dimension of the PC controversy, however, led to the "regrettable" consequence that the question "Whose First Amendment is it, anyway?" resulted in a response that it is the "American people's," with America being defined by the PC controversy as embodying the norms of Western civilization. Amazingly in light of massive and increasing concentration of media ownership, the explosion of money spent in political campaigns, and the privatization of public spaces in the United States, *this* was taken to be the most pressing First Amendment issue *America* then faced. And so perhaps it was.

6

The Governmentality of Discussion

I believe that the political significance of the problem of sex is due to the fact that sex is located at the point of intersection of the discipline of the body and the control of the population.
—Michel Foucault, "Truth and Power."

Much of this book speaks to the falsity of liberal claims regarding the abstraction or universality of rights, since the practice of rights is grounded in a finite empirical situation that has typically been the nation-state under the conditions of "modernity." This insight also carries implications for the way that liberalism is conventionally critiqued.[1] It is a commonplace of diverse forms of legal and political theory that the modern liberal subject is an abstract individual, unencumbered by social or cultural baggage. Critics since Marx have attacked liberalism for its seeming reliance upon a disembodied rights-bearing subject. They condemn liberalism for creating abstract, formalistic equalities among subjects. Critics argue that such fictions conceal or repress real differences among actually existing persons, the real social relations within which they are embedded, and the real bodies that they inhabit. The liberal rights-bearing subject, however, is not as abstract and disembodied as the critics claim.

Against the conventional criticisms of liberalism, I contend that rights are given meaning within a discourse that embodies subjects who can make legitimate rights claims. By staging my argument in the context of the First Amendment to the United States Constitution, I argue that law is a system of meaning that enables some to be recognized as authorized subjects exercising their right of free speech, while lending the expressive acts of others no particular significance or constituting them as social problems. Claiming a right within the discourse of American constitutional law rests, in part, upon claiming a subject position to which rights attach. In this chapter, I will extend this argument by examining the way that the legal discourse of free speech deals with the problem of sexual expression in order to elaborate the type of subject demanded and reproduced by the First Amendment. This is a subject position, moreover, that would become particularly hegemonic in the United States during the 1990s as concern over sexual expression heightened.

During the 1990s, controversies involving the First Amendment, sexual expression, and the question of decency and civility seemed ubiquitous. Reacting against National Endowment for the Arts (NEA) money being used to support art that was sexually explicit, Senator Jesse Helms led Congress to make NEA grants contingent upon the "decency" of the art, a condition many thought violated the First Amendment rights of the artists but that the Supreme Court upheld in the 1998 case *National Endowment for the Arts v. Finley.*[2] Congress continued to promote policies of civility and decency through such 1996 legislation as the Defense of Marriage Act and the Communications Decency Act, to say nothing of its attempt to impeach President Clinton for improperly governing his sexuality between 1998 and 1999. Since constitutional law places impeachment in a separate category from ordinary legal wrongs, aligning it with the most serious threats to national security, the question of sexuality and the nation's civility had apparently reached a crisis point by decade's end.[3] Although the attempt to impeach Clinton fell short, the two major political parties took the cause to heart as each pledged itself to "civility" in their party platforms for the 2000 presidential election. Indeed, George W. Bush made his pledge to bring civility back to national politics part of his regular stump speech.[4]

Through the 1990s, the Supreme Court validated the national policy of civility and decency by its legal support for the efforts of local and state governments to regulate the upsurge of nude dancing establishments known as "strip" clubs or places of "exotic" dancing. In 1991, the Supreme Court, in *Barnes v. Glen Theatre,* upheld Indiana's policy of regulating public indecency.[5] This followed a pattern of Supreme Court decisions since the 1970s giving governments greater leeway to regulate activities that are not even obscene but merely "indecent."[6] Based on the Supreme Court's ruling in *Barnes* that governments may regulate indecent public expression, federal and state courts upheld Mayor Rudolf Giuliani's efforts in the late 1990s to remove approximately 80 percent of the sex industry in New York City through various zoning regulations in order to promote "civility" in the city. As the 1990s came to end, the Supreme

Court reiterated its support for public decency regulations in its decision *City of Erie v. Pap's A.M.*[7]

As the different levels and branches of the U.S. government converge upon the problem of civility and decency and make the "trigger point" for regulation more sensitive, we are faced with two related questions. First, what is the logic or rationality of governance that makes indecent sexuality a problem (and what sort of a problem is it)? Second, what does it say about the logic of rights being put into play in these circumstances such that regulating the signifying practices around sexuality is not considered a violation of the First Amendment?

Conventional political and legal theory would describe this battle over the governance of sexuality as a manifestation of the opposition between those who value liberalism's individual rights and those seeking to promote their version of community values. Indeed, the *New York Times* has described the sex wars in New York City as pitting civility against civil liberties.[8] Critics of liberalism would agree with this description of the conflict, due to their argument that liberal legal rights draw boundaries around the individual, isolating this subject from external community norms. From this perspective, to enforce a right to free speech is to deny cultural values such as civility. In contrast, by examining the central place of "civility" in the legal discourse forming the background of these controversies over the sex industry that predominated during the 1990s, I shall build upon the arguments of earlier chapters to show how these struggles are in fact constitutive of an American subject that derives from racialized understandings of the American people. This is the problem that indecent sexuality poses for the American public. Thus, these struggles over civility help to embody, in a very particular way, the American subject who can claim its constitutional rights. The legal discourse that promotes a stricter regulation of sexual expression draws from a deep well of cultural meanings that distinguishes civilized subjects, who exercise their rights responsibly, from social problems that afflict the body politic. Therefore, a proper understanding of the logic of rights as manifested through these controversies over sexuality demonstrates that civility is not the antithesis of rights (although those who argue that liberal rights are disembodied may misperceive civility to be a limit to rights) but a mechanism by which subjects who are capable of exercising rights are produced. Indeed, even when public policies are found to violate a constitutional right to free speech, this finding does not follow from the anti-image of a disembodied holder of rights. It derives from understanding different commitments to follow from America's civilized identity.

As I discussed in chapter 2, Michel Foucault's perceptive analyses of the disciplinary interior to contemporary liberal societies and the normalization of "free" subjects who can be entrusted with the exercise of dispersed social powers heighten our attentiveness to the problems of governance faced by the American constitutional system. The U.S. Constitution decenters sovereignty from the state to the people. In so doing, it helps to inaugurate a form of politics to which Foucault refers in his essay on "governmentality." Governmentality comprises the three-way intersection of sovereignty, discipline, and government that converges upon a "population."[9] As contemporary thought comes to invent and discern specific national and racial peoples, the interests and security of the nation-state come to focus heavily upon the population to which the state attaches itself. Acknowledging the decentered nature of contemporary mechanisms of power, the modern state becomes accomplished at governing "at a distance." It coordinates and cultivates the powers of the population. Through his studies of diverse social institutions, Foucault explores the dispersed, subtle, and mundane ways in which power is exercised to encourage the construction of subjects appropriate for a given social formation.

This attention to the production of subjects by the institutions composing a given social formation is helpful to the project of understanding the practice of rights in a system that makes a national *people* sovereign. This chapter builds upon earlier ones by examining legal discourse as one mechanism of social discipline that helps to produce subjects capable of exercising rights necessary to the government of the people. As the cultural mechanism that authoritatively represents the norms of the American nation-state, the circulation of constitutional law facilitates the project of governance at a distance.

The cultivation and reinforcement of the American people's civic qualities are a key concern within a constitutional context that entrusts to the people the power of self-government.[10] Additionally, these characteristics can be used as signs to pick out the American people and its interests from the confusing and heterogeneous flux of those factions that put forward interests deriving from other social identities. Throughout modernity, when analysts seek to understand the American people better in order to improve their government, be those analysts the framers of the Constitution or pundits decrying the crisis of the moment, very often the quality of self-government extolled or thought to be in danger is the *civility* of the American people. And this was never more true than in the controversies over the government of sexuality in America as the 1990s came to an end.

Embodied Rights

Critics of liberalism frequently fault it for resting upon an inaccurate theory of the subject—the abstract, disembodied, isolated, or unencumbered individual. Michael Warner, for example, discusses the alienation caused by the bourgeois public sphere that derives public value through an inverse relationship with the substantive characteristics of one's body. The "we" of American constitutional law's subject "We the People," according to Warner, is a subject whose voice achieves validity by exiling its own positivity.[11] For Michael Sandel, the historical trajectory of American constitutional law is away from more communitarian and republican traditions and toward an embrace of the "procedural republic"—a neutral liberal state that puts into practice the concept of rights as trumps for unencumbered individuals. Because of this trend in American constitutional law, the nation is unable to address properly the problems that afflict it. As a result, the fabric of the community is unraveling. For Mary Ann Glendon as well, the liberalism of American constitutional law, resting as it does upon the unencumbered individual, erodes the social bonds that allow a community to address its collective problems.[12] While these scholars perceive the disjuncture between liberalism and their preferred concepts of the good life, they neglect the way that the practice of rights not only challenges certain modes of collective life but also helps to reconstitute positive forms of social identity.

The foundational texts of the liberal tradition and American constitutional discourse should make us hesitate before claiming that the liberal subject is disembodied. Indeed, these texts attach cultural meanings to bodies and prescribe different forms of government and freedom to those differently engraved bodies. We must be very deeply invested in the "repressive hypothesis" to fail to accord proper significance to J. S. Mill's introduction to "On Liberty." As I discuss in chapter 3, Mill contrasts a "civilized community," by which he means a community that is racially white, that is ready for the benefits of liberty to those "backward" societies where "the race itself may be considered as in its nonage." For those non-Western societies for which liberty is inappropriate, Mill states that "[d]espotism is a legitimate mode of government in dealing with barbarians."[13] Furthermore, to the degree that the British working class seemed to approximate less the norms of civility and more the identity of the non-Western savage or barbarian, to that extent it lost its voice in the polity through his scheme of representative government with weighted votes. In Mill's work we can see how the rights of subjects necessitate the production of subjects for rights.

Critics of liberalism rarely acknowledge how a discourse of rights can be productive of social formations that sustain the recognition of rights. In particular, critics of American constitutional law's liberalism fail to recognize how invoking legal rights not only disrupts, potentially, certain social relations, but also incites the production of the social basis that can lend authority to one's claim of right. This point becomes more clear as we examine the discursive rules of claiming rights in the specific context of American constitutional law.

Rather than locating sovereignty in the state, the U.S. Constitution is a reflection and creation of a new, governmentalized sovereignty—the American people. The rights guaranteed by the Bill of Rights are properly understood as the "rights of the people." The First Amendment, for example, protects the "right of *the people* peaceably to assemble." When one claims a constitutional right like freedom of speech, as I have been arguing throughout this book, one is interpellated as an American. This is not, however, an instance of a passive subject being acted upon or repressed by power. One gains a subject position that allows conduct. One seeks to invoke this form of discursive power in order to be authorized as a speaker—to be recognized as one who exercises a right to free speech legitimately. In the moment of claiming a right, one also hails others as Americans with the aspiration that this call will incorporate a public that will recognize the practice in question as an instance of "free speech" rather than as a social problem that must be contained or eradicated for the people's welfare. In this process much depends upon which elements that might constitute America are pieced together and which are expelled, and whether a given articulation can foster a self-recognition in one exercising judgment. Finally, much depends upon what sort of an identity the law fixes upon the one claiming a right.

To claim a right like freedom of speech is to seek to incorporate one's self into the American people. As I discussed in chapter 4, Martin Luther King Jr. mobilized a national discourse in support of equal rights for black Americans. In the process of embodying an American people that would authorize a right to protest and the goals of the civil rights movement, King aligned his American identity through the construction of an outside—communist totalitarianism. Being branded with the identity of "communist" was perhaps the most effective way to delegitimate the claims of the civil rights movement during this period, since communism was "un-American."[14] So, while the invention of the "American people" enables the possibility of claiming rights, "America" is distinguishable only by virtue of relations of difference—what is not American. American constitutional rights become recognizable through constitutive limits.

If constitutional rights are not as disembodied, abstract, or universal as they are sometimes theorized to be, then they cannot be as alienating or fragmenting as some communitarians fear.[15] Communitarians, construing rights as trumps for the isolated liberal individual, view rights as antagonistic to the social relations that hold together the community. Based upon an isolated individual, rights are hostile to the cultural makeup of actually existing persons. As an antidote to the detrimental effects of liberal rights, invocations of "our" tradition or current condition flow easily from the pens of communitarians. Privileged moral obligations constitute "us" as subjects, and "we" must recognize this.[16] Somehow, these deep identities lie below the vagaries of cultural change and struggle. Failing to recognize or acknowledge the essential contestability of the image of community upon which their arguments rest, communitarians do not understand legal rights to be a form of cultural production in the context of a society that is internally incomplete.[17] To adjudicate a question of rights is, in some measure, to adjudicate the identity of the American people and the requirements that flow from this identity.

Thus, I have argued in this book that questions of rights are not opposed to the centrality of a national or racial "people" in contemporary politics. Indeed, the practice of rights under current conditions reproduces forms of national power. Therefore, rather than continuing to argue that rights alienate "us" from our fundamental social identity, we should borrow a page from Foucauldian scholarship that challenges a narrowly repressive understanding of power with the insight that who we are is a contingent achievement that must always be reachieved in face of doubt. In relaying this insight to the arena of legal studies, we can conceive law as one space within which such achievements are made, contested, and enforced. Moreover, we might be more sensitive to the way that juridical rights have become thoroughly governmentalized in the American context. That is, legal rights have become a mechanism for the reachievment of national authority (in contrast to the conventional view of understanding individual rights as standing opposed to nationalism). While the constitution of a national people is the condition of possibility for American rights, this social entity is given new force whenever individuals cite their rights under constitutional law. As a form of power, claiming constitutional rights links a technology of the self with macrolevel government, exemplifying Foucault's insight that the power of governance in contemporary society is both individualizing and totalizing.[18]

Social Discipline: Empowering Public Subjects

Although the U.S. Constitution is a critical intervention that shifts sovereignty and legal rights toward the people as their ultimate referent, the implications of this shift emerged gradually and unevenly. For instance, through the early twentieth century, U.S. constitutional law permitted governments to treat public places much as a homeowner would treat his living room. That is, if someone said something that the owner did not like, the owner could kick the speaker off of his property. This legal reasoning derived from the older perspective that the state is sovereign over public places much as the homeowner is sovereign over his place. During the 1930s, however, a change occurred. The Supreme Court's rulings began to recognize more fully the implications inherent in making the people sovereign.

In *Hague v. CIO*, individuals associated with the Committee for Industrial Organization (CIO) complained that the government of Jersey City refused to allow any public meetings within the city to discuss the National Labor Relations Act. The individuals argued that these actions by the city government violated their rights of "free speech and peaceable assembly secured to them, *as citizens of the United States.*" The Court ruled in favor of the CIO, and in so doing, it diverged from the line of legal precedent that had permitted state governments to exercise ultimate authority over public places. Instead, the Court argued that "[c]itizenship of the United States would be little better than a name if it did not carry with it the right to discuss national legislation and the benefits . . . to accrue to citizens therefrom." Marking this revolution, the Court argued that public places are "held in trust for the use of the public." Public places, Justice Roberts stated, are to be used for the purposes of "communicating thoughts between *citizens*, and discussing *public* questions. . . .

The privilege of a *citizen* of the United States to use the streets and parks for communication of views on *national* questions . . . must not . . . be abridged or denied."[19]

Hague v. CIO continued the process of displacing sovereignty from the state to the people by empowering individuals to discuss national issues as citizens of the United States and by empowering persons to claim these rights as American citizens. In this way, the Court opened up a subject position that enables these acts, although such conduct is constrained by the necessity of acting as an *American* subject. When government is entrusted to the people, problems of discrimination and capacity emerge. That is, there must be some sign by which the American people can be identified and distinguished from other possible social identities. Additionally, the capacity of the American people for self-government must be cultivated, while those social problems that endanger these powers must be regulated for the nation's security. In sum, relevant subjects must be produced.

Disciplinary institutions are key mechanisms by which national subjects are created, subjects who will be capable of self-government.[20] The 1986 case of *Bethel School District v. Fraser* displays the relationship between the production of national subjects and the exercise of constitutional rights. As mentioned in chapter 3, this case involved a high school boy who was punished by a public school for giving a speech laden with sexual innuendo. The Court rejected his argument that the school's disciplinary action, based on the content of his speech, violated the First Amendment. In *Bethel*, the Court argued that the "role and purpose of the American public school system . . . [is to] prepare pupils for citizenship in the Republic." To constitute these subjects, it "must inculcate the habits and manners of *civility* as values in themselves conducive to happiness and as indispensable to the practice of self government." The Court stated that in order to educate America's youth for "citizenship," schools must teach "the shared values of a *civilized* social order. . . . The schools . . . may determine that the essential lessons of civil, mature conduct cannot be conveyed in a school that tolerates lewd, indecent, or offensive speech." The Court disposed of the student's contention that his right to free speech was violated with the argument that he was not yet an American subject who could make a legitimate claim to First Amendment rights.[21]

Tracking Mill's argument that savages have no claim upon inter*national* law or morality because they are not yet civilized, hence not *nations* properly understood, the Court indicated that education institutionalizes the civilizing process that leads to American national subjectivity as its telos. The sexual nature of Matthew Fraser's speech merely proved his lack of civility or decency, and it constituted him as a social problem that demanded regulatory reform in a civilized social order. *Bethel* therefore presents decency or civility as a sign of American subjectivity. Decency or civility refers to a form of self-governance that America demands of its subjects who are to be entrusted with a right of free speech. As we can see, being civilized is a necessary form of self-discipline for those seeking incorporation within the American body politic as a civilized social order. Civility thus plays the double role of being both a technology of self and a rule by which the American people governs itself. It links self-discipline with the regulation of a population.[22]

Government by Discussion

From within a society that fashions itself as civilized or decent, the meaning of civility or decency as social norms may appear neutral if not necessary for society's future. When placed in historical context, however, the racial content of these norms surfaces. As we have also seen in chapters 2 and 3 particularly, the meaning of a civilized identity is given through its opposition to those who are savages or barbarians.[23]

Historically, the terms decency and civility or being civilized have been used interchangeably. The terms refer to the social importance of outward bodily propriety. Treatises on manners tell one how to govern every aspect of bodily relations in a way that conforms to the norms of civility or decency, from snot on the nostrils, to how to sit, greet, drink, dip one's fingers into the broth, to how to fart, whether to greet a man taking a shit by the side of the road, how to share one's bed, or how to deal with questions of nudity and sexuality. Certain forms of self-governance are cultivated for appearing in public, before the eyes of others, that are different from what one might do when not in public.[24] The treatises foster specific technologies of self, practices of the self that articulate with larger changes in the social order between the Middle Ages and modernity in Europe. Although a treatise like Erasmus's of the sixteenth century might use wolves or peasants as negative points of reference to inspire self-discipline, by the eighteenth and nineteenth centuries, as we have seen in earlier chapters, civilization had gathered meaning in relation to those peoples the West was driven to colonize.[25] Thus, civility gives specific content to the norms by which American subjects like Fraser are disciplined and gives specific cultural meaning to the American body politic.

Civility in nations that interpret themselves as part of Western civilization thus becomes significant in its opposition to the savage or barbarian of the non-West. It is also intimately concerned with the regulation of the body; in particular, its sexual regulation. Indeed, as one editorialist helpfully translated during the 2000 presidential campaign, when Bush stated that the 2000 election was about restoring civility to politics, he was using code words for "I won't have sex in the Oval Office."[26] Decent sexual practices often act as a sign of the racial progress embodied by Western civilization. While civility and decency have long provided the context for the regulation of sexuality in the West, the particular prominence in American law and politics of sexual propriety today may be yet another symptom of a national reformation post–cold war.[27] The American nation today is haunted by different demons than from those at mid-century.[28] Instead of mapping its place in the world according to the logic of communism and anticommunism, America today seems to understand itself according to the more overtly racial logic of the West versus the Rest.[29] The ever frequent sexual disputes that occupy the national attention are indicative of this reconstellation of the American national formation. This shift is both manifested and reproduced in contemporary legal discourse.

Legal scholarship has taken renewed interest in the conceptual break produced by the American Constitution regarding the question of sovereignty and what this means for governance.[30] These interpretations of American constitutional law work to produce a particular culture of liberal rights. They incite technologies of self as they seek to educate their readers on the meaning of their rights and how they are to be exercised responsibly. The forms of social discipline that inhere in the liberties these texts extol emerge clearly through an examination of how these texts have found newly useful one element of the liberal tradition, the concept of "government by discussion." By tracing the genealogy of "government by discussion," we can see how rights adhere to specifically encultured subjects rather than to abstract individuals. That is, women must confine their sexuality to the patriarchal family, while men and women must be heterosexual with moderate sex drives. These forms of decent self-control and civilized social organization are indicative of Western civilization's racial progress. They are the conditions that make for the productive exercise of speech rights.

According to Cass Sunstein, a leading constitutional scholar who became a familiar face through his legal commentary on CNN during the attempt to impeach Bill Clinton, one "of the most important liberal innovations [is] the commitment to 'government by discussion.'" For Sunstein, the "placement of sovereignty in 'We the People,' rather than the government, may well have been the most important American contribution to the theory of politics." By locating sovereignty in the "People," the U.S. constitutional system "carried important lessons for freedom of speech. It created an ambitious system of 'government by discussion,' in which outcomes would be reached through broad public deliberation."[31] By linking "government by discussion" to the American Constitution's location of sovereignty in the "people," Sunstein sounds as if he could be channeling simultaneously the spirits of Woodrow Wilson and John Burgess. And as we shall see by tracing his use of "government by discussion" to its source, he very well might be.

Sunstein believes that current American law "protects much speech that ought not be protected. It safeguards speech that has little or no connection with democratic aspirations and that produces serious social harm." Sunstein advocates in favor of "distinctive protection to political speech" and a system that is "readier to allow regulation of nonpolitical speech." One example of the sort of contemporary free speech problem that the system must solve, and which he invokes repeatedly, is the problem of "nude dancing" at the "Kitty Kat Lounge."[32]

Sunstein refers his readers to Samuel Beer for a fuller understanding of what is meant by the concept "government by discussion." Beer, in *To Make a Nation*, argues that the American Constitution, and the Anglo-American constitutional tradition in general, is guided by rational deliberation or "government by discussion," a concept he borrows in turn from Walter Bagehot, whom we have met in chapter 2 as one of Wilson's intellectual heroes. Beer, paraphrasing Bagehot, argues that "government by discussion" is opposed to the

> typical "parley" in a traditionalist society . . . which dealt with particular "undertakings." In government by discussion the interchange took place on a higher plane of generality, dealing with "principles" under which many particulars could be classed. . . . In this process, Bagehot saw the central expression of the rational spirit of modernity. . . . In his Darwinian scheme, government by discussion greatly added to the survival power of

a society, enabling it to surpass and overcome other societies still stuck in the "cake of custom."[33]

Walter Bagehot begins the chapter in *Physics and Politics* that introduces the concept "government by discussion" by stating that the "greatest living contrast is between the old Eastern and customary civilizations and the new Western and changeable civilizations." The passage that Beer paraphrases, when he distinguishes the "parley" of traditionalist societies stuck in the cake of custom from the principled discussion of modern and progressive societies, makes the racial division that constitutes government by discussion explicit through its devaluation of the speech of racial subordinates: "But the oratory of the *savages* has led to nothing, and it was likely to lead to nothing. It is a discussion not of principles but of undertakings."[34]

For Bagehot, one sign of racial backwardness is female sexual activity outside of patriarchal governance.[35] In fact, he places a premium upon harnessing female sexual agency to the patriarchal family. Bagehot makes the patriarchal family a precondition for government by discussion, which in turn leads to further progress. According to Bagehot, certain conditions can be "traced to the nation capable of a polity, which suggests principles of discussion, and so leads to progress." His primary condition is patriarchal marriage, which he argues makes home education and discipline both "probable and possible." For Bagehot, "[w]hile descent is traced only through the mother, and while the family is therefore a vague entity, no progress to a high polity is possible."[36] Nations are formed from this patriarchal base. The aggregation of patriarchal families makes clans, and the aggregation of clans makes nations.[37] Upon this foundation, the capacity for discussion arises.

Bagehot is concerned to regulate the sexual agency of women in order to serve the goal of nation building which in turn provides the social conditions for government by discussion. Sexuality, however, must be normal along potentially infinite additional dimensions according to this scheme. In particular, Bagehot argues that a specific economy of sexual desire indicates civilized progress. While in less civilized contexts the most successful races are those that can reproduce fastest, in the context of Western civilization the reverse is true. Bagehot states that where "exceptional fertility exists there is sluggishness of mind," and he goes on to argue that there is "only a certain quantum of power in each of our race; if it goes one way it is spent and cannot go in another." Furthermore, because "nothing promotes the intellect [as opposed to sexual desire] like intellectual discussion, and nothing promotes intellectual discussion so much as government by discussion," Bagehot argues with delightful Victorian indirection that "free government has . . . been shown to tend to cure an inherited excess of human nature." Thus, "two things which seemed so far off have been shown to be near."[38] The capacity for being a speaker and producing speech is created through a strict discipline of sexual desire, while discussion in turn regulates sexual desire, thus reproducing the conditions for free speech. In a broad sense, therefore, government by discussion describes a set of *economic* relations that reproduces a national people capable of exercising its rights of free speech. This liberal subject is hardly abstract. Indeed, Bagehot demonstrates great concern over the constitution of the rights-bearing subject.

While Bagehot uses this economy of sexual desire as yet another proof of England's superiority over the savages of the "East," and seeks to instigate greater self-discipline amongst its population, there are seeming differences even within the "West." Bagehot manages these by fixing such differences in a particular class of people and by locating this type of person within urban space.[39] He then uses these forms of difference to incite his audience to govern themselves properly through the haunting association of difference with the savage. Bagehot argues that "the lower classes in civilized countries, like all classes in uncivilized countries . . . lack a *sense* of morality." He states that a "walk in London," to witness the "great sin of great cities," is all that is necessary to establish the truth of his argument.[40]

Government by discussion uses race to think social difference, sexual deviance to signify racial alterity, and sexual normality to represent the possibility of free speech. Sunstein's use of the term retreads the narrative footsteps of Bagehot, Wilson, and Burgess by reiterating that the American people are part of Western civilization, an identity formation constituted in racial opposition to the savage or barbarian of the non-West. The semiotics of government by discussion represents who shall count as a speaker. As a system of governance, government by discussion seeks to cultivate the formation of subjects who will, in turn, produce the correct effects by their exercise of speech rights. Through normalizing strategies of comparison, Bagehot inspires technologies of self—practices upon one's self and knowledge of one's self—that make one's interpellation within this regulatory framework all the more secure.

Like Bagehot's representations of excessive sexuality, the references to nude dancing that pepper Sunstein's texts also serve to represent "ungoverned" sexuality inappropriate to a civilized society.[41] This legal discourse incites technologies of self similar to those incited by Bagehot. Indeed, Sunstein argues that "government should . . . be allowed to maintain a *civilized* society" by "guard[ing] against the degradation produced by . . . obscenity," and he endorses the Supreme Court's decision in *Barnes v. Glen Theatre* to uphold a public decency statute that forbids nonobscene nude dancing by Darlene Miller at the Kitty Kat Lounge.[42] In sum, Sunstein's free speech scheme furthers a strict discipline of signifying practices involved in the construction of subjectivities, and then provides for protection of the speech produced by authorized subjects.

Decency's Genealogy: Contemporary Legal Regulation

> A modern city can deteriorate into an urban jungle with tragic consequences to social, environmental, and economic values.
> —Justice Powell concurring in the Court's decision upholding the regulation of the sex industry in *Young v. American Mini Theatres* (1976)

In light of the prominent attention given by liberal legal discourse to the production of subjects who exercise rights, we must reject as "too easy" any analysis of constitutional jurisprudence on sexual expression that relies on the premise that liberalism fosters a repression of the body, and hence of sexuality. We would do better, I suggest, if we focus our attention on the specific sociosexual subjects that American law constitutes. To this end, I will examine the patterns of justification for the regulation of sexuality.

Justice Stevens argues that the First Amendment reflects the "profound national commitment to the principle that debate on public issues should be uninhibited, robust, and wide-open." Yet he also argues that society's interest in protecting indecent sexual expression is of a "wholly different, and lesser, magnitude than the interest in untrammeled political debate." If we were to understand the liberal rights protected by the Constitution to refer only to an abstract individual, these statements of law might seem to contradict one another. On the one hand, Stevens appears to protect the neutral principle of freedom of speech for anybody, while on the other he seems to advocate the repression of speech for those who wish to express themselves sexually. Former Chief Justice Earl Warren provides the key to understand the compatibility of Stevens's assessments of First Amendment law in a way that links to *Bethel*'s distinction between subject formation and freedom of speech, as well as the reemerging interest in government by discussion. As Warren argues, governments can regulate obscenity in order to maintain a "decent" society.[43] The right of free speech is protected for American subjects. American subjects, however, are identified by their decency. The regulation of decency cultivates subjects who can then exercise the rights of self-government while controlling indecencies that threaten the body politic.

The problem with an indecent or obscene expression is not that it refers to sexuality. Nor is the problem one of maintaining a boundary between a disembodied public sphere and the private sphere to which the body's particularities are confined. As Justice Brennan puts it, "Sex . . . is one of the vital problems of human interest and *public* concern."[44] The problem is that indecency is a sexual practice that is improperly governed. The norms that define properly governed subjects are those of civility and decency, norms that are given content by the cultural context provided by Western civilization. The Supreme Court's opinion in *Ginzburg v. U.S.* demonstrates the importance of regulating sexuality to promote a civilized racial identity, and the important link between this racial identity and the right of freedom of speech.

In *Ginzburg v. U.S.* the Court upheld Ralph Ginzburg's obscenity conviction although the materials he distributed were not literally obscene in themselves. The materials, which included articles and photo essays on the subjects of love, sex, and sexual relations, were marketed to appeal beyond professional therapeutic and social science circles to the prurient interests of the general public. For soliciting interest in these publications without discrimination, Ginzburg was convicted under a federal obscenity statute. In other words, Ginzburg's crime was not to possess or to disseminate obscene materials. His crime was to incite the production of improperly governed subjects through a misuse of sexual expression that, if it had been used to reinforce the norms of civility, would have been perfectly legal.

Brennan sums up the Court's judgement:

The works themselves had a place, though a limited one, in anthropology, and in psychotherapy. They might also have been lawfully sold to laymen who wished seriously to study the *sexual practices of savage or barbarous peoples, or sexual aberrations*; in other words most of them were not obscene per se. . . . However, in the case at bar, the prosecution succeeded . . . when it showed that the defendants indiscriminately flooded the mails.[45]

Brennan uses the discourse of Western civilization versus the savage or barbarian to describe and contain sexual difference. Insightfully, he also understands that a text receives its meaning and value through the economy of its circulation and use. In this case, the circulation of the texts does not discriminate—it is "indiscriminate." This lack of discrimination constitutes the social problem that demands regulation because it threatens to erode the difference that sustains the American people. Should the materials have circulated in a way that represented the sexual difference of savage or barbarous peoples as a deviation from the social norms that mark the progress of Western civilization, then they would not have been found obscene. In other words, Ginzburg's crime was not that he engaged in sexual expression. His crime was to threaten the constitution of civilized American subjects by inciting alternative sexual interests.

Thus, we can find within First Amendment doctrine a great deal of concern for the American body politic. First Amendment law culturally constitutes and regulates the national subject as the substantive referent for rights. Recent concern over public decency also shows that these contemporary struggles over legal rights do not pit an unencumbered individual against the social norms of the community so much as they present contrasting views of the commitments that follow from the embodiment of the American subject as decent and civilized.

In *City of Erie v. Pap's A.M.*, the Supreme Court took up Erie, Pennsylvania's, attempt to regulate a "recent increase in nude live entertainment within the City" by adopting "the concept of Public Indecency prohibited by the laws of the State of Indiana, which was approved by the U.S. Supreme Court in Barnes vs. Glen Theatre Inc."[46] Although the Supreme Court in *Barnes v. Glen Theatre* had upheld Indiana's public decency law, the Pennsylvania state supreme court struck down the Erie ordinance on First Amendment grounds. *Barnes v. Glen Theatre,* in which a majority upheld Indiana's regulation of nude dancing, was the most recent Supreme Court precedent on public decency and was used to support Rudolf Giuliani's sex war in New York City.[47] In other words, the Supreme Court in *Barnes* found no First Amendment problem with regulating public indecency. In *City of Erie v. Pap's*, the Supreme Court overturned the Pennsylvania high court decision and reiterated its support for *Barnes's* legal interpretation of laws promoting public decency.

In *Barnes*, Darlene Miller, with several other women and clubs such as the Kitty Kat Lounge, challenged Indiana's public decency statute for preventing nude dance performances. The Court in *Barnes* overturned federal appellate decisions finding for the dancers and upheld the Indiana statute. Chief Justice Rehnquist's plurality opinion refers to the Indiana state supreme court decision *Ardery v. The State* as a source of meaning for the law.[48] *Ardery* involves one Henry Ardery who, in a public place, made an indecent exposure of his person. Decency, according to Indiana's supreme court, involves concealing from public gaze the sight of one's "privates." Adam and Eve's example of "covering their privates," the court goes on to argue, "has been imitated by all mankind since that time, except, perhaps, by some of the lowest grades of *savages*."[49] As we can see, decency refers to a proper governance of one's body and to the norms of the public. Thus, the genealogy of Indiana's legal interest, hence of Erie's interests since the city refers explicitly to Indiana's law to contextualize its city ordinance's regulatory purpose and legal legitimacy, evinces concern for the racial embodiment of the public subject.

Barnes was extensively discussed at the appellate level by two well-known judges, Judges Easterbrook and Posner. Although they disagreed on the question of whether nude dancing is protected by the First Amendment, they shared a common understanding of America as an instance of Western civilization while negotiating this landscape differently. Easterbrook dissented from the appellate court decision ruling for the dancers and argued that the state should be allowed to regulate nude dancing. During the mid-1980s, Easterbrook had invoked the specter of "Totalitarian governments" and located the right to propagate opinions as "[o]ne of the things that separates our society from theirs" in ruling against an antipornography ordinance.[50] With the waning of the cold war, however, a new field of vision and new problems emerged. Easterbrook now territorialized America within Western civilization.

Using the category of class, Easterbrook differentiates reasonable and responsible citizens from undisciplined and ungovernable subjects. As did Bagehot, Easterbrook then links the tastes of the lower classes with the practices that Western civilization considers normal to other spaces, thereby justifying the demand for their regulation within America. He contrasts "[s]ophisticates" who go to museums or the opera with "Joe Six-pack" who may want to see "naked women gyrate in the pub." Easterbrook articulates these class-based divisions of value to a racialized frame of reference in his concluding point: "Darlene Miller wants to impress the barflies so they will ply her with drinks. . . . We may doubt the wisdom of requiring women to wear more clothing in the bars of South Bend than in the *Folies Bergere* or on the beaches of Rio de Janeiro without concluding that Indiana has exceeded its powers under the Constitution."[51]

Easterbrook justifies constraining the performance of female sexual agency by arguing that the regulated dances would be more appropriate to places that signify exoticism, racial hybridity, and sexual licentiousness. In so doing, Easterbrook distances nude dancing from the norms of Western civilization. This makes the claims of the dancers upon American constitutional rights look anomalous and out of place. Moreover, he justifies the regulation of nude dancing by denying the patrons and dancers First Amendment standing by assimilating their existence to the social problem of excessive consumption of alcohol.

Rather than defending the rights of the dancers by referring to an abstract, disembodied legal subject, Posner defends the dancers by linking nude dancing to the protection of Western high culture, while invoking America's difference from the "Orient." Posner reminds the American people that "[p]ublic performances of erotic dances debuted in Western culture in the satyr plays of the ancient Greeks." Additionally, Posner demonstrates a concern for Western high culture by stating that a "rule cannot be laid down that would excommunicate the paintings of Degas."[52] Posner recognizes the right claims for free speech at issue in the case by locating the American people within Western civilization.

In addition to establishing a vision of the public in which nude dancing fits, Posner argues that the regulation of nude dancing is un-American if America is understood as an instance of Western civilization. He holds up a mirror to the public for it to recognize itself. The mirror is a reference to the "Islamic clergy," whom "[m]ost of us do not admire." He again holds up the mirror so that the American public can see "a morals police patrolling the streets of South Bend with knouts, like the Saudis."[53] By evoking seemingly incongruous images like a Saudi in South Bend, he encourages the American public to recognize the regulation of nude dancing as out of place within a civilized America.

While Posner and Easterbrook differed over whether Darlene Miller had a right under the U.S. Constitution to dance nude, they agreed that the norms by which the American people are recognized are those provided by Western civilization. They interpreted differently the commitments that flow from this initial recognition, however. Thus, Posner's argument that Miller had a right to engage in nude performances does not

depend upon an unencumbered rights-bearing individual. Both his arguments and Easterbrook's rely upon encumbering the American subject
within the cultural predicament of Western civilization. The American
people, empowered by the Constitution to claim a right to free speech, is
embodied through the norms of Western civilization and its difference
from the savage or barbarian.

By situating *City of Erie v. Pap's A.M.* in a legal genealogy concerned
with the civility and decency of the American people, we can better understand the basis on which the Supreme Court upheld Erie's ordinance
against a hostile Pennsylvania high court ruling. The city of Erie passed an
ordinance to regulate public nudity and modeled its regulatory efforts on
Indiana's public decency statute and the Supreme Court's ruling in *Barnes
v. Glen Theatre*. The ordinance, however, exempted from coverage non-
communicative forms of nudity like a young child running around without pants or a mother breast-feeding, and it included those wearing clothing that *simulates* nudity. Moreover, the city did not apply the ordinance
against a stage performance of *Equus*, despite the fact that it involved nudity and it warned its audience of this fact. How could the U.S. Supreme
Court rule that this ordinance did not violate the First Amendment? Just
as Ginzburg's crime was not to have engaged in sexual expression but to
have threatened the constitution of the civilized American subject, the
crime of the nude dancing establishments in Erie was not nudity but to
have staged indecency out of place in a civilized America. In other words,
the determining question of the case was not whether the nudity was signifying something, and if it was, then it was protected under the First
Amendment. Instead, the relevant question was whether the nudity signified indecency, because if it did, then regulating this indecency was in the
American public's interest by securing its civilized identity. That is, we
have a replay of John Burgess's insight that preserving sovereignty does
not violate rights. How the American people is constructed determines the
perception both of legitimate rights claims and of problems that must be
regulated to preserve the identity of this people. It orders the constitutional meaning of this case.

The Erie city attorney claimed that the public nudity ban was not intended to apply to "legitimate" theater productions. Thus, the attorney's
defense of the ordinance illustrates how the case turned on who was perceived to have legitimate standing in the eyes of the First Amendment.
In order to be perceived as a legitimate speaker, one must show the signs
of American identity. Because the American people is constructed

against the indecent and the uncivilized, if one has such characteristics attributed to one's self, then one becomes representative of a social problem. On this basis, Justice O'Connor upheld the government's police powers to regulate nude dancing to redress "*public* health and safety problems."[54] Legitimacy was denied to the clubs, dancers, and patrons through their exclusion from the public and their construction as problems to be regulated in the interests of the public. Thus, Justice Scalia cut straight to the point when he claimed that the case actually presented no First Amendment issue whatsoever.[55] In other words, we have a question of *standing*, and those with interests in the type of nude dancing deemed indecent have lost any legitimate claim to membership in the public; they are not included within the people who can claim First Amendment rights legitimately; hence there is no First Amendment problem with the regulation.

Stevens's dissent in *City of Erie v. Pap's A.M.* gives content to the "public" that determines how the case is decided by further clarifying how the terrain of contestation for the problem of nude dancing is Western civilization, much as Easterbrook's and Posner's opinions did for the *Barnes* decision. To defend his position that the law violates the First Amendment, Stevens attempts to situate the practice of nude dancing within Western civilization by citing Posner's argument in the Indiana case that "nude dancing fits well within a broad, cultural tradition." But Stevens also quotes the view of council members who supported the ordinance by finding that the problem with the entertainment in the clubs was that it was "indecent," rather than involving nudity per se.[56] Thus, being able to lay a successful claim upon a Western and civilized identity is the key to being perceived as part of the American public whose expressive interests are protected by the First Amendment. While the norms of Western civilization do not determine the outcomes to these legal disputes, they do constitute the discursive parameters within which these disputes are engaged and the meaning of these disputes for America, as we can see from Stevens's citation of Posner and his quotation of council members. Whether through Stevens's citation of Posner or Erie's citation of *Barnes* and the problems indecency poses for the public's welfare, the genealogy of this case rests in the division of Western civilization from the savage or barbarian along the axis of public decency. Thus the governance of the American public's sexuality incited a governmentality of discussion as the century ended where it began for America.

Conclusion

Critics of American liberal constitutional law and its radiating effects condemn this legal formation for its focus on legal rights that they say function like trump cards for disembodied subjects against the rest of society. According to these critics, liberal legal rights force real persons to repress their fundamental identities, alienating themselves from their true selves, in order to play by liberalism's rules. Moreover, through a misconceived focus upon a disembodied individual, rights claiming does not allow sufficient attention to the good of the community, the community that makes individuals who they are. Such formulations lead us to understand the problem of maintaining community norms such as decency as distinct from or opposed to the individual right of freedom of speech.

These criticisms of American liberal legal practices neglect the specific ways in which American subjects are substantively embodied within liberal legal law. As I have argued here, rights like freedom of speech are protected under the U.S. Constitution as rights reserved to the American people. Therefore, claiming a right protected by the Constitution requires one to invoke a specific American imaginary and claim it for one's self. By claiming a constitutional right, one incorporates one's self within the American body politic.

The American Constitution, by locating sovereign power within the people, trusts that the people will be able to exercise those rights necessary to its self-government. The capacity of the people to exercise its rights must be nurtured and threats to its civic qualities contained. This capacity is produced through a regulatory concern for the civility of the American people. Today, the public's heightened attentiveness to sexuality as a social problem afflicting the body politic is manifested in an intense focus upon civility and decency. This focus calls up the racially significant discursive space of Western civilization to provide the means for understanding America's social problems and those values that are most at risk. Through the regulation of civility and decency, American subjects are produced who can claim their constitutional rights and are capable of self-government. As Matthew Fraser, Ralph Ginzburg, and Darlene Miller learned, civility is a capacity that is a necessary precondition to gain standing before the First Amendment.

Conclusion

The desire to belong to any community whatsoever, the desire for belonging *tout court*, implies that one *does not belong*. . . . I could not say "I want to be Italian, European, to speak this language, etc.," if that were already the case. *Accounting for* one's belonging—be it on national, linguistic, political or philosophical grounds—in itself implies a not-belonging. This can have political consequences: there is no identity. There is identification, belonging is accounted for, but this itself implies that the belonging does not exist, that the people who went to be this or that—French, European, etc.—are *not so* in fact. And they have to know this!
> —Jacques Derrida, "I Have a Taste for the Secret."

Conventional legal and political scholarship presents liberalism and nationalism as opposed systems of thought and practice. For liberals who value rights for their capacity to trump the community's pursuit of its vision of the good in favor of the individual, a liberal legal regime is the proper antidote to the dangers of nationalism. For communitarians who believe that the common good is too often sacrificed to individual liberty, however, rights alienate "us" from "our" deepest values—from who we "really" are. Individual rights fray the social bonds that hold together the community, diminishing the welfare of both the entire community and the individual who is alienated from the community that would otherwise nourish him or her. Both liberals and communitarians, therefore, share the same descriptive assessment of liberal rights as legal forms purposefully unresponsive to cultural, social, gender, or racial difference, although their normative assessments of rights vary. Liberals value rights for precisely the reasons that communitarians seek to limit their applicability—they protect the freedom of abstract individuals to pursue their own ends, even if those ends differ from the majority will or community interests. Because of this perceived opposition between liberal rights and the good of the social group, controversies over rights are frequently analyzed as a conflict between liberalism and nationalism.

Although political and legal scholarship posits an opposition between liberal rights and nationalism, liberalism and nationalism have, paradoxical as it may seem, coincided historically. This book has analyzed how liberalism and nationalism work together in a mutually reinforcing manner in the United States context by focusing on how an archetypical liberal right like freedom of speech can function in a way that reproduces national conditions of power. Moreover, I have described how placing a claim upon one's national identity acts as a precondition for having one's speech rights recognized, because these liberal rights are protected by a national constitution. In other words, the preeminent liberal legal right is not necessarily in conflict with nationalism, the archetypical form of community power in "modernity."

When one claims a constitutional right like freedom of speech, one is claiming a right reserved to the "people." Governments may not infringe upon this right because the will of the sovereign American people has not given them this power. By framing the question of rights in this way, the U.S. Constitution sets in motion certain discursive rules for claiming rights under this legal regime. As one claims a right to free speech, one simultaneously claims one's identity with the American people. Therefore, adjudicating controversies over the right to freedom of speech also requires the adjudication of the claim to American identity. The liberal right of free speech is put into relation with nationalism such that the two are mutually implicated in the practice of rights in the American context. Liberal government reproduces national forms of power, while an assertion of national identity enables a person to gain standing to have his or her claim to a right of free speech recognized as legitimate; it authorizes him or her as a speaker in the perception of the First Amendment. Thus, as the preeminent liberal legal regime, the United States relies upon and feeds the disciplinary and biopolitical forms of power Michel Foucault studied. Moreover, as the national formation shifts, changes in the meaning of America and its place in the world affect how rights are claimed and contested, with a correlated redistribution of advantages and burdens for those who must utilize this system.

This book presents a paradox, then, for debates in political and legal theory over the value of rights. On the one hand, liberal rights are hardly as abstract or universal as liberal philosophy likes to advertise, because when rights are inscribed within a national constitution like the U.S. Constitution, recognizing a claim to a right of free speech requires a simultaneous recognition of a claim about American identity. Thus, contrary to liberal P.R., rights do not rise above questions of identity. But, on the other hand, just because liberal claims are wrong, communitarians do not automatically "win" the debate. Precisely because practices of rights incorporate national identities, rights cannot be as destructive to social identity as communitarians claim. Unfortunately, the fact that neither liberal nor communitarian claims are correct does not mean that the best of both worlds is achieved. Individual rights are not reconciled with the value of community through a unique American exceptionalism, or theoretical compromise. So is this good or bad? The answer, again, is paradoxical. While the identity formation of the American people enables a right to free speech to be claimed, the act of claiming this right relies upon and fuels a simultaneously disciplinary and exclusionary politics of identity that constantly inhabits our practices of rights.

Although I have studied how, for example, racialized national formations have animated the practice of speech rights, one could find similar patterns in other areas of law because of the relation between law and its social situation.[1] Questions of due process of law and cruel and unusual punishment are thoroughly infused by the problem of America's racial identity with the civilized West. Legal procedures are evaluated according to evolving standards of "decency," whether they comport with being "civilized"; punishments must not be so "savage" and "barbaric" that they violate the Eighth Amendment injunction against cruel and unusual punishment.[2] Additionally, the discourse of international law constantly evokes the community of "civilized" nations as law's proper frame of reference, which is unsurprising given the colonial origins of international law.[3] Law is a cultural code of conduct that regulates practices and purchases legitimacy in part through the subject positions it creates and then relates to the social conditions and systems of cultural value within which law circulates and interacts.[4]

Although I have emphasized the significance of the "people" to questions of free speech, I hardly mean to suggest that the interpretive struggle over what it means to be American is the one key factor through which to understand or resolve a controversy over speech rights. Obviously other factors that the law makes significant can engender interpretive differences that can help determine particular disputes. For example, what counts as "state action"? What counts as a "restraint"? Is a group better understood as a criminal "conspiracy" or as an "association"? Is a regulation "content-neutral"? Does it regulate a "viewpoint"? Is the law "vague"? Is it "over-broad"? Is the space within which the speech act occurs properly defined as a "public forum"? If the state has opened a space to function as a public forum, must it include religious groups seeking to evangelize and worship, or does the First Amendment's Establishment Clause preempt this question? The answers to all of these queries help to determine the legal analysis that will follow. And increasingly today when so much of our lives is understood to be governed by different sorts of codes, how to construe "code," whether it can be owned, whether there should be a right of access to it and for whom, may become increasingly significant. That is, in the area of intellectual property, the question of what counts as "speech" and what counts as "property" may very well be the point upon which analyses will most advantageously focus.[5] (Although it is also possible that in some cases determining what counts as "property" or "speech" will rely upon racial perceptions, race-based assessments of what has "value" as a "creation," and racialized perceptions of who counts as an author of meaning. For instance, John Locke bases his theory of property upon labor, but the labors of the Native Americans were not valued in his view, and so they were legitimately expropriated by Euro-Americans. This problem continues to be reproduced in the global economy of intellectual property rights today.)

Freedom of speech is a right that is integral to the practice of democracy. This book, then, helps to open a window upon another paradox of "modernity," particularly the twentieth century. That is, how could the twentieth century be both a century of democratization *and* a century of genocide? My treatment of John Burgess especially bears this question in mind. By putting into practice the norm of popular sovereignty, we put into practice the salutary idea that the people ought to govern themselves and be able to determine their fate rather than being governed by external forces over which they have no control, be those forces a dictator or the manic, hungry logic of global capitalism that dictates rather miserable conditions of life for so many today. But another question and another politics constantly haunt democracy. If democracy means that the people should rule themselves, then the problem of identifying the people shadows democracy; a politics of identity constantly hovers over democracy. Who is included in the "We" of "We the People"? This very question presumes some are not included within this "We"; indeed, may threaten its existence, hence the sovereignty of the people. Policies of national security are mechanisms by which democracy is saved, but their police actions multiply—from weapons such as guns and tanks to immigration and naturalization law, to the constant police actions necessary to reproduce the national formation in the face of internal difference that can never be totally eradicated without death or until the end of time. This is why democracy's focus on the good of the people is never far from the dangers of the state's focus through its police powers on the population.[6]

So we are left with a question, Is it possible to disarticulate the will to democracy from the drive to genocide? Jodi Dean is beginning to make steps in this direction as she seeks to disarticulate democracy from the "public." For Dean, the disciplinary, exclusionary, and nationalist way that the public has been materialized in "modernity," along with the way that its logic becomes food for communicative capitalism, means that we need to de-link democracy from the concept of the public.[7] At this point in my thinking, I am more inclined to keep the concept of the public while trying to disarticulate the public from its nationalist presuppositions on the one hand, without falling into the trap of seeking after the impossibility of a universal public on the other, in order to cultivate and multiply nonidentical relations between the public and the nation. Dean's work nonetheless exemplifies the radically creative way that political and legal theory needs to proceed if the twenty-first century is to escape from the twentieth century's dangerous quandaries.

My argument about how legal rights reproduce national forms of power is premised upon "modern" conditions whereby the hegemonic political and legal structure is the nation-state. Rights claims, however, can also fit into feudalistic legal orders and reproduce feudal forms of authority and status. Because law exists in relation to an empirical situation, answering the question of whether or not rights will reproduce national forms of power is contingent upon whether or not the conditions of sociopolitical life that animate the practice of rights are nationally organized and inspired. And there are some signs on the horizon suggesting that possible changes may be afoot.

The emerging global movements challenging the power of global capital and the way that various governing bodies promote the interests of global capital over other values are helping to place issues relating to globalization in the popular media, especially when one of these governing bodies attempts to meet and faces protest. As various entities of the state attempt to police the protests in order to promote security and order, no matter in which nation-state or locality these events occur, some scholarship suggests that these variously singular events betray an overarching logic—a logic of global sovereignty and resistance. Now that the terrain of economics on the one hand and resistance on the other is truly global, the various state forces police in the name of a globalized sovereign force, what Michael Hardt and Antonio Negri call Empire.[8]

Whether or not one is persuaded by all of the empirical or normative positions implicated in Hardt and Negri's arguments, social practices do seem sufficiently globalized such that they are calling into being new legal orders for their representation and reproduction. Globalized economic and financial interactions are producing forms of law and legal practices to suit their needs.[9] Changes in the landscape like the Channel Tunnel to facilitate transnational patterns of social interaction are also inventing new legal spaces.[10] And rights claims and concerns for justice are frequently not limited by the borders of the nation-state.[11]

Another sign of potential change can be seen in the case *Zadvydas v. Davis*, decided in 2001 by the U.S. Supreme Court.[12] This decision consolidates cases involving two different resident aliens who were being deported, Kestutis Zadvydas and Kim Ho Ma. Congressional law provides for the detention of aliens in the process of being deported for a certain period, a period that can be extended at the discretion of the attorney general if the removal process takes longer than the ninety-day removal period. In these cases, however, the resident aliens challenged the legality of their custody because there was no reasonable chance of eventual repatriation—Zadvydas was born in a German displaced persons camp of Lithuanian parents, so that Germany would not accept him; and Ma was born in Cambodia, a country with which the United States does not have a repatriation treaty. Thus, these two were facing a potentially indefinite period of being in custody. In a 5–4 decision, the Court ruled that the detention of aliens for an indefinite period of time would violate the Constitution.[13] The Court attempted to limit the potential implications of this ruling by making it entirely possible that the same result of indefinite civil detention could occur with a governmental justification. The Court also drew distinctions that could conceivably reiterate the nationalist logic I have examined in this book, such as that difference between an alien who has not yet entered U.S. territory (who has no right to due process, according to the Court) and one who has entered. But bearing all of this in mind, the Court justified its opinion by quoting the language of the Fifth Amendment to highlight its use of the word "person": "The

Fifth Amendment's Due Process Clause forbids the Government to 'deprive' any 'person . . . of . . . liberty . . . without due process of law.'"[14] That is, the rights-bearing subject it based its ruling on was the "person," not the American people. While this subject clearly does not have the same rights as the American people (the Court argued that the choice presented by the case was not between imprisonment and the alien "living at large," but between imprisonment and "supervision under release conditions that may not be violated"), the Court's focus on "person" does indicate a potential crack in the nation's sociolegal armor.[15] In describing limitations on congressional power over immigration law, however, the Court once again invoked as one of these limitations the standard that governs "the conduct of all civilized nations."[16] Recognizing a fissure in the sure grounds of the nation, the Court resorted to the old, familiar grounds of race for "our" governing norms.[17]

Thus, the significance of this invocation of the legal subject as "person" remains to be seen. Will we only leap from the national frying pan into a racialized fire when a globalized imaginary governs legal practices? Will legal performances succeed in expanding the limits of legal rights beyond the nation, only to fail to achieve justice for the poor as we witness a reenactment on a global scale of the failures of the Fourteenth Amendment's rights of personhood, whereby incorporated businesses were recognized within the scope of its rights, but not black persons until the nation's second Reconstruction? After an unfortunate revisiting of separate and unequal in America's sociolegal practices, we are due for another "Reconstruction." As I end this book, U.S. unions and Mexico are working together to improve the plight of Mexican immigrants in the United States without proper documentation. One of their planned strategies is to reiterate a civil rights performance from the second Reconstruction. Called an "Immigrants Freedom Ride," and modeled on the Freedom Rides of the civil rights movement of the early 1960s, the hotel workers' union plans to drive buses carrying illegal immigrants from California and other states to Washington, D.C., daring immigration authorities to arrest them, while publicizing their present legal and economic limbo.[18] Will this legal performative have occurred? Will it have helped to enact a reterritorialization of America and a reinscription of available legal subjectivities? Only time will tell. The reader, at this point, knows more than I do.

Notes

<small>NOTES TO THE INTRODUCTION</small>

1. Ronald Dworkin, "Rights as Trumps," in *Theories of Rights*, ed. Jeremy Waldron (New York: Oxford University Press, 1984), 153–67.

2. Amitai Etzioni, *The Spirit of Community* (New York: Crown, 1993): 5–7; Mary Ann Glendon, *Rights Talk* (New York: Free Press, 1991).

3. Duncan Kennedy, *A Critique of Adjudication {fin de siècle}* (Cambridge: Harvard University Press, 1997), chaps. 12–13, p. 335 especially; Wendy Brown, *States of Injury* (Princeton: Princeton University Press, 1995), chap. 5 especially.

4. Robert Bellah, Richard Madsen, William Sullivan, Ann Swidler, and Steven Tipton, *Habits of the Heart: Individualism and Commitment in American Life* (New York: Harper and Row, 1985); Michael Sandel, *Democracy's Discontent: America in Search of a Public Philosophy* (Cambridge: Harvard University Press, 1996).

5. Michael Sandel places his initial discussion of *Lochner v. New York* in a chapter entitled "Rights and the Neutral State," and in a subsection entitled "After the Fourteenth Amendment: Rights as Trumps." See Sandel, *Democracy's Discontent*, chap. 2; *Lochner v. New York* 198 U.S. 45 (1905).

6. *Jacobson v. Massachusetts* 197 U.S. 11 (1905); *Muller v. Oregon* 208 U.S. 412 (1908). Thanks to Jonathan Simon who suggested I might find interest in *Jacobson v. Massachusetts*.

7. *Ex Parte Jackson* 96 U.S. 727 (1877).

8. *Trop v. Dulles* 356 U.S. 86 (1958) at 102.

9. *U.S. ex rel. John Turner v. Williams* 24 S. Ct. 719 (1904) at 723, emphasis added.

10. *Kleindienst v. Mandel* 92 S. Ct. 2576 (1972) at 2583.

11. Ibid., 2586–87.

12. Ibid., 2591–92. For further discussion of the intersection of the First Amendment and immigration and naturalization law, see Harry Kalven Jr., *A Worthy Tradition: Freedom of Speech in America*, ed. Jamie Kalven (New York: Harper and Row, 1988), chaps. 30–33.

13. Thus my starting point of inquiry is to interrogate the very premise behind Wendy Brown's research question, "And what does it mean to use a discourse of

generic personhood—the discourse of rights—against the privileges that such discourse has traditionally secured?" Brown, "Rights and Losses," in *States of Injury*, 96–97.

14. *Young v. American Mini Theatres* 96 S. Ct. 2440 (1976).

15. Benedict Anderson, *Imagined Communities* (New York: Verso, 1991).

16. As the Court put it in *Shaughnessy v. United States ex rel. Mezei*, 345 U.S. 206 (1953), "Whatever the procedure authorized by Congress is, it is due process as far as an alien denied entry is concerned."

17. *Foley v. Connelie* 435 U.S. 291 (1978); *Ambach v. Norwick* 441 U.S. 68 (1979).

18. Laurence Tribe, *American Constitutional Law*, 3d ed., vol. 1 (New York: Foundation Press, 2000), 975–76.

19. On the concept of biopolitics, see Michel Foucault, *The History of Sexuality: An Introduction*, vol. 1 (New York: Vintage, 1990); Michel Foucault, "The Birth of Biopolitics," in *Ethics: Subjectivity and Truth*, ed. Paul Rabinow vol. 1 of *Essential Works of Foucault, 1954–1984* (New York: New Press, 1997). See also chaps. 1 and 2 below.

20. Anderson, *Imagined Communities*. On this point, I have benefited from the discussion at the Law's Grounds conference at Cleveland-Marshall College of Law, April 7–8, 2000, where I presented chapter 1 of this book, as well as conversation with Jodi Dean.

21. *Plyer v. Doe* 457 U.S. 202 (1982).

22. 42 U.S.C. § 1981.

23. Thus I locate the debate over hate speech codes historically as part of a longer, ongoing politics of identity that is inextricably linked to the practice of rights in the United States, rather than as a displaced *ressentiment* over economic oppression symptomatic of a confused American left as other scholars have portrayed these controversies over rights. See Brown, *States of Injury*, 27, 59; Slavoj Žižek, "Class Struggle or Postmodernism? Yes, Please!" in *Contingency, Hegemony, and Ideology: Contemporary Dialogues on the Left* ed. Judith Butler, Ernesto Laclau, and Slavoj Žižek (New York: Verso, 2000), 97, 130 n. 17.

24. An important exception is Ann Laura Stoler, *Race and the Education of Desire: Foucault's History of Sexuality and the Colonial Order of Things* (Durham, N.C.: Duke University Press, 1995).

25. Bruce Ackerman, *We the People: Foundations* (Cambridge: Harvard University Press, 1991); Cass Sunstein, *The Partial Constitution* (Cambridge: Harvard University Press, 1993). Benjamin Barber's discussion is also relevant; see *A Passion for Democracy: American Essays* (Princeton: Princeton University Press, 1998), chaps. 5–6.

Notes to Chapter 1

1. See Roberto Mangabeira Unger, *Knowledge and Politics* (New York: Free Press, 1975): 82–83; Bernard Yack, "Reconciling Liberalism and Nationalism," *Political Theory* (February 1995): 166–82; Ronald Beiner, "Introduction: Nationalism's Challenge to Political Philosophy," in *Theorizing Nationalism*, ed. Ronald Beiner (Albany: State University of New York Press, 1999). Perhaps the opposition has been put most starkly by Carl Schmitt, *The Concept of the Political* (Chicago: University of Chicago Press, 1996).

2. Cf. Norberto Bobbio, *The Age of Rights* (Cambridge, U.K.: Polity Press, 1996), esp. 39–41 and 90.

3. Michael Sandel, *Democracy's Discontent: America in Search of a Public Philosophy* (Cambridge: Harvard University Press, 1996).

4. Beiner, "Introduction." One should note, however, that many scholars of nationalism understand the nation to be a uniquely modern phenomenon. See Ernest Gellner, *Nations and Nationalism* (Ithaca, N.Y.: Cornell University Press, 1983); Benedict Anderson, *Imagined Communities* (New York: Verso, 1991); Eric Hobsbawm, *Nations and Nationalism since 1780* (Cambridge: Cambridge University Press, 1992).

5. Ronald Dworkin, "Rights as Trumps," in *Theories of Rights* ed. Jerermy Waldron (New York: Oxford University Press, 1984).

6. Owen Fiss, "Foreword: The Forms of Justice," *Harvard Law Review* 93 (1979): 1.

7. Amitai Etzioni, *The Spirit of Community* (New York: Crown, 1993), 5.

8. Richard Morgan, *Disabling America* (New York: Basic Books, 1984).

9. Giorgio Agamben, *Homo Sacer: Sovereign Power and Bare Life*, trans. Daniel Heller-Roazen (Minneapolis: University of Minnesota Press, 1998), 174.

10. Ibid., 175, 170.

11. Ibid., 174, 171–72.

12. Carl Schmitt, *Political Theology: Four Chapters on the Concept of Sovereignty* (Cambridge: MIT Press, 1985), 13.

13. Ibid., 13, 6, 12. There are also occasions where Schmitt himself implies that sovereign decisions in a state of exception occur outside of law, but I shall prove that this is not the best reading of Schmitt.

14. Ibid., 7, citation omitted, italics mine.

15. Ibid., 12.

16. Jacques Derrida, "Declarations of Independence," trans. Tom Keenan and Tom Pepper, *New Political Science* 15 (1986): 7–15.

17. For a critical treatment of Agamben, see Peter Fitzpatrick, "Bare Sovereignty: *Homo Sacer* and the Insistence of Law," *Theory and Event* 5 (2001) (http://muse.jhu.edu/journals/theory_and_event/v005/.5.2fitzpatrick.html).

18. See Pauline Maier, *American Scripture: Making the Declaration of Independence* (New York: Knopf, 1997), 208, 214.

19. Jacques Derrida, *Of Grammatology*, trans. Gayatri Spivak (Baltimore: Johns Hopkins University Press, 1976).

20. Thomas Keenan, "Deconstruction and the Impossibility of Justice," *Public* 6, *Violence* (1992): 17–28.

21. For a discussion of the American appropriation of this script, see Bernard Bailyn, *The Ideological Origins of the American Revolution* (Cambridge: Harvard University Press, 1967); Gordon Wood, *The Creation of the American Republic, 1776–1787* (New York: Norton, 1972); H. Trevor Colbourn, *The Lamp of Experience: Whig History and the Intellectual Origins of the American Revolution* (Chapel Hill: University of North Carolina Press, 1965). Maier, *American Scripture*, compares the American declarations with their precedents in British constitutional history, particularly the 1689 Declaration of Right. For a discussion of the persistence of this discourse in early American politics, see Lance Banning, *The Jeffersonian Persuasion: Evolution of a Party Ideology* (Ithaca, N.Y.: Cornell University Press, 1978), and J. G. A. Pocock, *The Machiavellian Moment: Florentine Political Thought and the Atlantic Republican Tradition* (Princeton: Princeton University Press, 1975).

22. Cf. Christopher Hill, *Puritanism and Revolution* (New York: Schocken Books, 1958), 57; see generally J. G. A. Pocock, *The Ancient Constitution and the Feudal Law* (New York: Cambridge University Press, 1987).

23. Prasenjit Duara, "Historicizing National Identity, or Who Imagines What and When," in *Becoming National*, ed. Geoff Eley and Ronald Grigor Suny (New York: Oxford University Press, 1996), 168.

24. Cf. Richard Epstein, *Takings: Private Property and the Power of Eminent Domain* (Cambridge: Harvard University Press, 1985), chap. 2. The Lockean influence continues to be emphasized: see Ronald Hamowy, "The Declaration of Independence," in *The Blackwell Encyclopedia of the American Revolution*, ed. Jack Greene and J. R. Pole (Cambridge, Mass.: Basil Blackwell, 1991), 265; Maier, *American Scripture*, passim.

25. Charles Howard McIlwain, *The American Revolution: A Constitutional Interpretation* (New York: Macmillan, 1924), 43. See also John Phillip Reid, *Constitutional History of the American Revolution: The Authority of Law* (Madison: University of Wisconsin Press, 1993), 54.

26. Cited in Reid, *The Authority of Law*, 42; John Dickinson, "Letters from a Farmer in Pennsylvania" (1767), in *Empire and Nation*, ed. Forrest McDonald (Englewood Cliffs, N.J.: Prentice-Hall, 1962), 18; John Adams, *Novanglus and Massachusettensis* (1774–75) (Boston: Hews and Goss, 1819), 14.

27. McIlwain, *American Revolution*, 95. McIlwain is discussing the implications of *Calvin's Case* (1608), which addresses the relation of the Scottish to the English Parliament when the two realms were joined under one king.

28. Reid, *The Authority of Law*, 75. See also Maier, who cites a declaration of Natick, Massachusetts: "the glaring impropriety, incapacity, and fatal tendency, of any State whatever, at the distance of 3,000 miles, to legislate for these Colonies, which . . . are so numerous, so knowing, and capable of legislating . . ." (*American Scriptures*, 92). On virtual representation, see Wood, *Creation of the American Republic*.

29. Adams, *Novanglus*, 96–97, italics mine.

30. Ibid., 91.

31. Ibid., 34 and passim.

32. Ibid., 117.

33. John Phillip Reid, *Constitutional History of the American Revolution: The Authority of Rights* (Madison: University of Wisconsin Press, 1986), chap. 14.

34. A Bill of Rights [and] A List of Grievances" (1774), in *A Decent Respect to the Opinions of Mankind: Congressional State Papers, 1774–1776* ed. James Hutson (Washington, D.C.: Library of Congress, 1975), 52–54.

35. "A Declaration . . . Setting Forth the Causes and Necessity of Their Taking up Arms" (1775), in Hutson, *Decent Respect*, 91. In Jefferson's draft, this later reference to ancestry reads: "we should be wanting to ourselves, we should be perfidious to posterity, we should be unworthy that free ancestry from [whom] which we derive our descent, should we submit with folded arms. . . ." See *The Complete Jefferson*, ed. Saul Padover (New York: Tudor, 1943), 26 (bracketed text refers to words Jefferson himself crossed out).

36. Cited in Reid, *The Authority of Law*, 62, emphases in the original.

37. I qualify the racism of this discourse during this historical period because the lawyer James Otis could advocate equal rights for blacks and frame this argument entirely within the British constitution—if the rights of Englishmen are a "birthright," then one's color does not matter as long as one is born a British subject under the British constitution. See James Otis, "Rights of the British Colonies" (1764), in *Pamphlets of the American Revolution, 1750–1765*, ed. Bernard Bailyn (Cambridge: Harvard University Press, 1965), 446.

38. Thomas Jefferson, "A Summary View of the Rights of British America" (1774), in *Complete Jefferson*, 15, 6–7.

39. Ibid., 17. The emigration argument is referred to in the "Declaration of Independence," although it is a longer reference in Jefferson's draft than in the version Congress approved. In the final draft, the reference reads: "We have reminded them of the circumstances of our emigration and settlement here. . . ." "Declaration of Independence" (1776), *Complete Jefferson*, 33.

40. On the question of identity, see William Connolly, *Identity/Difference* (Ithaca, N.Y.: Cornell University Press, 1991).

41. Hannah Arendt, *On Revolution* (New York: Viking Press, 1963); Bonnie Honig, "Declarations of Independence: Arendt and Derrida on the Problem of Founding a Republic," *Rhetorical Republic: Governing Representations in American*

Politics, ed. Frederick Dolan and Thomas Dumm (Amherst: University of Massachusetts Press, 1993).

42. By viewing the rights claims of the Declaration of Independence as inescapably shot through with questions of identity, I take a different approach to the eighteenth-century declarations than my friend and colleague Costas Douzinas. See *The End of Human Rights* (Oxford: Hart, 2000). Or, are we focusing on two different moments in the process of rights claiming? See *The End of Human Rights*, 259.

43. Arendt, *On Revolution*, 198, 214; Wood, *Creation of the American Republic*, 44–45, citing John Adams in part.

44. John Adams, "Dissertation on the Canon and the Feudal Law," (1765), in *The Works of John Adams*, ed. Charles Francis Adams vol. 3 (Boston: Little and Brown, 1851), 462–63; Adams, "Novanglus," 38, 102.

45. Derrida, "Declarations of Independence."

46. I have used Maier (*American Scripture*) as my source for the Declaration of Independence (Appendix C). The bracketed portions are parts of Jefferson's version that Congress cut. The parenthetical portion is an insertion by me made necessary by my use of ellipses. Emphasis mine.

47. Ernest Renan, "What Is a Nation?" (1882), in Eley and Suny, *Becoming National*, 49.

48. Jefferson to Major John Cartwright, June 5, 1824, *Complete Jefferson*, 293–94.

49. James Wilson, "James Wilson's Opening Address," Nov. 24, 1787, in *The Debate on the Constitution: Federalist and Anti-Federalist Speeches, Articles, and Letters during the Struggle over Ratification*, pt. 1 (New York: Library of America, 1993), 801–2.

50. Jefferson to Francis Hopkinson, March 13, 1789, in *The Portable Jefferson*, ed. Merrill Peterson (New York: Viking, 1975), 436.

51. Adams, "Dissertation on the Canon and the Feudal Law," 456, 462.

52. Cited in Maier, *American Scripture*, 239.

53. Jefferson's views on blacks are discussed in Garry Wills, *Inventing America: Jefferson's Declaration of Independence* (Garden City, N.Y.: Doubleday, 1978). On the generality of these views, see Gary Nash, *Race and Revolution* (Madison, Wis.: Madison House, 1990), 48. St. George Tucker explicitly links his plan to Jefferson's in St. George Tucker, "A Dissertation on Slavery: With a Proposal for the Gradual Abolition of It, in the State of Virginia" (1796), in Nash, *Race and Revolution*, 151–58, citing Jefferson at 155. The reference to the "rights of the people" is in Maier, *American Scripture*, 237. John Adams also described the passages in Jefferson's "Notes on the State of Virginia" on slavery as worth "Diamonds." See "Adams to Jefferson," May 22, 1785, in *The Adams-Jefferson Letters: The Complete Correspondence between Thomas Jefferson and Abigail and John Adams*, vol. 1, ed. Lester J. Cappon (Chapel Hill: University of North Carolina Press, 1959), 21.

54. I have benefited in my thinking about politicization from conversations with Jodi Dean. Thanks to Christine de Denus for proofreading the chemical analogy.

55. Here I am provoked by Jacques Derrida. *The Politics of Friendship*, trans. George Collins New York: Verso, 1997), 161–64.

56. Jefferson to Kercheval, July 12, 1816, Padover, *Complete Jefferson*, 288; Jefferson, "Notes on the State of Virginia," in ibid., 625. Jefferson's political opponents at century's end shared this logic as Federalists attributed Republican political strength to "French" influence and sought to limit such sedition by tightening the regulation of aliens and naturalization. See James Morton Smith, *Freedom's Fetters: The Alien and Sedition Laws and American Civil Liberties* (Ithaca, N.Y.: Cornell University Press, 1956).

57. Jefferson, "Notes on the State of Virginia," in *Complete Jefferson*, 661.

58. Ibid.

59. Ibid., 632; see generally Anthony Wallace, *Jefferson and the Indians: The Tragic Fate of the First Americans* (Cambridge: Harvard University Press, 1999).

60. Jefferson, "Notes on the State of Virginia," 678–79, 684.

61. Jefferson, Third Annual Message, Oct. 17, 1803, in *Complete Jefferson*, 402–3.

62. Michel Foucault, *Discipline and Punish* (New York: Vintage, 1979).

63. Jefferson, "To the Choctaw Nation," December 17, 1803, in *Complete Jefferson*, 465.

64. Jefferson, "To the Chiefs of the Cherokee Nation," Jan. 10, 1806, in *Complete Jefferson*, 479.

65. Johannes Fabian, *Time and the Other* (New York: Columbia University Press, 1983). See also chap. 3.

66. Jefferson, "To the Chiefs of the Upper Cherokees," May 4, 1808, in *Complete Jefferson*, 494. Emphasis mine.

67. Ibid. For a more psychoanalytic discussion of the American reference to Indians as children, see Michael Rogin, *Ronald Reagan: The Movie and other episodes in political demonology* (Berkeley: University of California Press, 1987), 134.

68. Jefferson, "To the Chiefs of the Cherokee Nation," January 10, 1806, in *Complete Jefferson*, 479.

69. Cornelia Vismann has suggested to me in conversation that, particularly from a common law perspective, cultivation produces a legally recognizable spatial claim—plowing inaugurates law in space. Hence it is particularly appropriate that Jefferson should choose cultivation as his method of sociolegally incorporating the Indians within America. See Cornelia Vismann, "Starting from Scratch: Concepts of Order in No Man's Land," *War, Violence, and the Modern Condition*, ed. Bernd Hüppauf (New York: Walter de Gruyter, 1997), 46–47. For a discussion of how the symbolic link between law and modernity and their opposition to

tradition and the savage are key to Europe's modern racial identity, see Peter Fitz-patrick, *The Mythology of Modern Law* (New York: Routledge, 1992). For a discussion of narratives of property as strategies of governmentality, see Nicholas Blomley, "Cultivating the Self: Gardening and the Spaces of Property," paper presented at the 2000 Law and Society Annual Meetings, Miami, Florida.

70. James Madison distinguishes between the public interest and a majority faction in Federalist No. 10, Nov. 22, 1787, *The Federalist Papers*, ed. Garry Wills (New York: Bantam, 1982).

71. Jefferson, Seventh Annual Message, Oct. 27, 1807, *Complete Jefferson*, 437.

72. Jefferson, "To the Chiefs of the Upper Cherokees," 494.

73. Agamben, *Homo Sacer*, 178–79. This is one of the strengths of Michel Foucault's work against Agamben's.

74. Hannah Arendt, *The Origins of Totalitarianism* (New York: Meridian, 1958), 294.

Notes to Chapter 2

1. David Rabban, "The Emergence of Modern First Amendment Doctrine," *University of Chicago Law Review* 50 (1983): 1211.

2. Ibid., 1212.

3. Paul L. Murphy, *World War I and the Origin of Civil Liberties in the United States* (New York: W. W. Norton, 1979), 25, 46, 64.

4. Ibid., 36.

5. Ibid., 71.

6. Ibid., 54, 55.

7. Mark Graber, *Transforming Free Speech: The Ambiguous Legacy of Civil Libertarianism* (Berkeley: University of California Press, 1991), 51.

8. Ibid., 9–10.

9. The dissertation on which Graber's book is based won the American Political Science Association's award for best dissertation in public law for 1989.

10. Ibid., 7–10.

11. Howard Gillman, *The Constitution Beseiged: The Rise and Demise of Lochner Era Police Powers Jurisprudence* (Durham, N.C.: Duke University Press, 1993).

12. Robert K. Murray, *Red Scare: A Study in National Hysteria, 1919–1920* (Minneapolis: University of Minnesota Press, 1955), 224, 263; William Preston Jr., *Aliens and Dissenters: Federal Suppression of Radicals, 1903–1933* (New York: Harper and Row, 1963); Murphy, *World War I and the Origin of Civil Liberties*.

13. Graber, *Transforming Free Speech*, 79.

14. Ibid., 123–24.

15. Ibid., 146, 125, 165, 149, 124.

16. Ibid., 8, 18–19, 143, 26.

17. Ibid., 40. Graber uses conservative libertarians as his standard by which to measure subsequent efforts to protect free speech at pp. 105, 124–25, and 143. When subsequent libertarians protect free speech sufficiently in Graber's mind, he praises them by saying that they preserved the insights of the conservative libertarians (91). Graber notes that the conservative libertarian standard of protection in libel cases went unmatched by most civil libertarians until the 1960s (41). Graber discusses the suppression and distortion of the conservative libertarians at pp. 128–29, and the superior protection they would give to radical speech at p. 9.

18. Ibid., 18.

19. Ibid., 36.

20. Ibid., 24.

21. See "A New History of Libertarianism," *Harvard Law Review* 106 (1993): 1684 (Book Note); Gregory Magarian, "Transforming Free Speech," *Michigan Law Review* 90 (1992): 1428.

22. Cited in Thomas F. Gossett, *Race: The History of an Idea in America* (New York: Schocken Books, 1965), 91.

23. Cited in ibid., 95.

24. Michael Hardt and Antonio Negri, *Empire* (Cambridge: Harvard University Press, 2000), 4. The authors describe the United Nations as functioning as a "hinge" from which political and legal practices shift from a world based on mutually exclusive nation-states to the globalized logic of Empire.

25. Samuel Kliger, *The Goths in England: A Study in Seventeenth and Eighteenth Century Thought* (Cambridge: Harvard University Press, 1952).

26. Reginald Horsman, *Race and Manifest Destiny* (Cambridge: Harvard University Press, 1981).

27. Gossett, *Race*, 111.

28. Ibid.

29. Albert Somit and Joseph Tanenhaus, *The Development of American Political Science: From Burgess to Behavioralism* (Boston: Allyn and Bacon, 1967), 3, call Burgess the father of American political science and one of its truly great figures. On Burgess and American social science, see also Peter Manicas, *A History and Theory of the Social Sciences* (New York: Blackwell, 1987), chaps. 10–11 (see p. 208 on Burgess founding the first graduate program in the social sciences at Columbia), and Dorothy Ross, *The Origins of American Social Science* (New York: Cambridge University Press, 1991).

30. John Burgess, *Reminiscences of an American Scholar: The Beginnings of Columbia University* (New York: Columbia University Press, 1934). Burgess mentions founding *Political Science Quarterly* at p. 200, and mentions Theodore Roosevelt at pp. 211ff. The other graduate social science program of note was under Herbert Baxter Adams at Johns Hopkins University, where Woodrow Wilson, among others, received his education. Somit and Tanenhaus (*Development of American Political*

Science, 34) refer to Columbia and Johns Hopkins as the only two Ph.D. programs of consequence before the end of the nineteenth century.

31. John Burgess, "Germany, Great Britain, and the United States," *Political Science Quarterly* 19 (1904): 2.

32. John Burgess, *Political Science and Comparative Constitutional Law* (Boston: Ginn, 1893), 4.

33. Ibid., 5, 90–91.

34. Lee Epstein, "The Comparative Advantage," *Law and Courts* 9 (winter 1999): 1. To get us started along the comparative path, this essay asserts that the nations of the world follow one of two basic models in court organization—the American or the European. At the least, such a statement might be considered as begging the question *why*. Oddly, in its discussion of recent comparative work in the field of law and politics, this essay from the American Political Science Association section chair of law and courts does not cite Charles R. Epp, *The Rights Revolution: Lawyers, Activists, and Supreme Courts in Comparative Perspective* (Chicago: University of Chicago Press, 1998), which won the association's 1998 Pritchett Award and an earlier version of which won the association's 1996 Corwin Award. On the complex interdependencies between colonizing powers and colonies resulting in the development of new forms of governance, see Paul Rabinow, *French Modern: Norms and Forms of the Social Environment* (Cambridge: MIT Press, 1989); Nikolas Rose, *Powers of Freedom: Reframing Political Thought* (New York: Cambridge University Press, 1999), 110–11; Ann Laura Stoler, *Race and the Education of Desire: Foucault's* History of Sexuality *and the Colonial Order of Things* (Durham, N.C.: Duke University Press, 1995). On comparative methodology, Alasdair MacIntyre's essay "Is a Science of Comparative Politics Possible?" in *Against the Self-Images of the Age* (New York: Schocken Books, 1971) is still worth reading.

35. Burgess, *Political Science and Comparative Constitutional Law*, 60–61.

36. Ibid., 35–37.

37. Ibid., 37–39.

38. Ibid., 40.

39. Ibid., 177. Elsewhere, Burgess argues that it is "doubtless true, as a principle of political science, that the same fullness of civil liberty, as well as of political liberty, is not naturally appropriate to all conditions of mankind. . . . [A] larger measure of civil liberty, too, is safe and necessary among highly civilized peoples than among those of lower character and enlightenment." This passage occurs in an essay where Burgess discusses the constitutional implications of U.S. imperial acquisitions. See Burgess, "How May the United States Govern Its Extra-Continental Territory?" *Political Science Quarterly* 14 (1899): 14.

40. Johannes Fabian, *Time and the Other* (New York: Columbia University Press, 1983). For a discussion of how dialogue implies a relation of equality that can undermine hierarchy, see Jacques Rancière, *Dis-agreement: Politics and Philosophy*, trans. Julie Rose (Minneapolis: University of Minnesota Press, 1999).

41. Burgess, *Political Science and Comparative Constitutional Law*, 61.

42. Ibid., 45.

43. Ibid., 46–47.

44. Ibid., 42–43.

45. Ibid., 43.

46. Ibid., 54–55.

47. Ibid., 81–82.

48. Ibid., 45.

49. John Burgess, *Reconstruction and the Constitution* (New York: Charles Scribner's Sons, 1902), 244–45. Elsewhere Burgess maintains the same position: "American Indians, Asiatics and Africans cannot properly form any active, directive part of the political population which shall be able to produce modern political institutions and ideals. They have no element of political civilization to contribute. They can only receive, learn, follow Aryan example." Thus, he argues that attempts to "pollute" America with "non-Aryan elements" is a sin of the "highest order," since the American commonwealth, though national in its origin, is transcendent in its mission. See Burgess, "The Ideal of the American Commonwealth," *Political Science Quarterly* 10 (1895): 406–7.

50. For a discussion of Woodrow Wilson in the context of World War I's racial formation, see Michael Rogin, *Ronald Reagan, The Movie and Other Episodes in Political Demonology* (Berkeley: University of California Press, 1987), chap. 7.

51. Arthur Link, *Wilson: The Road to the White House* (Princeton: Princeton University Press, 1947), 12–17, 32.

52. Walter Bagehot, *Physics and Politics* (New York: Alfred Knopf, 1948), 161.

53. Ibid., 172, 175, 180–81.

54. Woodrow Wilson, "Character of Democracy in the United States," *An Old Master and Other Political Essays* (New York: Charles Scribner's Sons, 1893), 114, 116–17.

55. Ibid., 117–18.

56. Ibid., 118.

57. John Burgess, *Recent Changes in American Constitutional Theory* (New York: Columbia University Press, 1923), 13.

58. Ibid., 24–26.

59. Burgess, "Ideal of the American Commonwealth," 406.

60. Robert Goldstein, *Political Repression in Modern America* (Cambridge: Schenkmann, 1978), 28–30, 38–40; John Higham, *Strangers in the Land: Patterns of American Nativism, 1860–1925*, 2d ed. (New Brunswick, N.J.: Rutgers University Press, 1977), 49.

61. Sidney Fine, "Anarchism and the Assassination of McKinley," *American Historical Review* 60 (1955): 788–89; Higham, *Strangers in the Land*, 111–12. It is important to note that there is some question of Czolgosz's sanity.

62. Murray, *Red Scare*, 266; Higham, *Strangers in the Land*, 312–24.

63. David Kairys, "Freedom of Speech," in *The Politics of Law: A Progressive Critique*, 2d ed. (New York: Pantheon, 1990).

64. William Preston, *Aliens and Dissenters: Federal Suppression of Radicals, 1903–1933* (New York: Harper, 1966), 82, 99.

65. Murray, *Red Scare*, 196.

66. Murray, *Red Scare*, 219. Racial theories of the late nineteenth and early twentieth centuries visually fix on various physical traits like cranial structure and then infer qualities like intelligence from these outward traits. Prescott Hall, for example, uses similar terminology to describe likely effects of the influx of immigrants from southern and eastern Europe: "[T]he most likely effects of the change in immigration will be as follows: the skull will become more of the brachiocephalic type, the average stature will be lower and the average complexion will be darker." See Hall, *Immigration* (New York: Henry Holt, 1906), 105. On skulls, faces, and the history of racial thinking, see Cornell West, *Prophesy Deliverance!* (Philadelphia: Westminster Press, 1982), chap. 2. Michael J. Shapiro discusses racial presumptions within Progressive thought, and the use of visual racism that fixes on skulls and brows specifically, in his discussion of E. A. Ross in *Cinematic Political Thought: Narrating Race, Nation, and Gender* (New York: New York University Press, 1999), 41–44.

67. Murray, *Red Scare*, 184.

68. William T. Hornaday, *Awake! America: Object Lessons and Warnings* (New York: Moffat, Yard, 1918) (published under the auspices of the American Defense Society), 106; Higham, *Strangers in the Land*, 199.

69. Ibid., xi.

70. Ibid., 120, 128. In chapter 6 I explore the intersection between race and sexuality and its relationship with the perception of "free speech."

71. Ibid., 180.

72. Richard Mayo Smith, *Emigration and Immigration: A Study in Social Science* (New York: Charles Scribner's Sons, 1890), 88, 91.

73. Prescott Hall, *Immigration* (New York: Henry Holt, 1906), 38–39, 99.

74. Ibid., 101, 103.

75. Ibid., 156, citation omitted.

76. Ibid., 183, citation omitted.

77. Ibid., 273.

78. Ibid., 278.

79. The literacy test was a controversial issue for a quarter century, and it finally became law over Wilson's veto in February of 1917. Henry Cabot Lodge was a key proponent of this measure as a member of Congress who worked closely with the Immigration Restriction League. Lodge nicely illustrates the power-knowledge nexus I have been exploring here, since he received Harvard's first Ph.D. in Political Science, writing on Anglo-Saxon law. He made use of his Anglo-Saxon-centered racism in his advocacy for the literacy test. On passage of the liter-

acy test, see Higham, *Strangers in the Land*, 203. On Henry Cabot Lodge, see ibid., 96, 102, and passim; Edward N. Saveth, *American Historians and European Immigrants 1875–1925* (New York: Columbia University Press, 1948), 51–64; and Henry Cabot Lodge, "The Restriction of Immigration," *North American Review* 152 (January 1891) and "Lynch Law and Unrestricted Immigration," *North American Review* 152 (May 1891).

80. Burgess, *Reminiscences of an American Scholar*, 103–4.

81. Rose, *Powers of Freedom*, chap. 6, reviews both the critical and the optimistic literatures on the sociopolitical use of numbers in order to emphasize the positive aspects of statistics. On the influence of survey design upon its responses, see W. Lance Bennett, *Public Opinion in American Politics* (New York: Harcourt Brace Jovanovich, 1980). On the longer term influence of surveys upon respondents (panel conditioning), see Larry Bartels, "Panel Effects in the American National Election Studies," *Political Analysis* 8 (2000): 1–20. On the association of population and statistics, see also Michel Foucault, "Governmentality," in *Power*, ed. James Faubion, vol. 3 of *Essential Works of Foucault, 1954–1984*, (New York: New Press, 2000): 215–17; David Theo Goldberg, *Racial Subjects: Writing on Race in America* (New York: Routledge, 1997), chap. 3.

82. John Wigmore, "Abrams v. U.S.: Freedom of Speech and Freedom of Thuggery in War-Time and Peace-Time," *Illinois Law Review* (1920): 541. See generally Thomas Lawrence, "Eclipse of Liberty: Civil Liberties in the United States during the First World War," *Wayne Law Review* 21 (1974): 33–112.

83. Wigmore, "Abrams v. U.S.," 543.

84. Ibid., 553, 561.

85. Woodrow Wilson, September 2, 1916, in *The New Democracy: Presidential Messages, Addresses, and Other Papers, 1913–1917*, ed. Ray Stannard Baker and William E. Dodd, vol. 2 (New York: Harper and Brothers, 1926), 283. This is consistent with Wilson's perspective on political dissent and the problems immigration posed when he was an academic. In 1893, Wilson described the "anarchic turbulence" to America brought on by immigration, and the problems for "Saxon habits in government" when the nation's "temperate blood" suffered the "corruption of foreign blood." See Wilson, "Character of Democracy," 122, 126, 128.

86. *Gitlow v. New York* 268 U.S. 652 (1925). For a discussion of the process by which most of the Bill of Rights was held to be "incorporated" within the Due Process Clause of the Fourteenth Amendment, see Gerald Gunther and Kathleen Sullivan, *Constitutional Law*, 13th ed. (Westbury, N.Y.: Foundation Press, 1997), chap. 7.

87. Laurence Tribe, *American Constitutional Law*, 2d ed. (Mineola, N.Y.: Foundation Press, 1988); Gunther and Sullivan, *Constitutional Law*.

88. Westel Woodbury Willoughby, *The Constitutional Law of the United States*, vol. 2 (New York: Baker, Voorhis, 1910), 842–44.

89. Kairys, "Freedom of Speech," 237.

90. Burgess, "Uncle Sam!" in *Reminiscences of an American Scholar*, 397–98.

91. Chafee discusses the 1906 act in chap. 11, sec. 2. The act is listed on p. 573. Zechariah Chafee Jr., *Free Speech in the United States* (Cambridge: Harvard University Press, 1941).

92. Preston, *Aliens and Dissenters*, 67–73.

93. Higham, *Strangers in the Land*, 218. On Grant as vice-president of the Immigration Restriction League, see Gossett, *Race*, 354.

94. Higham, *Strangers in the Land*, 201.

95. John Burgess, "Germany, Great Britain, and the United States," *Political Science Quarterly* 19 (1904): 2–5, 14–16.

96. Ibid., 18–19.

97. John Burgess, "The Present Crisis in Europe" (New York: German American Literary Defense Committee and Geo. J. Speyer and Co., 1914).

98. John Burgess, "Our Interest in the War," *Germany's Just Cause*, Memorial Library, University of Wisconsin, Madison, Cutter Collection FO 814 .G31, c. 1914. In addition to this and an essay describing the causes of the war, Burgess also contributed a favorable biography of the Kaiser to the pamphlet.

99. Higham, *Strangers in the Land*, 271.

100. Hornaday, *Awake! America*, 156.

101. Both Bruce Ackerman's *We the People: Foundations* (Cambridge: Harvard University Press, 1991) and Cass Sunstein's *The Partial Constitution* (Cambridge: Harvard University Press, 1993) recognize that the U.S. Constitution makes the American people sovereign and consider this insight as mediating, to some degree, the debate in political and legal theory between liberalism and civic republicanism, suggesting that the U.S. system contains the best of both worlds. What these two scholars of law and politics do not consider are the biopolitical implications of making the *people* sovereign—implications that Burgess does not shy from engaging in his own work.

102. On technologies of government, see Andrew Barry, Thomas Osborne, and Nikolas Rose, Introduction, in *Foucault and Political Reason: Liberalism, Neoliberalism, and Rationalities of Government*, ed. Barry, Osborne, and Rose. (Chicago: University of Chicago Press, 1996): 1; see also Pat O'Malley, "Risk and Responsibility," in ibid., 189ff.

103. As we have seen, Teutonic origins theory was closely connected with political action during this era: Hornaday was linked to the American Defense Society; the Teutonic historian John Fiske and Prescott Hall were linked to the Immigration Restriction League; Henry Cabot Lodge, who received Harvard's first Ph.D. in political science writing on Anglo-Saxon law, was a member of Congress who strongly supported immigration restriction and the literacy test; and Woodrow Wilson was president of the United States. Not only is Burgess an important Teutonic origins theorist, but his work also directly influenced governance. Future president Theodore Roosevelt was his student, and his main work

of constitutional law was used as a handbook for governance by Sanford Dole when he deposed Queen Liliuokalani in Hawaii and the United States refused to recognize those who overthrew the government. In fact, Dole even sought advise for governing from Burgess in correspondence. See Sanford Dole and John Burgess, "Letters of Sanford B. Dole and John W. Burgess," ed. Henry Miller Madden, *Pacific Historical Review* 5 (1936): 71–75. Burgess responded to Dole's query with a numerical description of the racial breakdown in Hawaii, and then got right to the point: "I understand your problem to be the construction of a constitution which will place the government in the hands of the Teutons, and preserve it there, at least for the present" (73).

104. Michel Foucault, "The Subject and Power," *Critical Inquiry* 8 (1982): 777, 789.

105. Ibid., 790. Foucault's translator Leslie Sawyer notes that Foucault plays on the double meaning of the French verb *conduire*, "to lead" or "to drive," and *se conduire*, "to behave" or "to conduct oneself" (789).

106. Michel Foucault, "The Birth of Biopolitics," in *Ethics: Subjectivity, and Truth*, ed. Paul Rabinow, vol. 1 of *Essential Works of Michel Foucault, 1954–1984*, (New York: New Press, 1997), 73, 75.

107. Foucault, "Governmentality," 201, 219–20. The attentive reader will notice the slippage in Foucault's terminology from "The Birth of Biopolitics," where he refers to "society" as the end of government, to "Governmentality," where he refers to "population" as the end of government. I have remarked on this slippage in the work of those continuing the Foucauldian project in "Governing Sexuality: The Supreme Court's Shift to Containment," in *Between Law and Culture: Relocating Legal Studies*, ed., David Theo Goldberg, Michael Musheno, and Lisa Bower (Minneapolis: University of Minnesota Press, 2001). For a critical discussion of "governmentality" in the context of legal studies, see also Alan Hunt and Gary Wickham, *Foucault and Law: Towards a New Sociology of Law as Governance* (London: Pluto Press, 1994).

108. Burgess, *Political Science and Comparative Constitutional Law*, 53.

109. Ibid., 57.

110. Ibid., 178–83.

111. Ibid., 40–45.

112. Ibid., 56. For a more complex analysis of the relationship between freedom and power, see Graham Burchell, "Liberal Government and Techniques of the Self," in Barry, Osborne, and Rose, *Foucault and Political Reason*, 19ff.; Vikki Bell, "The Promise of Liberalism and the Performance of Freedom," in ibid., 81ff.; and Rose, *Powers of Freedom*.

113. Burgess, *Political Science and Comparative Constitutional Law*, 174–77, 88.

114. Ibid., 39.

115. Ibid., 82.

116. Ibid., 86–87.

117. Ibid., 87–88.

118. Ibid., 87–88, emphasis in original.

119. Michel Foucault, *Discipline and Punish: The Birth of the Prison* (New York: Vintage, 1979); *The History of Sexuality*, vol. 1 (New York: Vintage, 1990).

120. Burgess, "Uncle Sam!" p. 386.

121. Ibid., 390.

122. Ibid., 388.

123. And for that matter, this formulation misrepresents Wilson's thought as well—Wilson is praising free speech, framed as "government by discussion," in his essay "Character of Democracy." I take up the current revival of "government by discussion" in chapter 6.

124. James Wilson, "James Wilson's Opening Address," in *The Debate on the Constitution: Federalist and Anti-Federalist Speeches, Articles, and Letters during the Struggle over Ratification*, pt. 1 (New York: Library of America, 1993), 791; Ackerman, *We the People*.

NOTES TO CHAPTER 3

1. Michael J. Shapiro, "Moral Geographies and the Ethics of Post-Sovereignty," *Public Culture* 6 (1994): 479–502.

2. Mill's position that it is through the "collision of adverse opinions that the remainder of the truth has any chance of being supplied," has an echo in U.S. First Amendment doctrine through Justice Holmes's dissent in *Abrams*, when he states that "the best test of truth is the power of the thought to get itself accepted in the competition of the market." *Abrams v. United States* 250 U.S. 616 (1919). Another moment in the First Amendment canon that exemplifies the Millian paradigm is Justice Brandeis's famous concurring opinion in *Whitney v. California*, 274 U.S. 357 (1927).

3. Zechariah Chafee Jr., *Free Speech in the United States* (Cambridge: Harvard University Press, 1941), 30.

4. Ibid., 31.

5. Ibid., 33.

6. John Stuart Mill, "On Liberty," in *Three Essays*, ed. Richard Wollheim (New York: Oxford University Press, 1975), 65.

7. Chafee, *Free Speech in the United States*, 33.

8. Ibid., 29. Chafee cites 1 Kohler, *Lehrbuch des bürgerlichen Rechts*, vol. 1, sec. 38 as authority for this argument.

9. Chafee, *Free Speech in the United States*, 30, citing *Gompers v. U.S.* 233 U.S. 604 (1914).

10. Chafee, *Free Speech in the United States*, 107.

11. Ibid., 273.

12. Ibid., 149–50; see also Zechariah Chafee Jr., *Freedom of Speech* (New York: Harcourt, Brace and Howe, 1920), 169–71; *Chaplinsky v. New Hampshire* 315 U.S. 568 (1942) (defining categories such as "fighting words" to be outside First Amendment protection). Although the *Abrams* dissent, *Whitney* concurrence, and *Chaplinsky* opinions clearly resonate with the Millian paradigm, other legal opinions directly cite Mill—cf. *New York Times v. Sullivan* 376 U.S. 254 (1964).

13. *United States v. Carolene Products* 304 U.S. 144 (1938). C. Herman Pritchett, *The American Constitution* (New York: McGraw-Hill, 1977), 305–8, discusses the preferred position doctrine in the context of the First Amendment.

14. Robert McKay, "The Preference for Freedom," *New York University Law Review* 34 (1959): 1188.

15. Ibid., 1185–88.

16. Other examples that focus on the First Amendment as particularly important among a small subset of preferred freedoms include Edmund Cahn, "The Firstness of the First Amendment," *Yale Law Journal* 65 (1956): 464, and Justice Hugo Black, "The Bill of Rights," *New York Law Review* 35 (1960): 865. Cahn's essay speculates on the causes of the "unified, organic text" of the Bill of Rights— "Whether it was the arm of destiny or the finger of partisanship or only the impulse of professional competence"—but he also uses an evolutionary perspective to describe the American national identity because whatever the cause might have been, "the forces he [Robert Sherman] set moving in the summer of 1789 are more active and prominent today than ever" (470). In his Bill of Rights lecture, Black makes absolutely explicit what was an implicit assumption during his interview with Cahn. He discusses the amendments in reverse order, starting from the Tenth in order to climax at the First, and concludes that the "First Amendment is truly at the heart of the Bill of Rights" (881).

17. R. George Wright, "A Rationale from J. S. Mill for the Free Speech Clause," *Supreme Court Review* 1985 (1986): 149–78. Wright is writing at a time when it seemed clear that legal precedent dictated that nude dancing was protected by the First Amendment, despite his displeasure on this point (164–65). Wright argues that if the "'message' of commercial nude dancing is so shadowy and equivocal, however, it is too attenuated and insubstantial significantly to implicate Millian values. . . . A claim of free speech protection for a given activity may 'trivialize' the Free Speech Clause because of the Millian pointlessness of the activity, and not because the activity is judged immoral, or harmful, or lewd, or misleading" (166; citations omitted). Wright must be relieved at the recent turn of events regarding the Supreme Court's treatment of nude dancing. See chapter 6.

18. Harry Kalven Jr., *A Worthy Tradition*, ed. Jamie Kalven (New York: Harper and Row, 1988); Thomas Scanlon, "A Theory of Freedom of Expression," *Philosophy and Public Affairs* 1 (1972): 204–26; Murray Dry, "Free Speech in Political Philosophy and Its Relation to American Constitutional Law: A Consideration of Mill, Meiklejohn, and Plato," *Constitutional Commentary* 11 (1994): 81–100.

19. John Adams, "Dissertation on the Canon and the Feudal Law," in *The Works of John Adams*, ed. Charles Francis Adams, vol. 3 (Boston: Little and Brown, 1851), 447–64; Mill, "On Liberty" 28.

20. Jacques Derrida, *Of Grammatology*, trans. Gayatri Chakravorty Spivak (Baltimore: Johns Hopkins University Press, 1976).

21. The logic of censorship is usually based upon this model of consciousness as well. Censorship makes sense if one is attempting to prevent consciousness or reason from becoming contaminated by some biasing force. For an example of this, see Herbert Marcuse, "Repressive Tolerance," *A Critique of Pure Tolerance* (Boston: Beacon Press, 1970), 81–123.

22. Cf. Michael J. Shapiro, *Reading the Postmodern Polity: Political Theory as Textual Practice* (Minneapolis: University of Minnesota Press, 1992).

23. *Paris Adult Theatre I v. Slaton* 413 U.S. 49 (1973) (upholding state efforts to bar distribution of obscenity to consenting adults); *Roth v. United States* 352 U.S. 964 (1957), *Miller v. California* 413 U.S. 15 (1973) (cases defining obscenity standards).

24. Frederick Schauer, "Speech and 'Speech'—Obscenity and 'Obscenity': An Exercise in the Interpretation of Constitutional Language," *Georgetown Law Review* 67 (1979): 899–933.

25. *Barnes v. Glen Theatre* 501 U.S. 560 (1991); *Pap's A.M. v. City of Erie* 529 U.S. 277 (2000).

26. Derrida, *Of Grammatology*.

27. Edward Said, *Orientalism* (New York: Vintage, 1979), 211, 216; see also Edward Said, *Culture and Imperialism* (New York: Alfred A. Knopf, 1993).

28. Nicholas K. Blomley, *Law, Space, and the Geographies of Power* (New York: Guilford Press, 1994), 41, 51–52.

29. John Stuart Mill, "Considerations on Representative Government," *Three Essays*, 266. Further references to Mill's essays will be placed within the text. "On Liberty," abbreviated as OL, and "Representative Government," abbreviated as RG, are both found in *Three Essays*. "The Spirit of the Age" (SA), "Civilization" (Civ), "Tocqueville on Democracy in America, vol I" (T, I), "Tocqueville on Democracy in America, vol. II" (T, II), and "A Few Words on Non-Intervention" (NI) are all found in *Essays on Politics and Culture*, ed. Gertrude Himmelfarb (New York: Doubleday, 1962). "The East India Company's Charter," (testimony before the Select Committee of the House of Lords, June 21 and 22, 1852) is found in *Writings on India*, ed. J. M. Robson, M. Moir, and Z. Moir (Toronto: University of Toronto Press, 1990), and will be abbreviated as WI.

30. Mill's use of "spontaneous" suggests that European nations were able to progress independently, while non-Europe has needed to be stimulated by the presence of Europeans. Support for this comes from "On Liberty," where he argues that if China is to progress, then it will have to be at the hands of foreigners.

31. There is "no danger," Mill then adds, "of the prevalence of democracy in Syria or Timbuctoo" (Civ, 60).

32. This passage provides some support for Benedict Anderson's argument in *Imagined Communities* (New York: Verso, 1991), showing the historical linkage between print capitalism and modern nationalism.

33. This move is due to the position that a sense of history is associated with a belief in the openness of social phenomena to rational comprehension. This presents phenomena as open to study of cause and effect, and once this knowledge is mastered, events then become amenable to human intervention and control. Cf. J. G. A. Pocock, *The Machiavellian Moment: Florentine Political Thought and the Atlantic Republican Tradition* (Princeton: Princeton University Press, 1975).

34. Shapiro, *Reading the Postmodern Polity*.

35. *Bethel School District v. Fraser* 106 S. Ct. 3159, 3163–64.

36. Anne McClintock, *Imperial Leather: Race, Gender, and Sexuality in the Colonial Contest* (New York: Routledge, 1995).

37. *Whitney v. California* 274 U.S. 357 (1927) (Brandeis concurring).

38. Wright, "A Rationale from J. S. Mill," 161.

39. Thomas Spragens, *The Irony of Liberal Reason* (Chicago: University of Chicago Press, 1981), chap. 9.

40. Samuel Huntington, "The Clash of Civilizations?" *Foreign Affairs* 72 (1993): 22–49.

41. *Miller v. Civil City of South Bend* 904 F.2d 1081 (7th Cir. 1990) (Posner concurring).

42. Samuel Beer, *To Make a Nation* (Cambridge: Harvard University Press, 1993), 66, 401–2.

43. Jonathan Rauch, *Kindly Inquisitors: The New Attacks on Free Thought* (Chicago: University of Chicago Press, 1993), 12, 26–27.

44. Ibid., 22 and passim.

45. Ibid., 20–21.

46. Geoffrey Bennington, *Legislations: The Politics of Deconstruction* (New York: Verso, 1994).

47. This is consistent with my attention in the previous chapter to the late-nineteenth- and early-twentieth-century racialization of what we consider today to be class politics.

NOTES TO CHAPTER 4

1. Nicholas Blomley and Gordon Clark, "Law, Theory, and Geography," *Urban Geography* 11 (1990): 433; W. Wesley Pue, "Wrestling with the Law: (Geographical) Specificity vs. (Legal) Abstraction," *Urban Geography* 11 (1990): 566. I contest

this view of modern law in Paul A. Passavant, "Enchantment, Aesthetics, and the Superficial Powers of Modern Law," *Law and Society Review* 35 (2001): 601–22.

2. Nat Hentoff, *Free Speech for Me but Not for Thee* (New York: Harper, 1992).

3. Peter Fitzpatrick, "Law, Plurality, and Underdevelopment," in *Legality, Ideology, and the State*, ed. David Sugarman (New York: Academic Press, 1983); Passavant, "Enchantment, Aesthetics, and the Superficial Powers of Modern Law."

4. Blomley and Clark, "Law, Theory, and Geography"; Nicholas Blomley, *Law, Space, and the Geographies of Power* (New York: Guilford Press, 1994).

5. Productive efforts to study the problem of law and geography from which I have learned include Blomley, *Law, Space, and the Geographies of Power*; Ruth Buchanan, "Border Crossings: NAFTA, Regulatory Restructuring, and the Politics of Place," *Indiana Journal of Global Legal Studies* 2 (1995): 371; Eve Darian-Smith, *Bridging Divides: The Channel Tunnel and English Legal Identity in the New Europe* (Berkeley: University of California Press, 1999); Peter Fitzpatrick, *The Mythology of Modern Law* (New York: Routledge, 1992); Richard Ford, "The Boundaries of Race: Political Geography in Legal Analysis," *Harvard Law Review* 107 (1994): 1841; Bill Maurer, "Law, Writing, Immigration, and Globalization in the British Virgin Islands," *Indiana Journal of Global Legal Studies* 2 (1995): 413; Boaventura de Sousa Santos, "Law: A Map of Misreading: Toward a Postmodern Conception of Law," *Journal of Law and Society* 14 (1987): 279.

6. William Connolly, *The Ethos of Pluralization* (Minneapolis: University of Minnesota Press, 1995), xxiii, citing in part the *Oxford English Dictionary*.

7. Paul Carter, *The Road to Botany Bay* (Chicago: University of Chicago Press, 1987), 62.

8. Michael Shapiro, "Moral Geographies and the Ethics of Post-Sovereignty," *Public Culture* 6 (1994): 479.

9. John Stuart Mill, "A Few Words on Non-Intervention," in *Essays on Politics and Culture*, ed. Gertrude Himmelfarb (New York: Doubleday, 1962).

10. Peter Goodrich, *Languages of Law* (London: Weidenfeld and Nicolson, 1990), 296.

11. Michael Shapiro is well known for staging confrontations and juxtapositions for similar purposes. For instance, in *Cinematic Political Thought: Narrating Race, Nation, and Gender* (New York: New York University Press, 1999), he not only creates such confrontations but examines cinematically produced juxtapositions and their political effects as well.

12. As the controversy over *The Satanic Verses* circulated in Great Britain, it was understood to raise issues of multiculturalism in addition to free speech. In the United States, the controversy was understood to raise the issue of free speech almost exclusively.

13. *Dennis v. United States* 341 U.S. 494 (1951).

14. Michael Rogin, *Ronald Reagan, The Movie and other episodes in political demonology* (Berkeley: University of California Press, 1987), uses a periodized de-

monology to understand U.S. national politics and the significance of the cold war for post–World War II American politics.

15. Michael Omi and Howard Winant, *Racial Formation in the United States* (New York: Routledge, 1986); Edward Carmines, Robert Huckfeldt, and Carl Mc-Curley, "Mobilization, Countermobilization, and the Politics of Race," *Political Geography* 14 (1995), 601–19; Sidney Blumenthal, *Pledging Allegiance: The Last Campaign of the Cold War* (New York: Harper Collins, 1990).

16. Mary Dudziak, *Cold War Civil Rights: Race and the Image of American Democracy* (Princeton: Princeton University Press, 2000).

17. Brief for the United States, *Brown v. Board of Education*, in *Landmark Briefs and Arguments of the Supreme Court of the United States: Constitutional Law*, ed. Philip Kurland and Gerhard Casper (Bethesda, Md.: University Publications of America, 1954 and 1955), vol. 49, pp. 2–3 (emphasis added in first two quotes; references omitted).

18. Ibid., 5–6, citing President's Committee on Civil Rights, *To Secure These Rights* (New York: Simon and Schuster, 1947), 89, 95. Taylor Branch, *Parting the Waters: America in the King Years, 1954–63* (New York: Simon and Schuster, 1988), makes an interesting observation in the course of his analysis of the Truman administration's civil rights report that is fully consistent with the analysis of this project. He notes that with the publication of this civil rights report, public discourse registered its significance by shifting its conceptualization of the issue from the "Negro problem" to one of "civil rights" (66). Within my framework, when the question began to be defined in terms of the rights of Americans (as opposed to a social problem––Negroes—that plagues Americans), it lent standing to those claiming rights as well as legitimacy for their claims.

19. Brief for the United States, *Brown v. Board of Education*, 6.

20. Ibid., 7.

21. Ibid., 8.

22. Branch, *Parting the Waters*, 113.

23. Cited in ibid., 138–39, emphasis added.

24. I use the term "nonracial" with some trepidation out of fear that my remarks could become grist for the mills of current legal practices that seem to suffer severely from historical amnesia regarding past racial practices in the United States.

25. Ibid., emphasis added. In his book *The Hollow Hope* (Chicago: University of Chicago Press, 1991), Gerald Rosenberg argues that the impact of Supreme Court decisions is minimal. He also makes the *Brown* decision and segregation one of his case studies. Rosenberg's position is challenged by Michael McCann, *Rights at Work: Pay Equity Reform and the Politics of Legal Mobilization* (Chicago: University of Chicago Press, 1994), who argues that a more subtle understanding of the uses, effects, and meaning of law is required than Rosenberg employs. In his own work, McCann finds that court decisions do have an impact on rights and

social practices. King's speech here, coming only a year after the *Brown* decision, lends support for McCann's argument. Here, we can see how the *Brown* decision was given immediate circulation, and how King used it to mobilize citizens to protest for their rights. Not only was their struggle successful, but the boycott brought King and Montgomery international attention, catapulting King to the forefront of the civil rights movement ahead of many more established activists, as well as acting as an important stimulus for the rest of the civil rights movement. In fact, subsequent protests would be organized on the anniversary of the *Brown* decision. In his speech at the Prayer Pilgrimage for Freedom on the third anniversary of the *Brown* decision, King mentioned the Supreme Court's decision in his first sentence.

26. Martin Luther King Jr., "Give Us the Ballot—We Will Transform the South," in *A Testament of Hope: The Essential Writings and Speeches of Martin Luther King, Jr.*, ed. James Washington (New York: Harper Collins, 1991), 197

27. Ibid., 197–98.

28. Ibid., 199.

29. King, "If the Negro Wins, Labor Wins," in *Testament of Hope*, 201, 203, 207.

30. Ibid., 206; 202.

31. King, "The American Dream," in ibid., 208, 215. King also uses religion effectively in this and other speeches, arguing that God is interested in the freedom of the whole human race, and not particular races. Religion, as a discourse with universal aspirations and a basis in belief rather than population typologies, can be an effective antiracial intervention.

32. My impression of King's later speeches is that the nation as well as race lost its validity as a foundation for rights, suggesting the importance of returning to these later efforts for the sake of justice today. Having said this, we must also note that King tempered his national perspective with a sensitivity to global issues early in the civil rights struggle.

33. King, "If the Negro Wins, Labor Wins," 207, emphasis added.

34. John Brigham, *The Constitution of Interests* (New York: New York University Press, 1996).

35. Cf. King, "I Have a Dream," in *Testament of Hope*, 217.

36. King, "American Dream," 208. In another context, King's use of the masculine pronoun might be scrutinized for its role in upholding a masculinist national public sphere.

37. King, "Give Us the Ballot," 197.

38. Cited in Branch, *Parting the Waters*, 196

39. Here I am thinking of how the meaning of a mark arrives through a process of iteration and citation, and that citation or reiteration helps to determine the success of a performative speech act such as a claim about the law. King is seeking to generate and secure the context that will allow *Brown* to signify the legal obligation of equality and inclusion for blacks in the American public. See

Jacques Derrida, "Signature, Event, Context," *Limited Inc.* (Evanston, Ill.: Northwestern University Press, 1988); Judith Butler, *Bodies That Matter* (New York: Routledge, 1993), 14.

40. King, "American Dream," 208.

41. King, "I Have a Dream," in *Testament of Hope*, 217.

42. Ibid., 219.

43. King, "American Dream," 214.

44. Ibid., 216.

45. King, "I Have a Dream," 219.

46. Ibid., 219–20.

47. In other words, to "hail" them in an Althusserian sense in order to interpellate then within this dream. See Louis Althusser, "Ideology and Ideological State Apparatuses," in *Lenin and Philosophy and Other Essays*, trans. Ben Brewster (New York: Monthly Review Press, 1971).

48. J. L. Austin, *How to Do Things with Words* (Cambridge: Harvard University Press, 1962).

49. Branch, *Parting the Waters*, 144, 182, 564, 596–97.

50. "The Nation," *Time*, August 4, 1967, 12–21, 16, 18; "The Nation," *Time*, August 11, 1967, 9–19, 11.

51. "The Nation" *Time*, August 11, 1967, 11; "Who is Really to Blame in the Rioting?" *US News and World Report*, August 7, 1967, 10. Much of the coverage of the "urban riots" of the late 1960s, it should be said, was produced within a racial frame. To take examples from just one edition of one publication, *US News and World Report* (July 31, 1967) published an interview with retired Justice Whittaker, in which he made reference to the survival of "our *civilized* and cultured society" and referred to the United States as a "*civilized* nation" ("Can a Disorderly Society Survive?" 27, emphasis added). Another article within this issue described the cause of the "Plainsfield riot" (New Jersey) as "sheer, *savage* hatred, fanned and exploited by Negroes who are dedicated to war against the white race," according to a "city official" ("The Real Tragedy," 31, emphasis added).

52. Samuel Huntington, "The Clash of Civilizations?" *Foreign Affairs* 72 (1993): 22.

53. Homi Bhabha, *The Location of Culture* (New York: Routledge, 1994).

54. John Fiske, *Reading the Popular* (Winchester, Mass.: Unwin Hyman, 1989), chap. 3; Victor Turner, "Passages, Margins, and Poverty: Religious Symbols of Communitas," *Dramas, Fields, and Metaphors* (Ithaca: Cornell University Press, 1974).

55. Turner, "Passages, Margins, and Poverty," 232.

56. G. Marzorati, "Salman Rushdie: Fiction's Embattled Infidel," *New York Times Magazine*, January 29, 1989, 24 (online: Lexis/Nexis).

57. Ibid.

58. Salman Rushdie, "In Good Faith," *Newsweek*, February 12, 1990, 53.

59. J. Banville, "An Interview with Salman Rushdie," *New York Review of Books*, March 4, 1993, 34.

60. "An Exclusive Talk with Salman Rushdie," *Newsweek*, February 12, 1990, 46–47.

61. Jonathan Rauch, *Kindly Inquisitors: The New Attacks on Free Thought* (Chicago: University of Chicago Press, 1993), 163. It seems odd for Rauch to urge his readers to "fight" in a book that takes aim at the twin evils of religious fundamentalism and "force" and as in favor of "reason." For a discussion of how those who take themselves to be exemplars of rational deliberation rely on force and preemption, see Jodi Dean, *Aliens in America: Conspiracy Cultures from Outerspace to Cyberspace* (Ithaca: Cornell University Press, 1998).

62. Rauch, *Kindly Inquisitors*, 20, emphasis added.

63. Salman Rushdie, *The Satanic Verses* (Dover, Del.: Consortium, 1992), 6.

64. Bernard Bailyn, *The Ideological Origins of the American Revolution* (Cambridge: Harvard University Press, 1967), 49 n. 37.

65. H. Trevor Colbourn, *The Lamp of Experience: Whig History and the Intellectual Origins of the American Revolution* (Chapel Hill: University of North Carolina Press, 1965).

66. John Adams, "Dissertation on the Canon and the Feudal Law"(1765), in *The Works of John Adams*, ed. Charles F. Adams, vol. 3 (Boston: Little and Brown, 1851), 462.

67. Rushdie, *Satanic Verses*, 132–40.

68. Rauch, *Kindly Inquisitors*, 21, 12, emphasis added.

69. "Talk of the Town: Notes and Comment," *New Yorker*, March 6, 1989, 27; M. Peretz, "Embroiled Salman," *New Republic*, March 20, 1989, 50.

70. B. Crozier, "Islamic Wasteland," *National Review*, March 24, 1989, 17, emphasis added; R. Rosenblatt, "Zealots with Fear in Their Eyes," *US News and World Report*, February 27, 1989, 10; P. Berman, "What the West Learned about the East (and the West) in the Rushdie Affair," *New Republic*, October 8, 1990, 37.

71. On Orientalism, see Edward Said, *Orientalism* (New York: Vintage, 1979).

72. Patrick Buchanan, "Clinton-Rushdie Session Puts Americans at Risk" (editorial), *Houston Chronicle*, December 3, 1993, 37A (online: Lexis/Nexis), emphasis added.

73. Leslie Gelb, "Rushdie's Death Foretold" (editorial), *New York Times*, December 29, 1991, sec 4, p. 9 (online: Lexis/Nexis) (emphasis added).

74. "Two Cheers for Blasphemy" (editorial), *New Republic*, March 13, 1989, 7.

75. Midge Decter, "The Rushdiad," *Commentary*, June 1989, 22; M. Peretz, "Embroiled Salman," *New Republic*, March 20, 1989, 50.

76. Roger Rosenblatt, "Zealots with Fear in Their Eyes," *US News and World Report*, February 27, 1989, 8, 10.

77. "Midnight's Conversion" (editorial), *New Republic*, January 21, 1991, 10, emphasis added.

78. For being a Muslim?

79. "Midnight's Conversion," 10.

80. Bhabha, *Location of Culture*, 2, 5.

81. Peretz, "Embroiled Salman," 50.

82. B. Parker, "Stanford Seeks Only to Curb Insulting Epithets; Free Speech Threat" (letter), *New York Times*, May 17, 1989, 26A (online: Lexis/Nexis); E. Cherney, "Where the Chicago Flag and Rushdie Affairs Differ" (letter), *New York Times*, April 4, 1989, 26A (online: Lexis/Nexis); I. Wilkerson, "Veterans Protest Flag Exhibit at Art Institute," *New York Times*, March 2, 1989, 19A (online: Lexis/Nexis).

83. J. Lindsay, "Threat to Arts Is a Threat to All Our Freedoms" (editorial), *New York Times*, August 11, 1989, 26A (online: Lexis/Nexis); T. Wicker, "In the Nation: Art and Indecency" (editorial), *New York Times*, July 28, 1989, 27A (online: Lexis/Nexis); P. Darrow, "Public Funds Need Not Support Private Tastes; Purse and Sword" (letter), *New York Times*, June 30, 1989, 28A (online: Lexis/Nexis).

84. Jonathan Rauch, "In Defense of Prejudice," *Harpers*, May 1995, 37, 42.

85. Ibid., 46.

86. "The Speech Police," *ABC 20/20* (May 12, 1995) (online: Lexis/Nexis). All quotes from this source.

87. A position that is not "on point" with regard to this case, since Rogers was to be tested on the material in question—the incident occurred in a classroom setting rather than a debating forum.

88. V. N. Vološinov, *Marxism and the Philosophy of Language*, trans. Ladislav Matejka and I. R. Titunik (Cambridge: Harvard University Press, 1986).

89. Geoffrey Bennington, *Legislations: The Politics of Deconstruction* (New York: Verso, 1994).

90. Rushdie, *Satanic Verses*, 53.

91. Within the British identity formation, he might be positioned racially as a "black," contrary to American notions; cf. Stuart Hall, "Signification, Representation, Ideology: Althusser and the Post-structuralist Debates," *Critical Studies in Mass Communication* 2 (1985): 91, 108–9.

92. Rushdie, *Satanic Verses*, 60–61, 132–40.

93. Ibid., 142, 141.

NOTES TO CHAPTER 5

1. Ironically, the exorcisms of the specters of PC have had more staying power than Rushdie's death sentence, see Ian Black, "Rushdie's Nightmare Is Over; Iran Disavows Fatwa and Bounty," *Guardian* September 25, 1998 (online: /Lexis/Nexis). Bill Maher's late night television show *Politically Incorrect* was born during this period and continued to run until recently; and John Leo, a frequent polemicist

against PC during the 1990s, published his book *Incorrect Thoughts: Notes on Our Wayward Culture* in 2000 (New York: Transaction).

2. Karl Klare, "Critical Theory and Labor Relations Law," in *The Politics of Law: A Progressive Critique*, ed. David Kairys, 2d ed. (New York: Pantheon, 1990), 65–67, discusses this paradox. For an overview of cls that emphasizes this question, see Paul A. Passavant, "Critical Legal Studies," in *Legal Systems of the World*, ed. Herbert Kritzer (Santa Barbara: ABC-CLEO, 2002).

3. I shall be concerned only with hate speech regulations promulgated by institutions of the state or federal government, such as the public Universities of Michigan and Wisconsin, since the U.S. Constitution requires only that state or federal governments not violate the right of free speech.

4. National Association of Scholars, "The Wrong Way to Reduce Campus Tensions," in *Beyond PC: Toward a Politics of Understanding*, ed. Patricia Aufderheide (St. Paul, Minn.: Graywolf Press, 1992).

5. Richard Delgado and Jean Stefancic, *Must We Defend the Nazis? Hate Speech, Pornography, and the New First Amendment* (New York: New York University Press, 1997), 46, 69.

6. On the plurality of First Amendment values as opposed to a singular "free speech principle," see Robert Post, *Constitutional Domains* (Cambridge: Harvard University Press, 1995). Other scholars have also emphasized the complexity of First Amendment values when placed in a context of social practice; see Steven Shiffrin, "The First Amendment and Economic Regulation: Away from a General Theory of the First Amendment," *Northwestern University Law Review* 78 (1983): 1212.

7. *Grayned v. City of Rockford*, 408 U.S. 104 (1972) at 116, internal quotations and citations removed, emphasis added.

8. For a discussion premised on the analogy of the university to the workplace, see Mary Ellen Gale, "Reimagining the First Amendment: Racist Speech and Equal Liberty," *St. John's Law Review* 65 (1991): 174; John Shapiro, "The Call for Campus Conduct Policies: Censorship or Constitutionally Permissible Limitations on Speech," *Minnesota Law Review* 75 (1990): 205. For a discussion premised on the idea that the university is the place where speech should be freest, see Henry Hyde and George Fishman, "The Collegiate Speech Protection Act of 1991: A Response to the New Intolerance in the Academy," *Wayne Law Review* 37 (1991): 1469; Benno Schmidt Jr., "False Harmony: The Debate of Freedom of Expression on America's Campuses," *Vital Speeches of the Day* (speech delivered at the Nation Press Club, Washington, D.C., January 4, 1991): 45–48. For a discussion of the significance of the "public forum" to First Amendment jurisprudence, see Harry Kalven Jr., "The Concept of the Public Forum: Cox v. Louisiana," *Supreme Court Review* (1965): 1, and the way that Kenneth Karst builds on Kalven's ideas in Kenneth Karst, "Equality as a Central Principle in the First Amendment," *University of Chicago Law Review* 43 (1975): 20.

9. Amy Gutmann, "Is Freedom Academic? The Relative Autonomy of Universities in a Liberal Democracy," in *Liberal Democracy*, ed. C. J. Roland Pennock and John Chapman (New York: New York University Press, 1983). See also Frank Michelman, "Universities, Racist Speech, and Democracy in America: An Essay for the ACLU," *Harvard Civil Rights-Civil Liberties Law Review* 27 (1992): 339; Shapiro, "Call for Campus Conduct Policies," 202–3 (discussing how the principle of academic freedom requires that courts defer broadly to universities in upholding reasonable regulations).

10. Gutmann, "Is Freedom Academic?"

11. Jonathan Rauch, *Kindly Inquisitors: The New Attacks on Free Thought* (Chicago: University of Chicago Press, 1993), 48–51.

12. This is similar to the argument that Frank Michelman makes against the Hyde bill that proposed to prohibit hate speech codes in places of higher education that receive federal money. See Michelman, "Universities, Racist Speech, and Democracy in America." The argument that striking down a hate speech code enacted by a university violates academic freedom becomes less persuasive to the extent that the campus is not governed democratically or a code is imposed on students who have no voice in university affairs. That said, we should note that a corporate freedom says nothing one way or the other about the methods of governance internal to the corporate body. Therefore, a resort to individualist premises must be made to address this issue of academic freedom and hate speech codes. Some may defend a corporate freedom in the area of higher education as an enactment of group pluralism to provide a marketplace of ideas and to enable choice in the context of diversity (regarding what university to work for or to attend as a student).

13. Cases providing guidance in the area of discrimination and harassment include *Rogers v. Equal Employment Opportunity Commission* 454 F.2d 234 (1971); *Meritor Savings Bank v. Vinson* 477 U.S. 57 (1986); *Robinson v. Jacksonville Shipyards, Inc.* 760 F. Supp. 1486 (M.D. Fla. 1991). In *Connick v. Meyers* 461 U.S. 138 (1983), the Supreme Court found no First Amendment violation when an employee of the city of New Orleans was terminated for raising questions within the office about how the agency was run. Since Sheila Meyers was speaking not as a citizen upon a matter of public concern, but as an employee on a matter of merely personal interest within the office, the termination of Meyers was upheld.

14. *Frisby v. Schultz* 487 U.S. 474 (1988).

15. Cass Sunstein, *Democracy and the Problem of Free Speech* (New York: Free Press, 1993): 199–200.

16. Post, *Constitutional Domains*. See *Board of Education v. Pico* 457 U.S. 853 (1982) (noting permissibility of "educational suitability" as a factor in the removal of books from the school library).

17. *Brown v. State of Louisiana* 86 S. Ct. 719 (1966); see also the discussion of *Brown* in *Grayned v. City of Rockford*. Note the Court's discussion of disruption

while upholding the First Amendment rights of the students protesting the Vietnam War to wear black armbands to school in *Tinker v. Des Moines Independent Community School District* 393 U.S. 503 (1969).

18. *Board of Education v. Pico*.

19. Sunstein, *Democracy and the Problem of Free Speech*, 200–201.

20. *Edwards v. Aguillard* 482 U.S. 578 (1987) struck down a Louisiana state law mandating "equal treatment" for creation "science" and evolution in public school instruction.

21. *Chaplinsky v. New Hampshire* 315 U.S. 568 (1942) excludes from First Amendment protection language directed at another that is either injurious by its very nature or likely to incite an immediate breach of the peace; Kent Greenawalt, *Fighting Words: Individuals, Communities, and Liberties of Speech* (Princeton: Princeton University Press, 1995), discusses how harassment is commonly regulated without violating the First Amendment; *Wisconsin v. Mitchell* 508 U.S. 476 (1993) finds that penalty enhancement laws that increase penalties when crimes are motivated by bias do not violate the First Amendment.

22. On judicial experience with torts, see Richard Delgado, "Words That Wound: A Tort Action for Racial Insults, Epithets, and Name Calling," *Harvard Civil Rights-Civil Liberties Law Review* 17 (1982): 133.

23. *Madsen v. Women's Health Center* 512 U.S. 753 (1994) (upholding in part and striking down in part a Florida state court injunction regulating antiabortion protestors on public streets outside a clinic); *Schenck v. Pro-Choice Network of Western New York* 519 U.S. 357 (1997) (reviewing a federal district court's injunction against antiabortion protestors, upheld fixed buffer zones but struck down floating buffer zones); *Hill v. Colorado* 120 S. Ct. 2480 (2000) (upheld a statute regulating antiabortion protestors).

24. Key to Justice Harlan's Opinion of the Court protecting the rights of the individual wearing a jacket inscribed with the words "Fuck the Draft" was that onlookers could easily turn away from Cohen's jacket and choose not to consume his message. See *Cohen v. California* 403 U.S. 15 (1971). Likewise, when Justice Stevens wrote for the Court in *Reno v. American Civil Liberties Union*, 521 U.S. 844 (1997), he emphasized how the Internet is a virtual public forum and the affirmative steps one needs to take to reach sexual expression in striking down the Communications Decency Act of 1996—in other words, one is not a captive audience to "indecent material," but a willing viewer. In *FCC v. Pacifica Foundation* 438 U.S. 726 (1978), however, the major difference of opinion between the majority upholding disciplinary action against Pacifica for airing George Carlin's "seven dirty words" monologue and the dissenters was over how to describe a listener's relation to broadcast media. The majority argued that broadcast media are uniquely invasive, likening them to an intruder disturbing one's right to be let alone in the home. The dissenters, however, described affirmative acts by the individual who, when listening to broadcast communications, is essentially choosing to enter the

public and can deal with any unwanted messages simply by turning the radio off. In all three of these cases, a key variable is whether the individual can choose not to hear a particular message. In *Miami Herald v. Tornillo* 418 U.S. 241 (1974), the Court struck down Florida's right of reply statute because it violated a newspaper's First Amendment right to convey its message through editorial discretion by forcing the paper to publish undesired speech—this case makes more obvious the First Amendment interests of one forced to associate with a message against his or her will (as opposed to some purely private interest). See also *Wooley v. Maynard* 430 U.S. 705 (1977) (protecting the First Amendment rights of a Jehovah's Witness couple not to be turned into a "mobile billboard" by the state of New Hampshire for its motto "Live Free or Die").

25. Paul A. Passavant and Jodi Dean, "Laws and Societies," *Constellations* 8 (2001): 376, 383. There is a long line of Supreme Court precedent recognizing the "public forum" as the space in which one's First Amendment rights are on their strongest grounds and governmental regulations most suspect. For an overview, see Kalven, "Concept of the Public Forum," and Karst, "Equality as a Central Principle in the First Amendment."

26. *Cox v. New Hampshire* 312 U.S. 569 (1941).

27. Charles Lawrence discusses "silencing" in "If He Hollers Let Him Go: Regulating Racist Speech on Campus," *Duke Law Review* 1990 (1990): 431.

28. In the wake of racist incidents on college campuses in the late 1980s and early 1990s, enrollment increased at historically black colleges. Linda Shrieves, "More African Americans Choosing Black Colleges," *Milwaukee Sentinel*, January 14, 1994, 2C.

29. *Young v. American Mini Theatres* 96 S. Ct. 2440 (1976). See also Cass Sunstein, *The Partial Constitution* (Cambridge: Harvard University Press, 1993); Sunstein, *Democracy and the Problem of Free Speech*; and chapter 6 below.

30. Nancy Fraser, "Rethinking the Public Sphere: A Contribution to the Critique of Actually Existing Democracy," in *The Phantom Public Sphere*, ed. Bruce Robbins (Minneapolis: University of Minnesota Press, 1993). Jodi Dean, however, in *Publicity's Secret* (Ithaca, N.Y.: Cornell University Press, 2002), argues that conceptualizing politics around the idea of the public sphere is the problem with politics today.

31. Gutmann, "Is Freedom Academic?"

32. Laurence Tribe, *American Constitutional Law* 2d ed. (Mineola, N.Y.: Foundation Press, 1988), 851–54 (discussing "hostile audiences" and the "heckler's veto").

33. There are other constitutional issues than the First Amendment issues with which I have dealt. I have not focused on equal protection arguments on behalf of hate speech codes, I have not addressed legislative attempts to hold private colleges and universities to the same standards to which public institutions have been held by courts, and I have not focused on the question of how a given code might or might not be administered in accordance with due process of law.

34. "Speech Therapy" (editorial), *New Republic*, July 13 and 20, 1992, 7; "The Speech We Hate," *Progressive* (editorial), August 1992, 8.

35. Hyde and Fishman, "Collegiate Speech Protection Act of 1991," 1472, citing Jerry Adler et al., "Taking Offense, *Newsweek*, December 24, 1990, 48. Emphasis added.

36. Adler et al., "Taking Offense," 48–49; Hyde and Fishman, "Collegiate Speech Protection Act of 1991," 1474.

37. Brigitte Berger, "Multiculturalism and the Modern University," in *Our Country, Our Culture*, ed. Edith Kurzweil and William Phillips (Boston: Partisan Review Press, 1994), 17, 19, 24; Schmidt, "False Harmony," 45, 47, emphasis added.

38. Arthur Schlesinger Jr., *The Disuniting of America* (New York: Norton, 1992); Kurzweil and Phillips, *Our Country, Our Culture*; Robert Hughes, "The Fraying of America," *Time*, February 3, 1992, 44; John Leo, The Academy's New Ayatollahs," *US News and World Report*, December 10, 1990, 22; Dinesh D'Souza, "The Visigoths in Tweed," in Aufderheide, *Beyond PC*, 11–22, emphasis added; Adler et al., "Taking Offence," 49, emphasis added. That the titles of the publications on the topic of PC were indicative of the nature of the conflict was suggested to me in conversation by Tira Grey, an undergraduate at the University of Wisconsin, Madison, writing her undergraduate honors thesis on the topic of PC.

39. Of course, Stanley Fish is well known for arguing that absolute free speech is impossible since the value of "free speech" is always limited by other fundamental values. See *There's No Such Thing as Free Speech . . . and It's a Good Thing, Too* (New York: Oxford University Press, 1994). Evidence of his point is especially easy to find when reading the arguments against hate speech codes.

40. George Will, "Literary Politics," *Newsweek*, April 22, 1991, 72.

41. Ibid.

42. Lynne Cheney, *Humanities in America* (Washington, D.C.: National Endowment for the Humanities, 1988), 12, 14, emphasis added. By utilizing a discourse of birthright, Cheney also echoes her predecessor at the position of culture czar, William Bennett, who, as secretary of education before the controversy over PC, issued a report assessing the state of the humanities in higher education. In this report, Bennett relies upon biological metaphors to describe the cultural process as he refers to the task of "transmitting a culture to its rightful *heirs*," considers the founding of America as the "result of ideas *descended* directly from great epochs of Western civilization," and argues that the humanities are relevant to a "civilized society" for their "civilizing effect." Indeed, even the title suggests that biological reproduction is the proper model to understand cultural questions: *To Reclaim a Legacy* (Washington, D.C.: National Endowment for the Humanities, 1984), 1, 30, 4, 18, all emphases added.

43. Wilcomb Washburn, "Liberalism versus Free Speech," *National Review*, September 30, 1988, 39, 42, emphases added.

44. "Talking Dirty," *New Republic* (editorial), November 4, 1991, 7.

45. John Taylor, "Are you Politically Correct," *New York,* January 21, 1991, 40.

46. Arthur Schlesinger Jr., "Multiculturalism vs. the Bill of Rights," in Kurzweil and Phillips, *Our Country, Our Culture.*

47. George Bush, "Remarks at the University of Michigan Commencement Ceremony in Ann Arbor" (May 4, 1991), *Public Papers of the Presidents: George Bush I* (Washington, D.C.: Government Printing Office, 1992), 469, 471.

48. *Doe v. University of Michigan* 721 F. Supp. 852 (E.D. Mich. 1989), 862–63.

49. In addition to popular commentaries, see also *UWM Post v. Board of Regents of the University of Wisconsin System* 774 F. Supp. 1163 (E.D. Wis. 1991).

50. Actually, there was a three-way division on the future of the two-level architecture of First Amendment doctrine based on categories of speech. Justice Scalia, speaking for five Justices, would seemingly jettison this approach which has governed the Court's twentieth-century free speech jurisprudence. Justice White, speaking for himself, and Justices Blackmun and Souter, would keep it and would not rule out the possibility of a constitutional hate speech regulation. Justice Stevens would move away from the two-level categorical approach to a more contextual approach but would also leave open the possibility of a constitutional hate speech regulation.

51. The Rehnquist Court has been known to give more protection to commercial speech than has been true in the past. See 44 *Liquormart, Inc. v. Rhode Island* 517 U.S. 484 (1996).

52. Frederick Schauer, "Speech and 'Speech'—Obscenity and 'Obscenity': An Exercise in the Interpretation of Constitutional Language," *Georgetown Law Review* 67 (1979): 899.

53. *R.A.V. v. St. Paul, Minnesota* 112 S. Ct. 2538 (1992), 2547. An example of content discrimination is when a government singles out speech based on its content for special treatment. Although this is constitutionally suspect (*Police Department of the City of Chicago v. Mosley* 408 U.S. 92 [1972]), the Court upheld a regulation of political speech in Tennessee within a certain distance of polls on election day earlier that term. See *Burson v. Freeman* 504 U.S. 191 (1992). An example of viewpoint discrimination is when one ideological view is singled out for discriminatory treatment at the expense, presumably, of another. For a helpful discussion of the *R.A.V.* case, see Sunstein, *Democracy and the Problem of Free Speech,* chap. 6.

54. *R.A.V. v. St. Paul,* 2548, emphasis added.

55. Ibid., Stevens concurring at 2569; 2542, emphasis added; Blackmun concurring at 2561; White concurring at 2553–54, citation omitted.

56. "Breaking the Codes" (editorial), *New Republic,* July 8, 1991, 7.

57. "Speech Therapy" (editorial), *New Republic,* July 13 and 20, 1992, 7.

58. John Leo, "A Sensible Judgment on Hate," *US News and World Report,* July 6, 1992, 25.

59. "The Speech We Hate" (editorial), *Progressive,* August 1992, 8–9.

60. Lisa Levitan, "WSA Senate to Recommend Speech Code Redraft to Regents," *Badger Herald*, November 8, 1991, 1; Ann Scott, "Legislators Request Review of UWS 17," *Badger Herald*, July 2, 1992, 1; Leah Pogatshnik, "Regents overturn Hate Speech Code," *Badger Herald*, September 14, 1992, 1, 2; Phil Brinkman, "'Hate Speech' Battle Is Focus at UW," *Wisconsin State Journal*, May 22, 1994, 1B, 2B; *Mitchell v. State* 169 Wis. 2d 153, reversed as *Wisconsin v. Mitchell* 508 U.S. 476 (1993).

61. "UWS-17, Our PC Enemy" (editorial), *Badger Herald*, April 27, 1992, 4.

62. Cary Segall, "State Hate Rules Face Test," *Wisconsin State Journal*, June 23, 1992, 1A.

63. "Repeal UWS-17" (editorial), *Badger Herald*, September 11, 1992, 3; Leah Pogatshnik, "Regents Overturn Hate Speech Code," *Badger Herald*, September 14, 1992, 1, 2; "U. of Wisconsin Repeals Ban on 'Hate Speech,'" *New York Times*, September 15, 1992.

64. Robert Cover, "Foreword: Nomos and Narrative," *Harvard Law Review* 97 (1983): 4.

65. Sarah Lubman, "Judicially Suspect: Campus Speech Codes Are Being Shot Down as Opponents Pipe Up; A Fraternity Sues and Wins over a T-Shirt; Alliances Target 'PC' Universities; Thought-Cops Get a Lesson," *Wall Street Journal*, December 22, 1993, A1; Brinkman, "'Hate Speech' Battle Is Focus at UW," 1B–2B; see also Barbara Kessler and Bill Marvel, "P.C. Wars Raging on Campuses: Traditionalists Battle Political Correctness," *Wisconsin State Journal*, May 22, 1994, 1B, 3B.

66. Andrew Altman, "Liberalism and Campus Hate Speech: A Philosophical Examination," *Ethics* 103 (1993): 302–17.

67. See my discussion of *Doe v. University of Michigan* (1989) and the concurring opinions of Justices White, Blackmun, and Stevens in *R.A.V. v. St. Paul, Minnesota* (1992) above.

NOTES TO CHAPTER 6

1. See also Paul A. Passavant, "Enchantment, Aesthetics, and the Superficial Powers of Modern Law," *Law and Society Review* 35 (2001): 601–22.

2. *National Endowment for the Arts v. Finley* 524 U.S. 569 (1998).

3. The Supreme Court declared the Communications Decency Act unconstitutional in *Reno v. American Civil Liberties Union* 521 U.S. 844 (1997). Although the Defense of Marriage Act has not come before the Supreme Court, there are excellent arguments that it, too, is unconstitutional. See Andrew Koppelman, "Dumb and DOMA: Why the Defense of Marriage Act Is Unconstitutional," *Iowa Law Review* 83 (1997): 1; Laurence Tribe, *American Constitutional Law*, 3d ed., vol. 1 (New York: Foundation Press, 2000), 1247 n. 49. For an excellent discussion of impeachment, see ibid., secs. 2–7. See also Charles Black, *Impeachment: A Hand-*

book (New Haven: Yale University Press, 1974), and Alexander Hamilton, Federalist No. 65, in *The Federalist Papers,* ed. Garry Wills (New York: Bantam Books, 1982), 330. I have discussed the Supreme Court's decency decisions in Paul A. Passavant, "Governing Sexuality: The Supreme Court's Shift to Containment," in *Between Law and Culture: Relocating Legal Studies,* ed. David Theo Goldberg, Michael Musheno, and Lisa Bower (Minneapolis: University of Minnesota Press, 2001).

4. "The Republicans: Excerpts from Platform Approved by Republican National Convention," *New York Times,* August 1, 2000, 16A (online: Lexis/Nexis); "The Democrats: The Party's Program; Excerpts from Platform Approved by Democratic National Convention," *New York Times,* August 16, 2000, 26A (online: Lexis/Nexis). George Bush evoked "civility" in his speech accepting the Republican nomination, "Texas Gov. George W. Bush's Acceptance Speech; 'They Have Not Led. We Will,'" *Washington Post,* August 4, 2000, A20 (online: Lexis/Nexis), and constantly in his regular stump speech, as noted in Jena Heath, "Bush Assumes Attack Posture; Governor Defends Texas Education," *Atlanta Constitution,* October 27, 2000, 10A (online: Lexis/Nexis). Placing "civility" in the Republican platform was noted; see Thomas Mann, "Party Platforms Provide Glimpse into Future," *USA Today,* August 15, 2000, 17A (online: Lexis/Nexis). Civility was also the prism through which the election was analyzed; see "Candidates More Stately This Time" (editorial), *Chicago Sun-Times,* October 12, 2000, 27 (online: Lexis/Nexis), and Bush was perceived to have outcivilitied Gore, see Sabrina Eaton, "Bush Sails Past Gore on Wave of Civility, Confidence," *Plain Dealer,* October 18, 2000, 8A (online: Lexis/Nexis). On this basis, Bush garnered at least one endorsement; see "Times Endorsement: George W. Bush for president" (editorial), *Seattle Times,* October 22, 2000, D2 (online: Lexis/Nexis) ("This endorsement is founded on two bedrock differences between Bush and Vice President Al Gore: Integrity and civility").

5. For a discussion of *Barnes v. Glen Theatre,* see Alan Hyde, *Bodies of Law* (Princeton: Princeton University Press, 1997), chap. 7.

6. *Young v. American Mini Theatres* 96 S. Ct. 2440 (1976); *Renton v. Playtime Theatres* 106 S. Ct. 925 (1986); *Barnes v. Glen Theatre* 501 U.S. 560 (1991). I discuss these cases in Passavant, "Governing Sexuality."

7. *City of Erie v. Pap's A.M.* 529 U.S. 277 (2000).

8. Susan Sachs, "Civility vs. Civil Liberties," *New York Times,* July 6, 1998, A12.

9. Michel Foucault, "Governmentality," in *Power,* ed James D. Faubion, vol. 3 of *Essential Works of Michel Foucault, 1954–1984* (New York: New Press, 2000), 219–20.

10. Thomas Dumm, *Democracy and Punishment* (Madison: University of Wisconsin Press, 1987).

11. Michael Warner, "The Mass Public and the Mass Subject," in *Habermas and the Public Sphere,* ed. Craig Calhoun (Cambridge: MIT Press, 1992), 385.

12. Michael Sandel, *Democracy's Discontent: America in Search of a Public Philosophy* (Cambridge: Harvard University Press, 1996); Mary Ann Glendon, *Rights Talk* (New York: Free Press, 1991).

13. John Stuart Mill, "On Liberty," in *Three Essays*, ed. Richard Wollheim (New York: Oxford University Press, 1975), 15–16; "The East India Company's Charter," in *Writings on India*, ed. J. M. Robson, M. Moir, and Z. Moir (Toronto: University of Toronto Press, 1990), 51.

14. See Taylor Branch. *Parting the Waters: America in the King Years* (New York: Simon and Schuster, 1988).

15. Amitai Etzioni, *The Spirit of Community* (New York: Crown, 1993); Glendon, *Rights Talk*.

16. See Sandel, *Democracy's Discontent*, 317–51; Robert Bellah et al., *Habits of the Heart* (New York: Harper and Row, 1985).

17. Ernesto Laclau and Chantal Mouffe, *Hegemony and Socialist Strategy* (New York: Verso, 1985).

18. Michel Foucault, "The Subject and Power," *Critical Inquiry* 8 (1982): 782.

19. *Hague v. CIO* 59 S. Ct. 954 (1939). Italics mine.

20. Dumm, *Democracy and Punishment*; Michel Foucault, *Discipline and Punish: The Birth of the Prison* (New York: Vintage, 1979).

21. *Bethel School District v. Fraser* 106 S. Ct. 3159 (1986), 3163–64. Internal quotations removed. Emphasis mine.

22. Michel Foucault, *The History of Sexuality* (New York: Vintage, 1978), 139.

23. See also Ann Laura Stoler, *Race and the Education of Desire: Foucault's History of Sexuality* (Durham, N.C.: Duke University Press, 1995), chap. four.

24. Norbert Elias, *The Civilizing Process* (Cambridge, Mass.: Basil Blackwell, 1994), 156.

25. Cf. ibid., 462–64.

26. Robert Reno, "Let's Get Back Separation of Sex and State" (editorial), *Newsday*, October 31, 2000, A34 (online: Lexis/Nexis, Nassau and Suffolk ed.). In his successful use of symbolic code to racialize the Democratic party opposition as a mechanism for becoming president, Bush the younger follows quite successfully in Bush the elder's footsteps.

27. George Mosse, *Nationalism and Sexuality* (Madison: University of Wisconsin Press, 1985).

28. Michael Rogin, *Ronald Reagan, The Movie and other episodes in political demonology* (Berkeley: University of California Press, 1987).

29. Samuel Huntington, "The Clash of Civilizations?" *Foreign Affairs* 72 (1993): 22.

30. In addition to Cass Sunstein's work cited below, see Bruce Ackerman, *We the People: Foundations* (Cambridge: Harvard University Press, 1991); Samuel Beer, *To Make a Nation* (Cambridge: Harvard University Press, 1993).

31. Cass Sunstein, *Democracy and the Problem of Free Speech* (New York: Free Press, 1993), 248, xvi. See also Sunstein, *The Partial Constitution* (Cambridge: Harvard University Press, 1993).

32. Sunstein, *Democracy and the Problem of Free Speech*, xvii, xx, 164. Sunstein mentions nude dancing at viii, xii, 2, 14, 148, and 164.

33. Beer, *To Make a Nation*, 66, 401–2.

34. Walter Bagehot, *Physics and Politics* (New York: Alfred Knopf, 1948), 161, 172. Emphasis mine.

35. Ibid., 128.

36. Ibid., 189.

37. Ibid., 189–90.

38. Ibid., 202–6.

39. For a general discussion of the linkages of class, gender, sexuality, race, and urban space, see Anne McClintock, *Imperial Leather: Race, Gender, and Sexuality in the Colonial Contest* (New York: Routledge, 1995).

40. Bagehot, *Physics and Politics*, 122, 201.

41. See also Murray Dry, "Free Speech in Political Philosophy and Its Relation to American Constitutional Law: A Consideration of Mill, Meiklejohn, and Plato," *Constitutional Commentary* 11 (1994): 81; R. George Wright, "A Rationale from J. S. Mill for the Free Speech Clause," *Supreme Court Review* 1985 (1986): 149.

42. Sunstein, *Democracy and the Problem of Free Speech*, 7, 164. One might protest that Sunstein's interest in regulating the threats to "civility produced by racial hate speech" (7) cancels out the racial effects of his unqualified use of Bagehot's "government by discussion"; i.e., Sunstein is intentionally not a racist, and is unintentionally associated with the argument of racial progress made by the Social Darwinist Bagehot. While intentions can be significant in certain contexts, I am more interested here in how such cultural texts continue to inform constitutional discourse on questions of reason and value. Moreover, the very fact that certain forms of representation can be accepted unproblematically as constituting our legal reality without us thinking about it is precisely what I put in question here.

43. *Young v. American Mini Theatres* at 2449, 2452; *Jacobellis v. Ohio* 378 U.S. 184 (1964), Warren dissenting at 199.

44. *Roth v. U.S.* 354 U.S. 476 (1957), 487. Emphasis mine.

45. *Ginzburg v. U. S.* 86 S. Ct. 942, 948–49. Emphasis mine.

46. Preamble to City of Erie Ordinance 75–1994, cited in *City of Erie v. Pap's A.M.* 529 U.S. 277 (2000), Stevens dissenting.

47. *Barnes v. Glen Theatre* is cited in *Adele Buzzetti d/b/a Cozy Cabin and Vanessa Doe v. City of New York et al.* 1998 US App LEXIS 5609 (1998), which upholds the zoning regulations.

48. *Ardery v. The State* 56 Ind. 328 (1877); *Barnes v. Glen Theatre.*

49. *Ardery v. The State*, 329–30. My emphasis.

50. *American Booksellers Ass'n v. Hudnut* 771 F.2d 323 (1985), 328. Recall, also, that Catharine MacKinnon rejected the framework of obscenity in favor of "pornography." See "Not a Moral Issue," Catharine MacKinnon, *Feminism Unmodified* (Cambridge: Harvard University Press, 1987).

51. *Miller v. Civil City of South Bend*, 904 F.2d 1081 (7ᵗʰ Cir. 1990), Easterbrook dissenting at 1125, 1131.

52. Ibid., Posner concurring at 1089, 1096.

53. Ibid., 1100, 1104.

54. *Erie v. Pap's A.M.*, O'Connor speaking for herself, Chief Justice Rehnquist, Justice Kennedy, and Justice Breyer, emphasis added.

55. Ibid., Scalia concurring in judgment (speaking for himself and Justice Thomas).

56. Ibid., Stevens dissenting (speaking for himself and Justice Ginsburg).

Notes to the Conclusion

1. See Peter Fitzpatrick's engagement of this question in *Modernism and the Grounds of Law* (New York: Cambridge University Press, 2001).

2. Cf. *Furman v. Georgia* 408 U.S. 238 (1972) (striking down Georgia's capital punishment laws), Brennan concurring. Justice Brennan and the other Justices refer frequently to *Trop v. Dulles*, 356 U.S. 86 (1958), which also uses a discourse of civility and decency to adjudicate the question of whether a punishment (loss of citizenship) offends the national conscience.

3. Anthony Anghie, "Francisco de Vitoria and the Colonial Origins of International Law," in *Laws of the Postcolonial*, ed. Eve Darian-Smith and Peter Fitzpatrick (Ann Arbor: University of Michigan Press, 1999): 89–107.

4. Paul A. Passavant, "Enchantment, Aesthetics, and the Superficial Powers of Modern Law," *Law and Society Review* 35 (2001): 601–22.

5. For excellent introductions to this area of law that will have great influence over our lives and freedoms, especially to the extent that our lives are increasingly governed in terms of code, see James Boyle, *Shamans, Software, and Spleens: Law and the Construction of the Information Society* (Cambridge: Harvard University Press, 1996); Rosemary Coombe, *The Cultural Life of Intellectual Properties: Authorship, Appropriation, and the Law* (Durham, N.C.: Duke University Press, 1998); Lawrence Lessig, *Code; and Other Laws of Cyberspace* (New York: Basic Books, 1999).

6. Jacques Rancière, *Dis-agreement: Politics and Philosophy*, trans. Julie Rose (Minneapolis: University of Minnesota Press, 1999), 80. If the "people" and "population" appear on the scene at the same time, then saving democratic politics by separating the people from the science of population may be more difficult than Rancière allows (99–100).

7. Jodi Dean, *Publicity's Secret* (Ithaca, N.Y.: Cornell University Press, 2002).

8. Michael Hardt and Antonio Negri, *Empire* (Cambridge: Harvard University Press, 2000).

9. Yves Dezalay and Bryant Garth, "Merchants of Law as Moral Entrepreneurs: Constructing International Justice from Competition for Transnational Business Disputes," *Law and Society Review* 29 (1995): 27; David Trubek, Yves Dezalay, Ruth Buchanan, and John Davis, "Global Restructuring and the Law: Studies of the Internationalization of Legal Fields and the Creation of Transnational Arenas," *Case Western Reserve Law Review* 44 (1994): 407.

10. Eve Darian-Smith, *Bridging Divides: The Channel Tunnel and the English Legal Identity in the New Europe* (Berkeley: University of California Press, 1999).

11. Bruce Shapiro, "Dead Reckoning: A World Effort to Force an End to the US Death Penalty Is Gaining Strength," *Nation*, August 6/13, 2001, 14; Pam Belluck, "Clemency for Killer Surprises Many Who Followed Case," *New York Times*, January 31, 1999, 12 (online: Lexis-Nexis) (discussing how Pope John Paul II's request for clemency swayed Missouri's Governor Mel Carnahan to commute a death sentence to life without parole). Thanks to Stephanie Smith for locating the latter article for me.

12. *Zadvydas v. Davis* 150 L. Ed. 2d 653 (2001).

13. Thus the Court construed the statute to contain an implicit "reasonable time" limitation subject to federal court review and remanded the cases for reconsideration in light of its ruling that incarceration beyond a six-month period may be challenged and that the government must justify further detention if the alien can show that there is good reason to believe that there is no significant likelihood of removal in the reasonably foreseeable future.

14. *Zadvydas v. Davis*, p. 666.

15. Ibid., p. 670.

16. Ibid.

17. In fact, even the dissenting opinions in this case seem to show the effects of a nonnational basis for conceptualizing matters of justice. Despite repeated protestations that the cases before him involve an individual who does not have a "right" to what he asks for, Justice Scalia, speaking also for Justice Thomas, concedes that the aliens cannot be "tortured" (which is not a small concession for these two), leading one to inquire into the basis for this right not to be tortured. Justice Kennedy, joined by Chief Justice Rehnquist, worries about foreign nations causing the release of dangerous and unreformable aliens into the "American community," subtle underworld terrorist links, and stealthy and fraudulent fugitive aliens, but winds up agreeing with the majority in principle, if not the interpretation of the principle. That is, although he distinguishes the "liberty interests" and "liberty rights" of deportable aliens and citizens, reiterating a distinction made in Scalia's opinion, he also concedes that "both removable and inadmissible aliens are entitled to be free from detention that is arbitrary or capricious," citing

"international views" on the detention of refugees and asylum seekers. In other words, he accords them some due process rights, but presumably has a lower standard of due process rights in mind than does the majority (since the "arbitrary and capricious" standard is a minimal due process standard). Nevertheless, he cites United Nations documents to justify his perception of rights for non-Americans in this case.

18. Steven Greenhouse, "In U.S. Unions, Mexico Finds Unlikely Ally on Immigration," *New York Times*, July 19, 2001, A1, A21.

Index

Abortion clinic cases, 14–45, 220n. 21

Abrams v. U.S., 41–42, 70, 208n.2

Academic freedom, xiii, 9, 139–47; as corporate freedom, 140, 141–42, 219n. 12; as individual freedom, 140–41, 219n. 12. *See also* University

Ackerman, Bruce, 84

Acts of 1917/1918, 9

Adams, John, 20–23, 26–27, 30, 89, 91, 127, 130

Agamben, Giorgio, 14–17, 85

"Age of Discussion, The" (Bagehot), 60

Agriculture, as norm, 34–35

Amendments to the Constitution: Fourth Amendment, 29; Fifth Amendment, xii, 191–92; Eighth Amendment, 4, 188; Fourteenth Amendment, 49, 72, 139–40, 192. *See also* First Amendment

America: boundaries, 111–12; as civilized nation, 30, 102, 130, 133, 139; cold war identity, 114–15, 137; exceptionalism, 11–12; global imaginary, 125, 128, 147; international image of, 115–17; meaning of, 110–11; Millian paradigm and, 87–91, 106–9, 113; moral geography, 106, 111, 126–29; national space, 133–34. *See also* British Americans

American Civil Liberties Union (ACLU), xiii

American Defense Society, 66, 77, 206n. 103

American identity, 29–30, 172, 194n. 23; cold war, 111, 114–15, 137; contestation, 133–34; Declaration of Independence and, 25–28; legal dissemination and, 156–61; multiculturalism as threat to, 149–50; as multiple, 110–12; as nonracial, 117, 213n. 24; postcold war, 126–27, 157, 162, 181; production of, xii, 26–27, 69–70, 85; racialization of, 50, 149–52, 161, 166; reachievement of, 170–71;

rights claiming and, 17, 21–25, 55, 57; self-protection, 101–2; statistical production of, 69–70. *See also* American people; Subject

American people: as belonging to Western civilization, 138–39, 156, 162–63, 177; civility of, 30, 167–68, 183–84; as embodied subject, 166–67; free speech reserved for, 4–5, 84–85, 169–70, 177, 183–84, 187; normalization of, 37, 138–39, 177; politicization of, 31–32; sovereignty, 28–29, 45, 84, 86, 167, 174–75, 185, 189–90, 206n. 101. *See also* American Identity; Rights claiming; Subject

American Public Problems series, 67

Anarchists, 64–65

Ancient constitution, 18–20, 23–25, 51, 197n. 35

Anglo-Saxon liberties, 18–20, 24–25, 89

Anglo-Saxons, 51, 75

Anti-PC campaign, 138–39, 148–52, 154–63. *See also* Hate speech codes; Multiculturalism; Political correctness; University

Ardery v. The State, 181

Arendt, Hannah, 25–26, 39–40

"Are You Politically Correct?" (Taylor), 152–53

Articles of Confederation, 28

Art Institute of Chicago, 131

Arts, 130–31

Ashcroft, John, xiii

Associations, voluntary, 82–83

Authority, 141, 170–71

Badger Herald, 159–60

Bagehot, Walter, 59–60, 62–63, 69, 87, 89, 175–78, 227n.42

Bailyn, Bernard, 19

Barnes v. Glen Theatre, 165, 178, 180–83

Beer, Samuel, 108, 175–76

Bennett, William, 222n. 42